The Pacification of Humanity

Exposing the Ideological Contagions

Emmanuel S. John

THE PACIFICATION OF HUMANITY
Exposing the Ideological Contagions
Copyright © 2016 by Emmanuel S. John
Books for Your Head Publishing
Terry Carroll Editing (Johnson City)

www.emmaueljohn.com

ISBN 9780985189839
Ebook 9780985189846

Printed in the USA by Ingram/Lightning Source International

To Page 12 5:45 pm . 10-24-21
To Page 29 5:42 PM
To Page 54 10/26
To Page 68 10/27
To Page 95 10/28
To Page 119 11-1
To Page 140 158 11-5
12-8-21 START p.159 To Page 167
Page 189 p 196
12-9-21 START p 196 to P. 232

Dedication

This book in dedicated to every single man and woman who has dedicated their lives in the defense of our freedoms. To all those persons who have shared their family members' military service time in order to insure that Freedom exists for all peoples in the modern world both here and abroad. To all those individuals who selflessly volunteer their time and energy to help other less fortunate than themselves attain what so many of us enjoy in our free society.

This book is for all the people who defend the U.S. Constitution as it was written by our forefathers. My goal in writing this book is to insure that your sacrifices were not made in vain. This book is also written as a "thank you" to those persons who have sacrificed their personal stations in life and their reputations by telling the truth and by exposing the lies of the selfish and self-centered. To all those people who have worked hard to fight against tyranny and oppression of all types both emotional and political. Let Freedom Ring!

Preface

I think the best way to preface this is book is by telling you a little bit about me. I am very inquisitive. I am that person in class who asks the hardest questions and challenges the most renowned experts. I am the straight guy who will sit down with a group of gay men and lesbian women to talk about their perspectives. I don't do these things to challenge the beliefs of others; I do these things to challenge my own beliefs so that I can see things more clearly and understand issues more deeply.

While working in the Baltimore City Public school system, I was often the only "white guy" in the building. I cut my clinical teeth on having open discussions about race with young black kids from difficult neighborhoods. I conducted therapy groups with drug dealers talking about the real problems created by dealing while acknowledging that those enterprises were the only methods available for them to earn income.

I am the guy who will talk about greed with the rich or speak about entitlement with the poor. I have talked about liberalism with the liberals, the need for laws with libertarians and about true values with conservatives. Being unafraid has bestowed upon me invaluable insights that could not have been attained any other way. The truth is out there but we have to work for it. Being open-minded has gifted me with; truth, clarity, insight and enlightenment; gifts that I will treasure until my death.

The Spirit of the Universe allowed me to be born into an open-minded Christian family. I practiced atheism and then returned to my Christian roots. I've practiced mysticism and the dark arts. I have embraced Native American spirituality and seized the power of the Wiccans. Having faith and confidence in myself has allowed me to appreciate the traditions of Judaism while working in the Jewish Community, to feel the passion of

Islam, to embrace the connectedness of Buddhism and the calming simplicity of Taoism. I have known the heights of Tantra and the universality of the Druids. I now know the integration of "nothingness with oneness" and the "I-am-ness" of Ashtanga Yoga.

I love truth and I cherish clarity even more. I investigate improbability and inconsistency but still ponder possibility. I am one of the most "out of the box" thinkers you may ever have contact with. I avoid criticism when I can, but I embrace critical thinking. Growing up very poor, I have experienced abuse, loss and despair to depths many people cannot imagine. I have lived a life beyond my wildest dreams from casual social interactions with the rich and famous to inspirational meditations with rednecks; from combat techniques with lifers in prison to martial arts with Shaolin Monks.

I am a psychotherapist who has spent more than 30 years treating people with all types of emotional disorders. I have been court certified as an expert in addiction treatment and addiction forensics. I have testified in Senate Sub-committee hearings as an advocate/lobbyist for addiction treatment. I have participated in some of the most difficult discussions life can confront a person with and I have had some of the most contentious physical confrontations known to human existence.

I embrace having my perspectives challenged. I have lived in the inner city and I have lived on several farms. I have raised a child and even a few farm animals along the way. I believe that the biggest obstacle in the lives of most human beings is their own limited thinking. I am grateful for the many great minds throughout history that did not shrink themselves down beneath their capacities but instead stood strong to challenge the world. I believe the world is a better place because I am here and I believe that it will be a better place if you all show up too!

Table of Contents

Introduction

Human interaction has been infected by out of control ideology; maligned by people who will do anything to perpetuate their selfish agendas. Modern man has painted himself into a theoretical corner of how he would like things to be and the actual realities of human existence. The progressive quest for a Utopia of rainbows and Unicorns has resulted in a Dystopia of loathing, victimization, self-centeredness and entitlement.

It's no longer OK to be human; in fact if you act too human you can face hate filled labels, ostracism and social retaliation from cultural bullies. Truth is the new hate speech because truth dissolves ideology. If you speak out, you risk character assassination and social alienation. We have been conditioned to keep our mouths shut so the big mouths can talk. We have been told that our constitution, our traditions and our beliefs are old fashioned and obsolete. We have been bullied into letting the government tell us how to raise our children. A government that now determines what our children need to know and not know. We are professionally ruined if we don't comply with the regulations of that same out of control Federal Government.

We have not lost our way; it has been hidden from us by runaway ideologies. We have been purposely mislead about current events by a self serving over commercialized media that has forgotten its duty. We are paying the price for an agenda driven form of polarization that forces us to one side of the political spectrum or the other. It is no longer OK to be moderate or "in the middle" because, according to the ideologues balanced is no longer fair.

There are clear reasons why we think so differently from the way our parents did and why our children and grandchildren see the world so vastly differently than we do. Education has become indoctrination. Through repetitious messaging the definitions of words have been changed without justification or consensus. We are inhibited to speak our truth in a social setting even when we know in our hearts that our insights could make a difference. We won't speak out because it's more trouble than it is worth. Free speech is no longer free; we are being oppressed and repressed. A free people cannot fit into two little boxes designed to streamline political power.

In this book I will explain to you exactly how this repression and pacification have occurred. I will put forth clear and simple methods for building our immunity against the contagions spread by the progressive ideologues on both sides. I will explain why we are experiencing so much emotional turmoil in our hearts and in our world. I will explain why nothing is ever resolved or settled. I will explain how race is used to divide us and why. I will give you many needed, vital and valuable insights.

I suggest that you have been made pacifistic by the bullies who are now in control of our culture and that your withdrawal from the debate is a part of their sinister plan. They demand your silence then use that silence as consent to things you vehemently oppose.

While reading this book you will learn how you have been brainwashed by the control of information in the form of propaganda. You'll learn how the future of freedom in the modern world is being selfishly stolen from our children by people who wholeheartedly believe that they know what is best for you and yours. Your action is required. Remaining ignorant of these issues is your consent; one day they will stop asking for that consent and then one day it will not be needed.

Chapter One

THE CONTAGION MAKERS

The Ideology Problem: It's Contagious and Deadly!

The problems in the world today aren't about conflict, war or religion. Nearly every major struggle in the world today gets its origin from pseudo intellectual Petri dishes in the form of ideology. Ideology grows in the fantasy filled incubator of progressive academia where delusional dreamers cultivate imagined utopias of shiny cities on hills, without thought to probability.

The problem with ideology is actually quite clear, but the powers that be protect it because it's all they have to work with. Ideology is emotion over reality. Ideology dreams of changing reality but does not require feasibility or fact to fester. All ideology requires is your willingness to suspend reason, to be emotional and to limit your vision so you can dream their dream.

The fact is that the purveyors of most ideologies be it religious or academic, just need you to support their agendas and they will do anything necessary to gain your allegiance. They want you to embrace the possibilities of ideology but only theirs.

You were never taught about ideology in school, only about which ideologies you should subscribe too. Thanks to a process called "indoctrination" you probably didn't even notice it was happening to you. While they may have mentioned their ideals, what they neglected to mention to you was the possible fallout and repercussions of those ideas. You were never taught what happens when ideology meets reality or of the history that proves most social ideology implausible.

Previous ideologies have contributed to every problem that the new ideology attempts to remedy. Without ideology there would be no conflict, no war and no hate; only peace of mind and harmony. I will show you in the following pages how unresolved conflicting ideologies result in war. This happens because ideologies will always conflict; ideologies are the enemy of acceptance and a harmonious existence. Ideology left unchecked by truth, facts, and reality it festers. It becomes a pathological contagion spreading through the masses by half truths, coercion, revisionist history and the control of data and information in the form of propaganda.

Ideology in and of itself does not become a problem unless there is a lack of tolerance to opposing ideologies. Some ideologies are so weak and so easily dispelled if challenged that their purveyors often work very hard to keep you from closely examining the proverbial and mysterious, "man behind the curtain." Ideology quickly becomes more problematic when it is met with strong opposition by mutually opposing ideologies or theories: This is when ideology becomes deadly.

The Train to Can't Happenton

Let's see how the train to Can't Happenton runs. If we viewed war as being a train-car on a train called Ideology, then War would be the car just before the caboose. War is one of the last cars you would see as the train passes you; war is the rear end of conflicting ideals.

Ideology is the engine that powers that train and it is driven by a group of people who want things the way they think things should be; their vision. There are many other cars on the train. In order from front to back they might include but are not limited to; Ideology (the engine driven by the progressive,) agreement,

2

support, tolerance, acceptance, appreciation, dissention, disagreement, opposition, argument, conflict, threats, physical confrontation and towards the end; avoidance, alienation, separation, isolation and war. The caboose is called "aftermath" because that is all that you see when the ideology train has run its course. Politics and perhaps even religion (religion being the birthplace of politics) could not exist without ideology. (Atheism is an ideology because they have yet to disprove the existence of God.)

I can assure you of this; if you get hit by a train it will not be the caboose but the engine that kills you; the engine always powers and leads the charge. The train cannot move without the engine. War cannot happen without ideology. Just like every other car on the above train, war is merely a mechanism of resolving conflicting ideology. You can ride in any car for as long as you like, but the ideology train has no destination on its one way track to a place that does not exist.

When war happens and death occurs, the ideology gets reset until the next new ideological option occurs and then the whole vicious cycle starts all over again. This train runs through every child, woman, man, town, county, state, country and continent; it always has and it always will. Once the train is moving it's very hard to stop. Ideology has fueled every man-to-man conflict and every war since the dawn of man. Civil wars, religious wars, wars based on economics and even wars based on race. Without ideology, racism and hatred could not exist.

The problem with the ideology train is that it does not lead to a destination called reality or resolution. The train never stops; it is always running because it can never reach its fruition. The ideology train never needs to pass a station called evidence, truth or fact as these are not fuels required to power the train. In fact the train often speeds up and quickly ignores any tracks in those

3

directions. The train of ideology is fueled by passion, envy, fear, bitterness, resentment, victimization, entitlement and a need for more emotional energy.

More often than not, ideology itself is built upon other ideologies: A castle in the sand. These notions might seem like great ideas but they are rarely practical. For instance; the ideology that "no child should go hungry" sounds great but children will always go hungry. The facts are that there is enough food on the planet to feed everyone (and there always has been) yet here we are, with children not eating. Some ideologues might suggest that "if the world could get along (ideology) and people could be tolerant of one another (ideology) then we could put together a plan (ideology and socialism) and we could solve the problem together (fantasy).

Have you ever tried to get everyone in your own culturally similar family to agree on something important? How did that work out? Now, take your family across the street to convince your neighbors too; now take your two families down the road to the other side of town. Now let's do it with all the different people of the world. IT'S NOT HAPPENING! It's like herding cats, but more difficult.

Who says that children not eating is a problem or that by feeding all the children everything would be grand (ideology)? Some opposing ideology might say; it's not about food, it's about overpopulation (ideology) that personally, you should only have the amount of children that you can feed or that you can afford to care for yourself (ideology). What's next? Let's use birth control or infanticide and abortion to limit the amount of mouths, etc etc... (I'll stop there. If you don't get my point, there is no hope for you. In fact, you are a proof of my argument that it is impossible to get everyone on the same page.) The rest of you can jump off that train and we'll see where it goes. At this point

4

some of our readers are already being blocked by their ideological indoctrination via a little obstacle known as cognitive dissonance (defined later).

Opposing ideologies and the methods on how to resolve their differences is where most conflict is born. The only chance for there to be zero conflict is when there is zero opposition or only one option. A single option is almost never the case as ideology is also a form of fantasy. All that ideology needs to get started is a dream and there are more dreams than there are people. The real problem with the attempted elimination of conflict is that conflict is a part of human NATURE and, despite some beliefs to the contrary, man never wins in a battle with nature.

The bigger picture

Unfortunately I can't resolve the problem of ideology or change human nature. I can help you cope with, avoid being duped by and protect your psyche from becoming emotionally ill as a result of the propaganda methods employed by purveyors of selfish ideological quests. In the following pages I'll teach you how ideologues use confusion to manipulate and co-opt your support for impossible fantasies while using your emotional reactions both good and bad to fuel the train to their progressive ends.

In this book we will be seeking clarity in order to expose some popular ideologies. I will expose their methods and their madness. Before we do that, I would like to commend you for making it this far. I say this because many timid, confused and brainwashed people have been diverted by both topic and title. People want to believe what they want to believe and very few seek actual knowledge and awareness. For your open-mindedness you will get to take a journey with me through the landscape of modern day human perspective, motivation and emotional attachment. A lot of this journey will focus on language; words, definitions and perspectives. To do this, we have to examine the social forces at work that are trying to change our culture to meet their unrealistic ideological agendas.

Language is everything

Language isn't something, it's everything. Language is not only how we interact with the external world, it is also how we organize our memory and our internal machinations. Don't just believe what I say, let me prove it to you. Think of something in your mind that has occurred recently; good or bad, perhaps an event over the past week, at work, school, family; anything at all, the topic is not vital.

Now try to picture that event, thing or scenario without using any words to recall the event in your mind and memory. If a word comes to mind, you have to stop. Try to recall it without attaching words. You can't do it because everything has words attached to it. Words create labels that define everything in our lives, even our emotions. Recalling the topic you chose without words can't be done because words define and place value on all of our experiences thereby creating our perspectives. We use words to do these things even when we are alone in a quiet room. This process is called intra-personal communication or self talk. Self talk is healthy; everyone does it and it is the way we work out problems and dilemmas. It is how we decide on outcomes and even how we develop our opinions. We need to do this or we become lost and confused.

Some ideologues will suggest that certain thoughts are wrong and that they shouldn't be held in the mind or entertained. This is an attempt to manipulate you and limit your thinking. They say: "You shouldn't think that way." I say "Why not?"

Everything you can think, feel or believe has been processed and valued based on how you define words. Let's go a step further. Now try to process a feeling from any of the senses;

6

touch your arm and describe it without words, without language. Again, it can't be done because language is the base structure of everything in our minds. Without words we are like a newborn baby just staring at everything with a blank expression (Very Zen but not very productive). We also use language to store and grade all types of memories from traumas, to facts, to pleasurable experiences. This process is how we hold on to and feel things of an emotional nature. Our values are words.

As you walk with me through this process we are going to examine and experience firsthand how the use, misuse and distortion of language has contributed to a growing stream of social ills, social disequilibriums and personal anxieties. Many people are struggling to cope with the mad mad world we live in. I propose that this struggle is the result of our own, or another's, failed ideology; good intention paving a pathway to hell.

As we proceed, we will examine how the social control of language has created confusion for the individual. How the processing of things like; self-concept, self-worth, self-esteem and self-respect have been contaminated by unrealistic notions of how we should be. By the agendas of people who passionately and blindly seek their own selfish ends. We'll examine ways in which your perspectives may have been maligned and how your perspectives have been high-jacked.

Before we go any further, let's talk about the book's title. Its current rendering; "The Pacification of Humanity" is not the original idea inspired in the mind of this author. It was not an easy choice. You see, being a psychotherapist, published author of several other books and an educational designer I understand the need to "tailor" language to fit my target audience as well as how to present the subject matter being addressed.

While writing this book it became quite obvious to me that people are afraid to write about some of these topics. They have been made pacifistic with threats of professional ruin because they have challenged the status quo. Many writers who might expose these issues fear the reprisal they might experience on a professional and or social level so they give into the coercion of the bullies and keep quiet. They have become pacifistic!

Despite the importance of these insights, I was stunned to see how little direct conversation existed about the fallout of failed ideology. Many societies have been literally ruined by leaders with unrealistic agendas. Some writers have been censored by publishers and others have been censored by the fear of academic retaliation. They have been strong armed by "Cultural Bullies" (the people in society who attack them and make them pay for their supposed FREE speech).

These types of repression occur because "Political Correctness" has been perverted and maligned so that it can serve covert agendas. The whole idea behind free speech is that there should be no cost for speaking out and voicing an opinion. In contrast, Political Correctness suggests there is a cost for speech. Political Correctness suggests that people should be sanctioned for not towing the ideological party lines. The costs and penalties include, but are not limited to; shaming, blaming and labeling. Ironically these are the very things that the PC culture is supposed protect against! The PC culture uses its own precepts to quiet dissent and stifle objection. The truth is that at this point in my life I figure what the heck; someone's got to do it! (I guess that I really am that guy.)

As an author willing to place his career on the line for truth, I also know that communication and marketing start from day one of any published work and that some words are more marketable than others. There was a strong yearning in me to title this book; "The Pussification of Humanity" because I really wanted to rebel against censorship.

However; during the books evolution it became much more clear to me that we aren't wimps at all. That many people of good will are very strong indeed; strong people are just not as desperate as the progressive ideologues (from all sides) so they let people be. The weak people are the ones who live in a constant state of need. You, the strong people, are the silent majority who feel secure enough within yourselves to allow the lunatics to think that they are running the asylum. Unfortunately we have let them fantasize a little bit too long. Our strength has contributed to our pacification and our silence to their tyranny. They're now running the asylums known as national governments; systems and institutions built on delusions.

The strong have ignored important issues so long that the progressive ideologues have been able to program an entire generation via their indoctrination through the educational systems. The last few generations have been taught what to think, not how to think. The silent majority of mature and successful people have been manipulated and pacified by being fed selective outrage, talking points and faux distractions. The information age has developed the "Selective Information Generation"(SIG's) where their societal moral high-grounds are formed in the halls, offices and lounges of academia.

These academic elitists (people who think they are smarter than everyone else) have figured out that the masses can be pacified with occasional offerings and entitlements (bought). The irony is that most of academia could not survive in the real world without their college jobs. In the words of George Bernard Shaw "He who can, does. He who cannot, teaches." This is not a new perspective, he wrote that in 1903.

Fortunately for us real people we have not been changed at our core but we have instead been misled by unrealistic notions and empty promises of what we wanted to hear. Tricked by the desire for fast change, instant gratification and the assurance that things would be managed with our best interests in mind; they have not been!

One problem with insight in the modern world is that people will only give you about 10 seconds to turn them on or turn them off. Of this we are all guilty. Critical thinking has been removed from its place in human learning and practice. Sad but true! My only request is that you hold on for this entire ride. I will shock you and I will even make you mad at me at times but if you bear with me you will find the value in what I offer.

I know that some words become triggers for us. Words can turn some people away while those very same words draw other people closer. The difference in our reactions is most frequently determined by our current emotional state and by what I call "social inertias."

Sometimes people tune in to certain words because it's the "hip" thing to do (everyone's doing it), sometimes because it triggers a positive or negative memory. Sometimes it's simply because someone else programmed them to think that way; they usually don't even know why. (Watch a protestor interview.)

We are not holding back

There is a fine line between censoring, moderating, being courteous, being "social," being dishonest and the outright stifling of one's self-expression. We will not be holding back during this process. This is a free speech zone and all censorship has been lifted for this process. (How sad is it that I even have to say that?)

If you've ever had to "hold your tongue," then you've been censored and were therefore forced to distance yourself from yourself. If this has occurred, then you were put in a circumstance where you were forced to be different from how you are. You were coerced by a fear of reprisal or drama that

10

you did not want to experience. Because of these events, social inertia was redirected and all the people in the room falsely believed that what was actually spoken out loud was a true consensus. It was not; repression is contagion and emotional illness brought on by political correctness.

The reason why you did not speak your real mind was most likely because it was considered to be "politically incorrect" or insensitive in "polite" society. I'm sorry that happened to you and for all the other people in the room who were denied your insight. In the U.S. we are guaranteed the opposite of repression. Supposedly these freedoms and our diversities are the things that made us great yet here we are having our voices suppressed and our society in decline. Our social fabric has worn out. I know what it is like to interact with groups who think they are superior to everyone else; mostly because they say so. I call the people who create these conversationally limited environments, void of any real free speech; "Cultural Bullies."

CULTURAL BULLIES

Just because something is nice or kind it does not make it wise, smart or possible. Niceties do not equate to accuracy. In fact, niceties actually warp reality, create confusion, stifle personal development and even inhibit self-expression. Niceties are manipulations, simply proven by the fact that we practice them so that others see us in a certain light. In modern culture we have begun to hide from HARSH WORDS like they were some sort of plaque that might kill us, when in fact, the avoidance seems to be making us more ill and weaker.

We are plagued by this social contagion of correctness but we can develop immunity to it if we learn how to pay attention to what people are really saying. Most people of good moral character will agree that society has become too thin skinned; too sensitive. It's as if we are not strong enough to hear the truth or experience things as they really are.

I want to be clear here. I am not referring to curse words. I am referring to uncomfortable truths. My belief about foul language is just that, it is a foul in communication. In most cases foul language is nothing more than intellectual laziness and the result of an undereducated and undisciplined mind. Sometimes we do curse when we are upset but that is because during those times we lose our composure. Emotionally healthy people are able to maintain their emotional composure. Unhealthy people do not have control of their mouths. Most times the curser isn't mad at all they're just protesting something they don't like or something they don't agree with. They believe that by cursing you will somehow take them more seriously. (FYI; most listeners stop listening to you intellectually when you start cursing emotionally: They process only your emotions. When people giggle at cursing it is actually at your limitations and as a way to deflect their own discomfort.)

When it comes to curse words I wholeheartedly agree with the author Hugh Prather who said; "when I curse I am not trying to say something, I am trying to be something." The most important aspect of cursing is that it discredits you because it is obvious you are not speaking on an intellectual level: People will never take you serious when you do. When you curse you're simply not communicating as well as you might. In fact; cursing is actually a subconscious way to create distance, to push people away. If that is what you want, then fine. Curse words actually limit true expression. They're just lazy. If you "like to curse" then you'll love this book because, as a therapist, I believe that the growing trend of using curse words in social situations is in fact a form of rebellion against censorship and political

12

correctness. I do understand but cursing is an ineffective means of communication and at most an impotent rebellion.

Despite some convenient sentiments to the contrary curse words are not you being honest or real. They are you being lazy. They are not a productive communication technique and your actual points are rarely heard or taken seriously by others. You usually just come across like a drama queen. When you make fun of people who are offended by it then you are practicing the dark art of the cultural bully.

Internal censorship

My goal is not to censor you. In fact it's the opposite, I am trying to help you say what you really want to express; in more accurate terms. In regards to censorship, I have become convinced that most of the current censorship of the "self" externally to the world, inevitably leads to the censoring of our internal dialogue as well. This is repression and it is emotionally unhealthy. Thus the tone and topic of our external language ends up being how we see things on the inside, even if we are lying. Inconsistency of communication creates a major problem for the modern human animal. It can be a predisposition to self-deception, repression, violence and loss of emotional control.

Just because we believe things are a certain way does not make them so. It is an immature notion to think that just because something makes sense to us, that it is real or true. Just because we try to act a certain way it does not, in essence, mean that we are that way (more later). When we adjust ourselves in social circumstances we're just "acting" a certain way and acting is not a portrayal of the true self. Have you ever thought to yourself; "If they only knew what I was really thinking?" If so then what this means is that you weren't able to be you in that social setting. Sad! You may have been bullied into being different from who you are. Your silence became support for their

13

ideology. Cursing is merely a form or retaliation and rebellion. It accomplishes little.

I can say with absolute certainty that most of the psychotherapy clients who present for treatment (both individual and family) have perspective problems of some kind. It is my experience and the experience of many other therapists that these perspectives are most often distorted by the misuse of language (understanding). The confusion about what a word means or even the use of weak language (inaccurate understanding) creates internal uncertainty and inconsistencies. Words are our perspectives, they're everything.

One thing that has become quite clear to me during my 30 years of counseling people from every social class and from most of the major cultures in the USA is that "we feel the way we feel because we think the way we think." This is the foundation of a paradigm (school of thought) in psychology called "existentialism." Existentialism suggests that we think the way we think based on how we define words and how we process symbols and events. The use of positive language creates positive attitudes and the use of negative language creates negative attitudes etc...

I suggest to you that the inaccurate processing of feelings due to misbegotten concepts and ill-contrived thought patterns have led to the majority of your emotional struggles; that the continuity of the self is modern humanity's greatest emotional and social struggle at this time.

More words than ever

Along with the expanding technology for communicating in modern society, words have become an even larger part of our existence; more than ever before. Thanks to texting, emails, digital books, streaming video and instant news media feeds

14

mankind is rarely left to his own thoughts. If they are not your thoughts occupying your mind then they are someone else's.

We have the thoughts of others in our heads more than ever before in the annals of human history. Oftentimes we don't even know what we think to the point that we confuse others thoughts and experiences with our own. We don't even know what we really feel because the time to process our experiences and the time to form our perspectives has been overrun by input.

Not only are there more words being thrown at us than ever before but there is also less time to process what we receive before we are pressured to respond. Think about this; people used to write letter and wait days and months for the response; all the while processing the exchange. People would have to wait until the end of the day to tell their partners what they were thinking or even months to tell their friends. Then we got home phones and we could do it daily usually at the end of the day. Then we invented home based answering machines where we got the messages about what someone else was thinking during their day at the end of our own day. Then we could retrieve these messages from any landline. Now we can't walk down the street or go pee without outside intrusions into our state of mind. There is no time to process our thoughts by ourselves so we lose ourselves. We are becoming a collective.

When these rapid intrusions occur, the rate of our response times are now interpreted as how much we care about the sender and even how nice or polite we are. This is a lot of emotional pressure and it is creating emotional baggage in the form of more co-dependency. Layer on top of these emotional pressures the need to respond "appropriately" in a digital format that is very limited in regards to expression and it's no wonder we get misperceived and that we are often misperceived as well. Processing data accurately has become much more vital to our

15

emotional stability than ever before and the quality of doing so has become much more limited.

As a therapist I have growing concerns that these bombardments of input, social censorships, pressure to comply within culture norms and the human desire to "fit in" robs people of both contentment and fulfillment. There is evidence to suggest that these types of repressions and even falsehoods create anxieties. These pressures and judgments may also contribute to some of the explosive social violence we see happening with increasing regularity. These violent outbursts are extreme and exaggerated rebellions against a society that demands conformity. This is the result of pressure and repression. When people aren't heard, when people are stifled and when people can't talk freely without the fear of potential or actual rejection they act out with often disproportional responses. "I'll show them; they'll hear me now! (BANG BANG!!)" Forget the guns for now; the real problem is failed human interaction.

Acquired "Cultural Repression Disorder" (CRuD)

Unfortunately, it has become so important to be accepted in modern culture that we are all too often willing to change who we really are to fit into select social groups and organizations. Many of us change who we are at work and call it being professional. Some people change how they really are when they meet a romantic prospect then wonder why things didn't work out.

Obviously there are motivations and benefits for restraining ourselves in different places, but is it worth the cost to our own self-concept? Some of the obvious costs are; our forthrightness, our genuineness, the expression of our individuality and perhaps, even more importantly, our authenticity. When we aren't authentic we feel that we are not known by others; we feel alone.

Maybe you don't think this happens to you? Have you ever been in a situation where someone assumed your political leanings, religious beliefs or cultural background and they then made a statement that you were supposed to support but actually didn't? Did you feel known then? Did you speak your mind and face conflict and retaliation or did you hold your tongue and feel as if you sold yourself out just a little? If this has occurred then you were peer-pressured into compliance. You changed who you were to avoid conflict. That is pacification.

Here is a stark cultural contrast to consider when it comes to originality and individuality reflected in daily life. Twenty years ago any two people who would show up for a social event in the same outfit would have been mortified and perhaps even teased. By contrast it's now actually become a common practice; it is now seen as a form of unity (uni-form-ity) when people all look the same. The two people with the current mindset don't realize that this action and the feelings related to it are in itself a subconscious lock step uniformity that screams "We are alike," that "It's good to be alike" and that "Being like everyone else is a positive thing." Actually, it's a little desperate.

These practices may also suggest that in some way peer pressure and judgment is eliminated because the individual is not required to stand on their own presentation and expression. While this uniformity may be a generational trend, it does not make it a healthy habit. It's a little too "lock step" for this author, yet few can deny that having the same fashion item as another is somehow vogue by today's standards. Names like Apple, Prada, BMW etc... in today's modern culture suggest some level of social status or success. Having the "right car" and living in the "right neighborhood" with the kids at the "right schools" is supposed to mean something. Scary! It means you bought in.

17

Why might this be occurring and what is the point of it? How about safety in numbers? You can judge me alone, but we won't let you judge all of us. The problem is that people don't just "want" to fit in, they "need" to. Mostly because it is too costly to stand out and go against the tide. If an Irishman shows up in a kilt to work he will be singled out. For that matter any man who shows up to work in a dress will be judged both positively and negatively. Most people in society today are afraid to stand out and be an individual because they are afraid of being outcast, judged and even targeted for ridicule. Ryan showing up for work in his kilt or dress might be warmly greeted but he is probably not going to be considered for the promotion in corporate America. These scenarios are a travesty of self-expression in the truest sense of the word. Being afraid to be "me" is a pacification of who we really are.

This tiny little example exemplifies the contagious nature of cultural repression. By not feeling free to be our true selves we remain unknown and sometimes even lonely in a crowd. The truth is that Ryan probably won't even mention that he wants to come to work in his kilt, let alone show up in it. This is repression.

People can only fake who they are for so long before they pay a price. Eventually they start experiencing resentment, depression, anxiety/panic attacks, and out-right mental breakdowns; they may possibly find themselves self-medicating with chemicals. These cultural dynamics may even suggest a possible reason why so many social events are now more and more centered around substance use than ever before in human history. Without the chemicals (medication) as a social lubricant, many of us might not feel comfortable with or be able to tolerate each other without the use of said chemicals. Perhaps chemical intoxication is the only avenue left for creating a common bond (using the chemical together) when no other commonality really exists or is truly known. This is not to suggest that chemical consumption isn't just people having fun but the fun is over when the chemical is required. (Don't worry, take another sip of your wine, a hit of the pipe or drag of the smoke and keep reading.)

I strongly urge you to consider that this form of repression is why some people may see it necessary to commit heinous acts of violence in social settings. There is a reason why they don't just shoot themselves? It's because they are mad at society and not themselves. No matter what you believe, we are seeing these reactionary explosive events of self in social settings more and more often. People are having dramatic meltdowns on video as they crack under the pressure of unrealistic and unproven ideological social norms. These acts of violence are getting more and more deadly every day; from suicide to murder or both. You see; if I can't fit into your social parameters and definitions of success then I have to battle against them. I must either comply or separate myself from you. If I don't, I will become irrelevant and unsuccessful. If you won't let my voice be heard then I have to shout louder! If you still won't hear me then I have to do something so big that it will make you pay attention. This happens every time a child gets bullied at school; an employee becomes an outcast at work or even when a college student is smarter than his or her professor.

The incubation of the Cultural Bully

There are groups of people in today's society that I have already referred to as "Cultural Bullies." Instead of wanting your lunch money these bullies want your submission to their ideals and you allegiance to their causes. These bullies may act alone but when they do they use the weight of the entire popular cultural to beat you down.

19

These cultural bullies are both loosely held-together groups of people and clearly identified social organizations. You might find them on the local playground or advertising their party's candidate for the coming election. They are groups of people who band together to pressure others through the use of topic polarization; suggesting that you must choose one side or the other of an issue. Obviously they want you to adopt and support their agendas; there are always agendas. But that is not enough! They also want you to become a champion for their causes, often suggesting that if you don't back them up then there is something wrong with you and that you are inhumane, ignorant, uncaring and hateful.

These groups of cultural bullies see it as fashionable to voice support in every and any way possible, be it t-shirts, bumper stickers or under-organized protests. They create impulsive time-limited opportunities to show your support that keep people from having too much time to think about it; the flash mob mentality. The cultural bully will often use unfriendly labels and hate speech to shame and coerce those who do not respond. They will say and do whatever is necessary to gain either your allegiance or your silence. This is cultural bullying.

Through the use of a technique called "polarization" they often force your choice. They malign unimportant issues with what only seem to be vital causes. They will seek your support on issues that you don't give a damn about then use your desire to be socially accepted into their social group as a prerequisite for allegiance; just like on the playground. "Are you pro-choice or pro-life?" They will always maintain that you are either with them or against them. They will proclaim your right to choose then take it away reporting that being neutral is a sign of consent to the opposition. This is coercion.

Just like the schoolyard bully, they need you do things their way; it's the only way they can feel secure about themselves and their beliefs. They want you to get in lock step with them and follow their directions. Once you show them your weakness, your so called "out of the box opinions" are history.

It is my theory that this "cultural bully" phenomenon is actually a type of social dysfunction brought on by a society that sees democracy as more than a form of government. They believe that what is right is determined by a majority consensus; that when most of the people agree that an ideology is not only right but that it is also somehow realistic. Consensus is the only proof they need. That is why facts annoy them.

Many people in the modern world believe with every fiber of their being that if the majority of people in a group agree on something that it must be correct and valid. That somehow logic and reality are a math equation that evolves out of a majority rule. Whoever has the most voters at the end not only wins the argument but has somehow been proven to be right. This is a perversion of democracy and an ill-fated use of consensus. Their belief is that; "Most of us think this way so you should too! You'll have to anyway when we make it the LAW because we have the votes." Scary! This is a form of Fascism.

Ever been in a place where the majority of people decide something is right or wrong (without data) simply because they outnumbered those who might see something different; perhaps even in regards to a looming catastrophe like Hurricane Katrina? As if, because they are larger in number and because "we all" agree that it somehow makes the belief accurate.

This conundrum has always puzzled me because most people believe that the MAJORITY of people are stupid. So yes, even dysfunction can become the new normal and eventually the law. Ever seen people rejoice and feel they were right because

21

the Supreme Court said so? Heck, why do we even need science. Just poll the audience!

I get that some of the above is funny when seen in the light of day, but the light of day is not where these bullies operate. Instead, their operations are covert (hidden). They often do their planning behind closed doors using the self-righteous justification that they know what is best for the rest of us. Believing they know better is the heart of progressivism and this self-righteousness is not reserved for any one political party. For the most part progressives will figure out your needs without asking you and then give you a solution you didn't want. (I told you I would either challenge your thinking or validate it.) The problem is not their solutions as much as it is their methods. Before they advocate for a solution they should determine what problems those solutions will create.

In a somewhat dastardly fashion these bully groups are actually taking advantage of the yearning and even the need that many people in today's society have to be accepted, to fit in and to be relevant. Cultural Bullies only embrace individuals who share their sentiments and, in a very cult like manner, they ostracize the people who don't agree; usually beginning with personal attacks like: "You're stupid, you're a racist, a sexist, a homophobe, you're a religious nut, an atheist, a commie, etc..." Because people don't want to be called these names they suspend their objections. This is pacification at the hand of a bully!

THE ECHO CHAMBER
I think I heard that before

The above described groups known now as "cultural bullies" can only thrive in a vacuum. In order for them to make their ideologies seem feasible they develop "safe zones." (Heard that term lately?) These "safe zones" are not safe for you; they are safe for their ideology. These "safe zones" are a place for their

22

unchallenged ideas to fester. These incubators for baby ideologues are known by many sociologists as "echo chambers." This is a figurative place where the only voices that will be spoken and heard openly are the voices of people who perpetuate the same party lines. The only people the echo chamber's inhabitants ever hear from are the voices of those people who think like they do and subscribe to their same belief systems.

In these "echo chambers" ideas are safe from challenge and reality. It is a place where favored notions are enhanced and never refuted. Ideologues enjoy these chambers for the faux validation they receive as people of like mind regurgitate exaggerated and unsubstantiated notions of utopia. (Like a cult.)

In this safe place, the Echo Chamber ideals can be championed without scrutiny. The application of critical thought is never applied. The echo chamber is "in the Box" thinking personified. By operating in the dark quarantine of the chamber ideas are safe from challenge and doubt. They are safe from the light of scrutiny. In the chamber these ideological pathogens can fester in the minds of its inhabitants until an immunity to counter perspectives can be developed. Their seclusion allows the indoctrination process to fully develop as its carriers prepare to spread their agenda outward. In the chamber the birthing of the pseudo intellectual develops and they are raised up to be self righteous cultural bullies.

In essence these chambers allow for a foundation of thought to solidify before ever being tested or proven. Since there is no dissent in the chamber, there is no doubt, only validation. It is comparable to science without research; nothing but theory and no way to be proven wrong. Ironically enough the ideals that develop in the chamber become beliefs before they can even be improved upon. It's like bad cement made without all the right elements and proportions. It may seem strong but when the realities of the world and life itself apply pressure the notions crumble. These untested ideas often fail in catastrophic ways for the individual naive enough to have been co-opted into the cult structure.

The chamber allows for half baked ideas to seem very solid. The residents of the chamber are able to seemingly strengthen their resolve in regards to their beliefs simply by the support and validation they receive from other members. This lack of scrutiny is what makes them "feel" overly righteous in their beliefs. The pathetic part is that it makes them feel more intelligent and more informed then they are. The truth is that their quarantine has denied them the real growth potential of their ideas, the strength that scrutiny might have contributed. In science an idea must be tested and validated; most often by people who don't believe in the theory. The echo chamber guards against these counter perspectives just like a cult.

Politically, the chamber is a way to protect the party line and a major reason why cults of all kind separate themselves from the ideas of others. (Next time you watch a National Party Convention step back and just watch the members swirl in their little chamber of self righteousness.) Outside influences are very carefully vetted to make sure they will not "contaminate" the chamber with conflicting information. (Next time you're in a conversation about politics or on a college campus step back and just watch the members play out their mental masturbations of self reassurance.) Perhaps you'll see this occur at your job. In many of these groups there is a vetting process for those who are allowed to speak. The approval process is not a way to determine experience; the process is only concerned in proving that participants are "Like Minded."

The chamber is a means of preserving the self-deception of the inhabitants. These "Echo Chambers" are a serious

24

intellectual problem in the world today. The Wiki defines the media version of the echo chamber as follows: "an echo chamber is a situation in which information, ideas, or beliefs are amplified or reinforced by transmission and repetition inside an "enclosed" system, where different or competing views are censored, disallowed or otherwise underrepresented." I hope that this definition scares you a little but I'd rather it disturb you.

The concept of the echo chamber was originally popularized in the late 90's but due to the media's complicity in the problem they have squashed the insight lest they be found out. These echo chambers are overly represented in our modern lives. They are becoming a major problem for any group with opposing insights. Ideological clashes are now growing in number due to the increased frequency of social exchanges now taking place. The chamber has become too large to vet the inhabitants and they are now being confronted with the impossibility of their own delusions.

As alluded to above, the two most favored breeding grounds for the echo chamber are the college campus and the mainstream media on both sides. Large exposure or the "number of views" is not necessary; as the chamber also exists in the form of letters, emails, texting, page posts, word of mouth and good old fashioned leaflet propaganda. If one group were to control a country's information and data, the entire country could very easily become a Petri dish of these untested contagions.

The Echo Chamber is a form of mental and emotional segregation. Its existence weakens the notion of individuality to the point of irrelevance: It is socialistic. A brief example might be a group of people who claim to be racially tolerant yet live in a guarded and gated community where they restrict who can enter and even who might be able to live there. The community organization is a place where tolerance works unless you are on their undesirable list. People in these communities may even believe that there is less crime than is reported because they are not subjected to real world threats. No one in the community would suggest the locked gate is a form of segregation. The people living in that type of community may have even convinced themselves that they have no racial bias, yet they are quick to lock their car doors when they leave their compounds.

The darker side

I want to be clear here that these Echo Chamber groups can also be very extreme organizations ranging from the KKK to ISIS. Yes even terrorist groups operate in an echo chamber, they must. Their segregation is how they can come to believe such insane notions like modern day Jihad and that beheadings are beneficial to their cause. Their echo chambers have allowed them to remain 1500 years in the past! In fact these terrorist cults are a perfect example of how to get a group of people to follow you "blindly." Cut your members off from all media except your own, use intimidation, burn the other peoples' books, kill anyone who voices a contrary opinion or theory and repeat your ideology over and over again. Demand that your members repeat your ideology from memory or DIE! (Sound familiar?) Reward compliance and suggest a moral high ground or eternal place for the righteous in this life and the next. (Not sure how 72 virgins is paradise, but that is what they have been sold and that is what they have bought.)

Adjust the gain

Perhaps the scariest thing about these echo chamber groups is that once a person is ac-"cult"-urated into the group the newly embraced "groupie" experiences acceptance and regular validation for their allegiance and subjectification. From a behavioral standpoint this a reward process that continually reinforces allegiance; constantly strengthening the bond. This

26

behavioral conditioning becomes subconscious, meaning that the conditioned subject does not have to be conscious of their shift in loyalty or belief. Subjects of the chamber who start pressuring others to join the club or to get in lock step are venerated and moved to a higher level in the group's status. This creates a competition to convince and convert: A human pyramid scheme. This is the very same mechanism in place in the major political parties in the U.S. and elsewhere.

For all these reasons I use the term "Cult-ural Bullies." It is a cult like culture that is developing in the mainstream of America right now; right in front of your eyes. Today's internet trolls are the modern version of how cultish groups of the past spread their agendas. They are the same cult groupies that once lined airport terminals around the world and knocked on your front door. Now they man computer terminals where they push their beliefs from their mother's sofas all the way to the halls of justice. They peck at large groups looking to find unsure travelers whose only desire is to feel a part of something good and right.

In a cult-like fashion, some of these modern day cultural groups even require your financial commitment to prove you really support them; sometimes before you are allowed to enter the chamber. This coercion phenomenon is both a byproduct and end product of a democratic socialistic ideology where the group is more important than the individual. This is the opposite of what a free country is founded upon.

These cultural bully groups are in your life right now and you often enter their echo chambers without knowing it. You know you're in one when suddenly you are harshly criticized for a statement that seems honest, forthright or middle of the road. Facts and reality are usually a shock to the inhabitant's systems so they respond with a "fight or flight" type of panic reaction.

They use harsh language and labeling to make you feel bad for the way you think about a subject (sometimes just because you think).

The inhabitants of the echo chamber are not used to people who don't agree with them and they will see your disagreement as rude. They will interpret your challenge to their beliefs as you personally attacking them. When you are not in concert with their agendas, they attack you to protect their fragile emotionally-based beliefs which have been previously untested and unchallenged. They name-call, use personal attribute attacks, emotional segregation, emotional abandonment and, when they lose the logic argument based on facts they quickly brand anyone in disagreement with unrealistic and even irrational maxims. Their natural reflex is to see you as the "stupid one" because you don't agree with all the other people in their chambers. They can rarely stand alone. They cast you out of their little world, out of their echo chamber and un-friend you; not to get rid of you, but to protect their ideology. After their inner-sanctum is breached, they then quickly huddle together in their little covens and attack you when you are not there because they can't defend their ideology with logic. They create a consensus judgment of you and because there are no objections to their rants, they see themselves as the righteous victors. Does any of this seem familiar?

Is it clique-ing yet?

When I was a child they had another name for homogenized groups like the above; a name which seems to have been conveniently removed from the popular social lexicon; they were called "cliques!" A group of kids bullying a single child on the playground are a clique. They are most certainly a group of bullies with a clearly defined culture.

28

I would like to point out that no cult has ever developed without first being a clique or without having an echo chamber. Two of the largest cliques in American society today are the Democratic and Republican parties. Are you a member? No! Libertarian or an "Independent" maybe? Why? Because the other ones are so ------ (Insert hate speech maxim here).

You're being manipulated by their all or nothing language; by words that polarize and even by mild forms of coercion (if you're not with us you're uncaring or stupid). All the various sides of today's media are complicit in the formation of these groups. Every boardroom and conference room is a smaller version of an echo chamber; the more secret it is, the more cultish and the more intellectually limited.

Helping you resolve these manipulations and pressures for your own clarity is a major goal of this book and a hope of this author. I really don't care what side you are on. I prefer you be an individual and have no side at all, but unfortunately siding up is an act of human nature (explained later). I want you to give these groups the one thing that scares them the most; your right to your free speech and your original thinking without being afraid of their phony childish reprisals. I want to emancipate you from their bondage and control.

POLITICAL CORRECTNESS
The freedom of repression

If you live in the modern world, then the PC populace/police have already imprisoned your heart, your soul and your mind. The repetition of ideology that you have been exposed to by the media alone has tainted your vision. More specifically it has sterilized you of original thought and freed you from your freedom of expression; at least that's their plan.

The modern world we live in is an era of time where it is easier to be a victim than to stand up and call BS. You are not

29

weaker then you were ten years ago, but there is a side of you that thinks maybe there is nothing you can do. Somehow that impotent little voice inside us has convinced us that there is an easier way to live and that going along with the flow will help us avoid conflict and disharmony. I assure you that an easier softer way does not exist. Their visions of utopia just may have clouded our judgment.

We have been limited, but not just by forces outside of us, we have also been limited by our own lack of willingness and our acquiescence to the narrow visions of losers and lazy people who are not willing to exert the effort required or to spend the personal capital necessary, to challenge the status quo. The good news is that this is not our fault but we have been swept up in the current and are now having to choose to either ride that current of the masses or find our way to shore in order to walk it off.

Answer this simple question: Is it more comfortable to be around people who think like you or be around people who will outright disagree with you? It's obvious, right? We live in a world where potential discomfort is avoided at all costs. I guess you can call it a form of intellectual laziness, but it is actually emotional avoidance.

Let's use a big "no-no" topic (because we're not wimps) to examine the negative impact of political correctness. Let's use the concepts of Global Warming and Climate Change. Ever notice how most, perhaps all of your friends think the way that you do on such an issue? No? Some see it differently? If so, then I bet you all don't talk about it much or that you try to avoid the subject or keep it brief, right? This silence is the end-state desired by the keepers of the Echo Chambers and the creators of unrealistic ideologies. In the chamber, supposed truths are refined and barriers are built to guard against any proofs that might invalidate their ideology. There is no proof of man-made climate change either way. We eventually avoid the counter arguments that might change our minds and we end up choosing our connection to people over truth and common sense. This is how we self-deceive.

This isolationism is an attempt to reduce anxiety and be safe and secure; it's human nature. Before the global warming scare, talk about the weather was a safe subject, the safest. Let's take some time to learn a little about why we are predisposed to avoid conflict. You see, there is a little thing called "stress" that we are conditioned to avoid. Eons ago, we either ran or fought when we were stressed or threatened; now we ignore, run and avoid.

So let's talk global warming; or, wait it's not called that any more, now it's called climate change? It used to be called the weather. One Echo Chamber says man is the cause. Contrary to the left view of the right, the right does not deny climate change; it only doubts that man is responsible or that he is able to control it. Most believe it is a long-duration natural cycle.

I'm not going to attempt to give you a science lesson and I am not going to try to convince you either way. I am only using the topic because it is the favorite of the polarizing powers in control of information. We all know about the "Carbon Footprint." Simply put it is the amount of carbon dioxide and other carbon compounds emitted due to the consumption of fossil fuels by a particular person, group, etc. The claim of the alarmists is that we are making the Earth's levels of carbon dioxide (and other compounds) in the atmosphere too high.

Right now the CO2 levels are about 400 ppm (parts per mil) up from 275ppm 100,000 years ago, before the industrial revolution. That is a 32% rise. When the global alarmists show you graphs to support their ideology, they go back about 80 thousand years and according to their own numbers there were regular spikes every 100,000 years. In their numbers, they show

31

the current level in a group that includes evidence from more than the past 1000 years. We have to admit that it sounds pretty significant when you look at it that way.

Did you know that before homosapians (mankind) the levels of carbon were much higher. No, they didn't tell you? Well I will. Atmospheric CO_2 levels reached spectacular values in the past, possibly topping over 5000 ppm in the late Ordovician Era (around 440 million years ago). That is more than 12 times higher than it is now. (No humans were involved in the making of these events.) I could argue that it has decreased since man became involved but I would have no evidence, only ideology.

In the early Phanerozoic era (540 million years ago) solar output (heat from the sun) was about 4% less than current levels. What this means is that the sun has been heating up. The Pleistocene Epoch is typically defined as the time period that began about 1.8 million years ago and lasted until about 11,700 years ago. The most recent Ice Age occurred then. Yep, it was only 12,000 years ago that glaciers covered huge parts of the planet Earth. We didn't have cars, yet the planet was warming much faster than it is now. There were glaciers in New York City. Maybe they are shrinking or just shifting to other parts of the planet now, but there is no actual proof that man is the cause. Here is a secret they don't want you to think about. If the sun warms up, so will everything in our Universe. Nothing that you can try will ever affect the sun's output. They talk about solar flares like we did it somehow; that is just arrogance and trickery.

People will believe what they want to believe but, more often than not, people are being connived to "want to believe" things that they have no real investment in. As a therapist I think it is a little egotistical and controlling of man to think that he can affect nature on this level. If the sun heats up the planet will too. The ozone has been in much worse shape in the past. When the

32

sun cools down cyclically it will take many years for the Earth to cool back down so the cycles won't match. It works just like the water in your swimming pool, local lake or ocean.

Despite all this climate change over the past Billion years the Earth has recovered without our help, without our permission and without our knowledge. Why have you been made to care about this? Because it polarizes people and puts their fear (emotions) over their logic. If you think its true then you become a liberal and you must therefore vote left. If you vote for free enterprise you vote against the Earth (NOT). This is intellectual polarization and the forced forming of sides. Thus you vote their way. It's an intellectual slight of hand.

The indoctrination hype

We teach our children not to fall prey to peer pressure but then we are forced to pay for a school system that forces our children to believe one-sided principles and ideologies that are most often favorable to the government's agendas. The education system in every developed country reinforces compliance to the party line with good grades and the prospect of a rewarding career. If a dissenting student doesn't comply with their agenda or doesn't go along with the assimilation process, they are cast out into the supposed dread of future failure. "If you don't think like us you're stupid or bad and you will never be happy." I know that is very simplistic but, like it or not, that is essentially how our children are programmed and conditioned. Sounds like a bully tactic right?

If you choose not to go along in the modern world you are called a rebel. This tactic is called Social Emotional Isolation, or abandonment and it is an attempt to coerce a person to comply or be cast out. This is the reason why today's small government Southerners are always seen as rebels; they were cast out of the system by the system, because they disagreed.

33

Your own indoctrination began when you were just a child. When you were born your family probably had a political leaning and they taught you to lean in the same direction; that's indoctrination. When you were able to watch TV or listen to the radio, you were experiencing the agenda of the media station executives. When you went to school you were taught what the government regulators deemed as "need-to-know information." You were told it, had it repeated to you, were forced to read it and then you were tested on it to prove your indoctrination was thorough. Finally, you were rewarded with a nice piece of paper showing your social prowess and compliance. (More later)

PROPAGANDA

We'll tell you what you need to know

Remember the Nazis? I'm sure that you remember the sociopath named Hitler but do you also know the name Joseph Goebbels (pronounced ger-buls)? If you're Jewish, you do. He was considered by many to be the most influential man in Germany, possibly even more than Hitler himself. He was considered the architect of the entire thought process that engulfed Germany and much of Europe during that time.

Do you know what his job title was? Many people think he was a soldier but his role was not even military. He was the Reich Minister of Propaganda. Did you know that? That wasn't one of his titles, that was his only title. He was the spin-doctor for the entire Nazi party and movement. He was the press secretary for Hitler and Nazi Germany. He made the man whose designs damn near destroyed the world.

Goebbels was an evil genius when it comes to propaganda. In case you don't know, propaganda is the control of information, especially of a biased or misleading nature, used to promote or publicize a particular political cause or point of view. It is also the withholding of information by providing only information

34

that molds the perception in the target audience in a favorable way, so that it reinforces an ideology. The control of information made the Nazi Party and all of its atrocities possible.

I want you to think seriously here for a second. Who controls the information where you live and work? Is it Facebook, your local TV news, the mainstream media or do you get information emailed or sent to you that is "tailored" to your way of thinking? If you do, then there is no way you are getting the full story because these information outlets have no legal responsibility to provide you all the data.

If it has an editor it has a bias; either minor or extreme but it has a bias. When we had no media we didn't have the problems of left or right leaning information because the only information we needed to know then was how to survive and take care of our basic needs. Now we live in the modern world where either we educate ourselves and our children or someone else does it for us. Passive learning is not leaning. It is indoctrination.

I will expand on these issues in the coming chapters. I will teach you how to clarify your vision and perspective, even how to avoid becoming self-deceived by the human desire to believe what you want to believe. I will show you how to avoid believing what has been prepared for you in order to meet someone else's needs and designs. Prepare yourself; some of the topics we will discuss will be hard to digest at first because you have been conditioned not to discuss them. You might even want to take a break from the book now and go listen to or read some of that specially seasoned news and opinion. I promise that you will now start seeing the slanted and one-sided perspectives being presented for you.

Chapter Two

TRUTH: THE SOCIAL ANTIDOTE

Words about feelings

Due to the role that the truth and reality play in the remedy for confusion, there will be no apologies for words or terms discussed in the remainder of this book. I have become immune to intimidation tactics and I will not be coerced by talking points or party lines. The reason that party lines exist are to warn you of your pending ouster if you cross them. It's the party's guide for keeping you in LINE.

Write me if you like but don't bother complaining to me. I won't join your cult or your echo chamber because they're way too crowded and they don't make practical or logical sense. I'm an individual. If you need to whine call your mother or your cult leader instead. I'm sure they'll listen and then tell you exactly what to think and what to do.

I will provide only as much clarification for my points as "I" deem necessary to make "MY" points. I am not trying to start a cult. If you think I should have said something differently; write a book. Maybe I'll write another one for you later or maybe I already have. I've written some great stuff on denial and self-deception.

Right about now you're either seriously judging me or cheering me on based on a couple of thousand words. Do you like me? No matter! If you don't like me, ask yourself why you are so threatened by another person's free expression. I'll tell you why, because the people who want us all to be polarized (on one side or the other) have conditioned you into choosing sides; usually quicker than you should. They like snap judgments because their ideals don't stand the test of time.

With all that being said, I have been and will be, painstaking in my word choices but I will also be freely expressing myself in hopes of empowering you to do the same. If you're confused or uncertain use a dictionary; something the cultural bullies never do because they like having their own definitions. Looking up the words that I use will aid in your understanding of my points. As a therapist my words have always been carefully chosen for impression, accuracy and intent. I am trying to give you my perspective not make my perspective your perspective. If we agree and you have increased clarity then great; pass it on!

Taboo topics

As we proceed there will be language and subject matter that you may have been conditioned to believe is harsh, hateful or even taboo. I've been a therapist for 3 decades and a yogi for more than 10 years (at the writing of this book). I promise you that there is very little hate in me and that the little bit of dislike remaining is reserved strictly for those who steal innocence and manipulate with lies. There will be frank and direct discussion about social and emotional truths that may feel awkward at first. I encourage you to explore why these awkward/taboo feelings have presented in you and to then figure out who programmed you to react so dramatically to them. Trust me when I say with 100% conviction, it is never bad to think critically about issues, not even the ones I raise. It can however, be unhealthy to be critical of people and or things you don't fully understand. That is "contempt prior to investigation" (William Paley).

If you can't handle straightforward truth and open discussion then I suggest you stop now and go buy a book from the fiction section. The truth will set you free and I will probably piss some of you off. If you can't handle uncomfortable words or having your notions challenged then you can't handle the truth. If you can't handle words then life is going to kick your butt if it hasn't already.

If you've been caught up in an echo chamber or even if you've been a cultural bully yourself in the past no worry. We all have; that's how they win. You may even feel anxious or be afraid of what improved insight might mean to your world view. GOOD! I promise the world won't spin any different because you change your mind on an issue. People will still assume they know what you think.

It's better to build a strong logical foundation now than have it crumble when you least expect it. If you live a life where you try to insulate yourself from uncomfortable words and ideas then you live a life where you have been insulating yourself from the truth and reality too. You may be living in an echo chamber; maybe I can show you a way out. If you stay in that chamber you will undoubtedly one day find yourself lying to some therapist; telling them what you think they need to know. Trust me, I'm a clinical professional with decades of experience and a license to prove it; inconsistencies of thought create anxiety and depression; sometimes even worse.

Political Science

Ever wonder about the term political science? It basically suggests that they have figured out how to co-opt you into their way of thinking. They have figured out the science of how to infect you with their ideology. Since "political correctness" is an invention of the political structure and their ideologues, some of your political views may be challenged but I promise not to do what they do and box you into one perspective or another. Please don't do that to me! No matter what happens during this discourse your remaining votes will be more freely cast.

I won't tell you what I am politically because I am me, I'm not a little box label. By nature neither are you, not really. I am not this or that. Neither are you. Like many others I may vote a certain way but that is only because I am usually voting against something that I consider more a dangerous threat to freedom. Don't waste your time trying to figure me out because I reserve the right to change my mind without notice. That is freedom and that is something I cherish. The freedom to change your mind is something the cult leaders don't want you to be too invested in.

There will be no placating here and being able to speak directly to the subject matter is crucial. This book will make you think and rethink and that is all I am really trying to achieve. You see, I want you to have your thoughts, not someone else's.

Pacification

The word "Pacification" is indeed what we speak of when we reference the changing of oneself to fit the rules, whims, insecurities and fancies of others. I did not coin the phrase or invent this term but I have given some amplification and specific context to its modern day meaning. Merriam Webster defines PACIFICATION as: "the act or process of pacifying: the state of being pacified and the act of forcibly suppressing or eliminating a population considered to be hostile." Basically the last aspect of the word is suggesting that a person or population can be stifled by oppression or even violence; not just quieting them but eliminating their voice. This is the same coercion that created the "Silent Majority."

Being manipulated into being pacifistic is a form of oppression and even abuse. The title chosen for this book clearly represents our current societal and personal struggles with intrapersonal communication (that is the voice we use to talk to ourselves). We are so afraid of being rejected, targeted, ostracized or just made uncomfortable that we have begun to use avoidance of a problem as a way of solving the problem. It doesn't solve it. Avoidance may temporarily reduce current anxiety but the contagion only festers when it is not treated. Just like an infection.

Modern society has begun to generate personal discomfort at the mere potential of becoming uncomfortable later. I'll say that again, "We become uncomfortable before we actually are uncomfortable." We become uncomfortable because we might be uncomfortable later. We worry too much about how a possible occurrence might make us feel later. We suffer now, before it has even occurred only to suffer again IF it happens. Preemptive suffering has never changed an event that might occur later and it does not spare us later suffering.

When we don't confront a person we believe to be wrong and we "let them believe" that they are right we are, through our silence, consenting to their point of view or their act. Yes, we should choose our battles wisely but this mindset does not suggest that we won't have any battles.

When we keep our opinions to ourselves to avoid conflict and confrontation we may actually be afraid that our own notions won't stand the test of a challenge or the scrutiny of a back and forth debate. This is how we remain ignorant and self-deceived. Our viewpoints are formed and sharpened by scrutiny and debate. This is how we learn. Practice makes better.

Being afraid and avoidant are both aspects of pacification. We become pacifistic when we accept what others demand even if we don't like it or believe it. While often guised in the delusion that we are being nice, being too pacifistic is unhealthy for the human psyche. We need balance. Repressing ourselves or allowing ourselves to be repressed, is a formula for emotional illness. Sigmund Freud, the father of modern psychology believed repression to be one of the major causes of our most deep-seated emotional problems.

The above apprehensions we have are not heartfelt feelings, they are actually cognitive in nature. Recall the early phrase credited to the Existentialists; "We feel the way we feel because we THINK the way we think." These future based feelings are not real feelings but are instead an anticipation (thought) of "potential discomfort." They only bother us because we think they do, because we are afraid of being uncomfortable later.

Somehow we have developed a societal norm that suggests that no one should have their feathers ruffled or be made to face unpleasant truths in public. Certain cultural groups have suggested (without evidence) that the world would be a better place if confrontation and discomfort were outlawed. Some ideologues believe that we would all get along better if we just didn't talk about difficult things; real things. That is very convenient for people who don't want to be challenged.

Directly related to these ridiculous notions is a new emotional illness that has evolved. This new illness is brought on by the "anti-discomfort police" who are now infecting us with a new set of anxieties centered around the above referenced "potential inconveniences." This is a fear that we may be uncomfortable later so it is better to be uncomfortable now. This is lunacy! We must speak out against lunacy but only when we are actually experiencing it. When we feel an illusionary event that hasn't happened yet, we feel it for nothing. We make it real when it might not have ever occurred. The really crazy thing is that what we fear occurring may actually be a resolution to an ongoing dilemma. Avoidance brought on by pacification is an attempt to control without resistance; it is core political science.

The more we try to avoid potential discomfort the more anxiety ridden we become. It is a vicious cycle. It is actually less costly emotionally if we deal with problems as they occur, not before.

A battered wife is pacifistic in her current nature and that pacification keeps her in danger. We suffer greater emotional torment and a greater loss of self-respect when we avoid important and necessary action. The pacification of humanity presents in many ways. We can resolve it if we are willing to face some harsh realities.

Self-concept suffers when we don't stand up for what we know is right. It is healthier to just deal with the real fallout here and now; to avoid living in apprehension. It is healthier to assert ourselves and let the bullies know that we aren't going to sit back passively and allow their foolish rule to continue. Assertiveness is a lost art but it exists inside of you right now. It always has.

Just to be clear here, most of the pre-suffering we do is completely unnecessary because the things we worry about the most rarely occur. We often look back and ponder; "I felt all that for nothing, what I was worried about never even happened, what is wrong with me." This is needless and costly self-talk.

When I work with people with major anxiety and panic disorders I ask them this simple set of questions. What do you fear the most? "Heart attack," "losing control" or "dying," they say. Then I ask "Has that ever happened?" "No" they say. They seem quite shocked at the realization that the feared event has never occurred. This is False Evidence Appears Real (F.E.A.R.).

I am going to attempt to show you how to heal from all this confusion and misdirection. It can be done alone but for some of you it may require help from an outside source. No matter how you achieve it, resolving these missteps and confronting the things you've avoided is essential if you want to be happy and whole.

Chapter Three

TIME TO CHANGE THE WORLD

Your world first

We may not be able to change the world single handedly but we can change our world all by ourselves. You can start repairing your perspectives today. You start by refusing to live from someone else's limited view of the world and by using your own eyes to see as well as your own mind to think. You purposefully look for both the bad in the good and the good in the bad. Open-mindedness is the key to emotional liberation and to a reduction in anxiety. Being judgmental is Judge-Mental.

We have to change this overly sterilized and overly sensitized world we live in back into something more realistic. We need to get REAL about the world we actually live in and stop trying to pretend that bad things and discomfort aren't real and that pain can somehow be avoided. This is a real world where people will always starve and freeze to death. It's a world where blacks do hate whites, where some people hate gays and where some gays hate heterosexuals. This is a world where; people get beat up trying to save someone, where people get murdered by the people they love, get raped by their parents, run over by drunk drivers, experience domestic violence, get beheaded by hatred cults, drown in floods, get blown up and even get bullied into being people they are not. Welcome to reality! Trying to pretend these problems aren't real does not make them go away. It fact it actually leaves us underprepared and ill-equipped when these difficulties really do arise. The little boy whistling in the dark routine is no longer working.

Some of things we worry about are real but many are not. Many of the things we don't think about are problems that need attention. Many of the things we do think about are a waste of energy. An example: It is true that many black people from urban areas would feel worried if they had to walk down a dark country road at night. So would white people. The real truth is that most country folks would just see if you needed help and give you a ride where you needed to go. What is real is that there are hundreds of streets in America today that a white person cannot walk down without being victimized. These are just examples of how limited our perspectives can be.

There are positives and problems with both of the above circumstances but they are reality nonetheless. Ideology that people shouldn't "fear or hate," does not change what is in the hearts of man and neither does legislation against hate or speech. Thinking you can stop hatred by the use of a law is foolish. You can't outlaw emotional reactions; you can't make hate illegal any more than you can make love a requirement. In the real world people do horrible things to one another; they always have and they always will. Pretending that everyone loves one another will not keep you safe. Ideology of how things SHOULD BE won't keep you from harm no matter how good it sounds. This is one way ideology fails; how it can be potentially more harmful.

In a strange way, much like in the world of immunology, avoidance and lack of exposure to pathogens actually makes the system less resilient. Repression and the avoidance of real life dynamics actually makes them more disheartening when they do occur. It is said that acceptance is the answer to all our problems because once we accept something we transcend it. This is where words, definitions and perspectives really begin to matter. You see, you have to accept what is but it doesn't mean that you can't change things. Change is in fact, a constant in the

Universe: The problem is that man might not have the best plans for how things should occur.

Changing your environment

Before we start changing our world we have to determine what is real in our worlds, what is possible and what is not. We will become unsettled and uneasy if we continue to believe that mankind can be a way that he has never been. While world peace may be possible, it is unlikely since there is no proof that it has ever existed. Had there ever been peace on Earth we could have a reference to work from, but there has always been violence in both man and animal. Peace on Earth is an unrealistic ideology that only leaves us frustrated and annoyed.

We can become emotionally upset and ill if our ideology gets smacked in the face by reality. If we think that another race doesn't hate us and we experience a hate crime firsthand, the shock of it can cause life long suffering like, PTSD. The emotional trauma of such an event (PTSD) is hard to overcome. We are actually shocked by truth when our ideology fails us.

A man walking down a street trying to avoid harm is less surprised and upset than the person who foolishly thought he was safe. This is not being worried about things that may never happen, this is protecting oneself from reality and harm. The awareness of reality (not ideology,) allows us to take precautions to protect ourselves from experiencing harm. It is evidence based. We live on planet Earth, not on planet "If," Earth not "If."

I am not suggesting that you start by being paranoid, only that you start by not being stupid or delusional because someone told you that Utopia exists in some safe zone. This does not mean you should be afraid, it means you need to be wise and realistic. The man walking down the street did not make the unfortunate event occur but he did take the risk. If you're black you might not presume that everyone in a room of mostly white

47

people will like you but a mature black man in a room of black people doesn't think everyone there likes him either. His perception is that there is a difference in a room of white people because they are white people. This is racial stereotyping on his part. In fact, there is usually more dislike in a room of one race (any race) then in a room of two or more. Words, definitions and perspectives. As I mentioned, my goal is to broaden your perspectives with doses of awareness, reality and perspective.

We are going to use the issue of race more later on but I have one last perspective for now. There is a PC (politically correct) cultural expectation that if a white person hates one black person they are racist. Think seriously about this if you are black. Why is there an expectation that white people must like all black people or be racist, but then all black people don't like all black people either; what are they called?

The PC culture and the Cultural Bullies suggest that people aren't allowed to rightfully judge a man, as Martin Luther King said; "on the content of his character." Excuse me, but if you're a jerk I'm not going to like you. In fact, it would be racial bias if I treated you differently (even favorable) because you are of a certain race. We'll examine some of these issues more in later sections because hatred, bigotry, race, gender and socio-economic issues are our major social stumbling blocks in the modern world. These issues have always been at the heart of society's struggles and always will be. Only in some fantasy world built on ideology is there extinction thought possible. These issues of division and polarization will always be with us because they are valued commodities for the power brokers.

Passive inaction

Passivity and inaction will not change the world. In fact inaction only allows negative emotion and momentum to increase because there is nothing to slow it down. I can promise

48

you this: The world won't change if you don't start demanding something different; if you don't start being different. It won't change at all if you don't change how you operate. The world won't become anything different if you don't start responding differently to it. You must begin by demanding authenticity no matter how ugly it is. Speak truth to lies and be genuine to the people around you and you will always be true to yourself.

Resistance

There will be resistance. The shift in the presentation of self that I am suggesting is not an easy task but you will feel more secure in yourself and your relational dynamics once you start the process. You will feel more genuine and authentic, almost immediately. As a therapist, I can tell you that these changes are not only possible but they will be the greatest gifts you can give yourself or anyone in your life.

To stop the lies and take off the masks ordered by the cultural bullies is very emancipating and it is the beginning of any true source of personal freedom. If you want to be a gay conservative or religious liberal, if you want to be pro-choice conservative or pro-life liberal, be it. I support you but it means nothing if you don't stand up for yourself. You are not required to pick a side. You can be the resistance that stops tyranny. Know that many people have died for your right to choose without coercion, pressure or retaliation. This change process may even help you find out who your real friends are.

Sitting in your chair right now you will begin to feel the difference if you make the decision to be more real and authentic from this point forward. The truth is that because so many other people won't have this information, they will most likely respond more passively to your pushback. They may even compliment your increased assertiveness. They may be surprised at first

49

because they are suffering with the same confusion and lack of social confidence that you are struggling with; share this book.

Once other people see the options available they will actually begin to follow you because you have given them a choice just by your choosing. If you do not plan to speak up and speak out then you can't complain later when nothing changes or when things have gotten worse. I'm not sorry I ruined your comfort zone and you won't be either.

Even with your new attitudes and your new perspectives, there will still be resistance. There have always been bullies and there always will be. Ideology won't disappear because you shine light on it. In fact you may see the real people behind the masks once you take yours off. What we need to do is learn how to navigate through these lost people in intelligent ways. Simple responses to remember when faced with the bullies: "I'm OK with us not agreeing" or "I don't think that way any longer." They work great and are very effective. Even; "I'm changing and trying out something new" or "I'm no longer restricting myself to little talking point boxes."

When you start making these changes you will really notice the bullying. If they bully you, just remind them that tolerance only exists when we disagree and that tolerance cannot exist when we do agree. Then ask them if they are tolerant of your differences (THEY HATE THAT). Remind them that none of us "know what we don't know." Taking the equilibrium away from a bully is quite effective and even therapeutic at times. If they resort to name calling then you just found out how they really are. It might be worth the risk.

Getting faux real

We live in a real world where people fail and people win, where your kid might actually be intellectually slow and physically uncoordinated or even unattractive. Your kid may suck at a sport and if he does he shouldn't get a trophy or an award. These are the REAL problems and once we focus on the real ones the faux problems fade away. The faux problems are usually just an untimely distraction from the important things in life. Faux problems are usually the things that other people want us to put our energy into, usually for their agendas.

Ideologues of all types love to create distractions. They use these distractions to take you off the important subjects and fill your mind with nuisance considerations that you only kind-of care about. Some people call this "intellectualization." Here is an example; I was once talking to a felon about his drug crimes in Maryland only to have him begin mentioning other states like California where federal drug laws aren't enforced. He seemed to get distracted from the reality that he still broke a MD law while in MD and that the laws in California are irrelevant. In his head he still used this erroneous comparison to distract himself from his MD violation as if "ideologically/theoretically" it wasn't a real crime; that he was somehow a victim of the system.

People who purposefully use these types of mind games, like intellectualization, are quite unhealthy people to be close to. They are usually extremely manipulative and deceitful. The ones who don't know they're doing it are just lost. "Intellectualization" is the use of another subject they have facts about to suggest that somehow they have credibility for their argument on a different issue. Sometimes this is reflexive and even sub-conscious. This defocusing often happens because phony people have a hard time with people who talk about real things. Their lack of self-esteem and personal responsibility requires that they maintain their victim status so they are always looking for an exemption from their responsibility. They struggle to relate to people with true humility because they don't have any self-esteem to spare. Reality makes them uncomfortable and their intellectualizations become activated as a desperate attempt to reduce their feelings of shame and guilt.

Hidden allies

I hope you understand that just because people aren't saying things out loud in the public arena, it doesn't mean they aren't thinking about issues the same way that you do. The majority is silent. Many of them have been bullied into passive submission without their knowing it. Common sense suggests that if you can believe something then others can too. Thanks to the Cultural Bullies people now fear possible reprisal for speaking out. People worry about how they will be viewed by others or about what other people will think if they speak out. Some people even fear professional retribution that can cost them their jobs and careers.

This faux fear of potential inconvenience results in people holding back. This apprehension is a tactic of the ideologue. People respond and react to false fears just like they do to legitimate fears; most often in an unhealthy way. Their reaction to their fear makes the fear seem that much more real. Humans are creatures of habit. Something that is not real can seem to be more real due to the frequency of an experience. There is always something comfortable in the familiar; even if it's unhealthy.

Critical thinking

Critical thinking is the intellectual vetting of information and opinion. It is the objective analysis and evaluation of an issue in order to form a reasonable judgment.

There is a difference between thinking too much and critically thinking. Critical thinking does not usually require a big investment in time or energy but it does require a commitment to examine information differently. Few people take the time to seriously evaluate what they hear. Many people struggle to be objective about what they're being told. There are people who never consider additional reasons for an event beyond what they are told. Only a small number of people use their imagination to think outside of the limited scope of their own experiences. IT'S TIME TO START!

The way most people think through things can be easily compared to searching for something that is lost. The old saying goes; "that it's always in the last place you look." Have you ever analyzed that statement? Well, of course it is in the last place you look because you don't keep looking once you find what you're looking for. Beliefs work the same way; we stop when we find what we are looking for; as soon as we hear what works.

For most people there is no reason to figure anything out once they think they have found their answer. The problem is that we may be settling for an understanding too soon. Not analyzing information thoroughly makes us vulnerable to being duped and mislead. "We don't know what we don't know;" sometimes we need to look deeper to see if we can find out what we don't know. We need to expand our vision and put forth intelligent effort to determine if there are any options to what we comprehend. The opposite of critical thinking is under-thinking.

Leadership is usually held by people with alternative perspectives on issues. Out-of-the-box thinking is appreciated in this segment of our society. Unfortunately due to the effect of pacification on our society we rarely risk extending ourselves to provide alternatives to initial insights. We go with the flow. The cultural bullies have coerced us into believing that critical examination of what we hear is mean spirited or negative by nature. It is not! It's just good common sense.

From the WIKI; "Critical thinking, also called critical analysis, is clear, rational thinking involving critique." Its details vary amongst those who define it. According to Barry K. Beyer (1995) "critical thinking means making clear, reasoned judgments." During the process of critical thinking, ideas should be reasoned and well thought out/judged. The National Council for Excellence in Critical Thinking defines critical thinking as "the intellectually disciplined process of actively and skillfully conceptualizing, applying, analyzing, synthesizing, and/or evaluating information gathered from, or generated by, observation, experience, reflection, reasoning, and communication, as a guide to developing beliefs and actions." Critical thinking is not judgmental thinking but is instead using good judgment. I doubt there are many people reading this book who would deny the world could use some more common sense.

The negativity of ideology

Let's use our critical thinking and consider how negative behaviors form from negative perspectives. We are all familiar with the "power of positive thinking" yet few realize the possibilities of positive perspectives and how fanciful ideology has made us all, too negative. While ideology can be a positive view of the future, ideology is almost always inherently negative.

By suggesting how the world should be, you must first determine that it is currently flawed or underperforming. Ideologues, especially progressive ideologues, always see the world as needing to be better than it is right now. That's obviously negative. This negative perspective is necessary in order to motivate and cultivate people to support issues emotionally. This is done by focusing on the current possible failures at play.

Ideology suggests that the world is not doing as well as it could be doing and that progress is moving too slowly (this is progressivism). This way of viewing the world is not critical thinking per say; it is judgmental thinking with an ulterior motive that is extremely manipulative and always agenda driven.

It becomes really unproductive when the desired state of things recommended is not attainable or realistic.

For example: When I was a young adult in college I ended up becoming a "Democratic Socialist" mostly because that is what academia creates by teaching its one-sided view of the world. Young minds go to school trusting that they will be given all of the information necessary to form an honest opinion but due to academia's liberally slanted hiring practices, this is impossible. (We'll cover this more later.) Academia is perhaps one of the largest echo chambers on Earth. It indoctrinates people into socialism by teaching only pacifistic socialist ideology that demands the student contribute to the collective. It does not discuss all the failures related to socialism. (Cultish)

The ideology or the idea of socialism is great but the reality is that it just doesn't work. It never has; technically it can't because eventually you run out of other people's money. Creating an environment where people feel like they have to protect their money kills incentive, innovation and growth. It kills the economy because big spenders stop spending.

The public educational system only teaches the ideology of socialist perspectives and not the potentiality. In a socialist setting the government becomes too powerful once it takes over the free market and it becomes so controlling that the only way to counter it is with the creation of huge unions that can peacefully rebel against the government's failings. When the cost of everything goes up, the system collapses in on itself. The end result is, socialism fails. Personal freedom is eviscerated.

In Europe at the end of the WWII, most the countries there had a chance to reinvent themselves politically. They built on the visions that Hitler manipulated them with and most formed democratic socialist style governments. Poland's failure in the 80's is a great example of the infeasibility of socialism and free enterprise. The problems with these smaller socialist countries eventually led to the collapse of the Berlin wall and the dissolution of a little place once called the USSR "Union of Soviet Socialist Republic," in case you forgot. The USSR was a socialist USA. (Many students coming out of college never hear the name USSR because it is a great example of an epic failure.) Socialism has been tried and it has failed every time! Many colleges don't teach that the USSR ever existed. (I bet there are some young people Googling it right not.)

Socialism and personal freedom are incompatible; it's right there in the name. Socialism is an ideology that sounds just great but it is only a theory. It has never been successfully proven except for cases where human rights violations are the norm. The real truth is that socialism is a disproven ideology/theory with a 100% failure rate as evidence. China has considered itself to be a Republic since 1912. Even China is moving toward a free market economy but it is still fairly totalitarian or communist. For the majority of its existence China had an emperor who had a mandate from heaven. People are not taught these realities because they interfere with current progressive agendas.

In order for an ideologue to validate that something in the world is flawed and that it needs "fixing," they must first find a source that has committed a miscarriage of function. They need someone or something to blame. They must have a crisis or failing of some kind to reference because they must have a "thing" that needs "fixing" or a victim who needs reparation.

In this way, ideology requires that a state of victimization exists (they screwed us) and then a sense of righteous entitlement that things should have and could have been better if only those "other stupid people" did things right. Ideology complains about

56

the how and why, while not having a feasible method of its own. It demands fantasy be made real while living in the land of "IF."

Ideologues believe that suffering is a result of what someone else did wrong or because someone else didn't do something they should have. This sought after discord is very likely the cause of a lot of the generational and racial divide we are now experiencing. This is an ideological contagion.

The new ideology or "flavor of the day" targets the past. It usually seeks and even needs there to be, a causal factor; such as a group, race or prior ideology that has failed. (Sound familiar?) "Change" they shout, "progress" they whisper. If the prior ideology is in place and we are not satisfied with our current status (whoever is?) then we reflexively hop aboard the conflict-ideology train to "Can't Happenton" described in the opening.

Remember that the engine of the train is Ideology then the cars; agreement, support, tolerance, acceptance, appreciation, disagreement, opposition, argument, etc... and then war.

One of the biggest ideological distraction tools in modern society today is supposedly the problems left over from slavery. REALLY??? That is a problem now? Do you really see a lot of racism (not hatred) around you now, because I don't!

Critical thinking was not applied to slavery during its inception or during its existence because if it was, it would have never been instituted in the USA. The ideologues of the day (progressive democrats) formed an ideology around racial superiority that allowed them to think that slavery was "OK." People may have known the truth but they didn't want it getting out because of the nearly free labor workforce they would enjoy. Slavery is the result of ideological thinking that suggested Africans were not as human and therefore not owed the God given rights of humanity. (No real proof was ever given) The

57

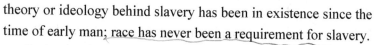

theory or ideology behind slavery has been in existence since the time of early man; race has never been a requirement for slavery.

Let's examine the ideology and genesis of slavery real quick since I know that this subject hangs a lot of people up. In ages past, slaves were the spoils of war; right after the killing, raping and pillaging were completed. Whenever a tribe or village was vanquished the survivors had two choices; slavery or death. These enslavements occurred long before the US ever struggled with the problem and even before "white men" as we label them today were identified. Yes, the North Africans of Egypt had slaves and so did the Romans. It was not until the Middle Ages that Northern Europeans even considered the institution in the form of servitude. Many servants were born into a lower class of families but many children were also given to repay financial debts or in exchange for property. This is when people really started hating the rich land barons because they were taking their children. This was the initial genesis of economic class tension.

Slavery actually took flight and was institutionalized in the Middle East by Muslims. Slavery had already taken place in the communities of the Incas and Mayans where they would keep punished criminals or prisoners of war as slaves. This was the evolution of the prison work camp. All of these problems stem from ill conceived ideology.

Creating crisis

In order for an ideology to present itself as necessary, it has to either identify or create a problem where one was not noticed or where one did not previously exist. Creating racial tension, threatening gun rights and things like threatening to make abortion illegal are great focal points that get public sentiment riled up. These emotional issues create the motivation required to get people (the masses) to create outrage and demand change; these are polarization techniques.

58

Ideology uses the negativity of a crisis to create passion, fear and outrage. Ideologues often suggest to you that you should be angry about something that was done to you or to someone you care about; even when you didn't notice that it had occurred. This is the politics of fear. It is the creation of separation and division. Progressive Ideologues create feigned outrage and then demand reparation and remedy. The bully tactics get mixed in and the outraged populace hops on board the train to Can't Happenton. This is the same way the Jewish people were demonized via the propaganda machine of the Nazi party. It is a very dastardly method of gaining support and it is alive today!

Progressive ideology starts by suggesting that if you care about people and human rights you'll join them. That if you don't join them in their cause then you don't care about important things. They shout with "bull-y" horns to make sure you hear the message and respond. They will call you names if you don't join them; from uncaring and apathetic to xenophobes (or worse). Anything they can do to threaten and thereby coerce you into action on their behalf.

Ideology creates discomfort in ways that might not have been felt otherwise and sometimes it creates emotional responses to issues that aren't even real. Remember the old adage; "what you don't know can't hurt you?" While it is certainly not true in all cases it is possible that the original context was in reference to issues of a political and propaganda nature.

You can be affected by ideology at your kitchen table and knowing the signs will prevent division and discord in your family. Your kids will not only be taught what the system wants them to know it will also direct them to take it home in order to set you straight. Because anyone can get caught up in the cultural bully cycle it will eventually land at your dinner table; the only question is, will you notice it for what it is when it does.

59

Proponents of any specific ideology seek to alert people to how they have been are victimized by selfishness and bias.

Personally the greed of the rich has never affected me in a negative way. In fact, I have gained from being near them and many of them have given me jobs and rides on their fancy boats. I invite the rich people of the world to befriend me right now. The only people who are not getting what they want from the rich are the government enablers and the tax collectors who have insatiable thirsts for other peoples' money. When the government says you're being cheated, what they are really saying is that we would have more stuff to give away if we could get more money from the rich so let's raise taxes on success. They lend victimlogy to being poor. Remember, money is the ultimate power; no matter who has it. That's why governments want more of it.

Their machine

By controlling data and information the ideologues automatically become propagandists. Just like the Nazis they provide the selective information necessary to formulate a specific line of reasoning. (This is the reason so many people make comparisons to Hitler in modern day politics; Ideology and propaganda is how the control of people is achieved.) When you hear them say, "Education is important" what they are really saying is; "We need people to follow our line of reasoning." The powers that be and the powers to be, want to educate you on how to be outraged, offended, wounded, robbed cheated and victimized. That is the machination of their success: Controlling information equals controlling the peoples' minds and bodies.

If you are using your intellect, you may even question if I am controlling information with this book. If so, then maybe you are getting my point. Maybe you are already thinking more critically. I would suggest that you not worry until I try to tell you what specific beliefs to have. I want you to have an

60

awareness of the processes and that will give you clarity. I am not suggesting any form of specific ideology but I do have my own conclusions; that's called free speech. I am trying to broadening your vision to see how the people in charge attained power and why. I am not trying to sell you a specific ideology here. That would have been easier before I told you about it because you were not as aware of the process as you are now.

My goal is to reveal to you the people who are trying to manipulate you into believing their ideologies. You see ideologues want to tell you WHAT to think and not HOW to think. I am giving you a "how to think" and not a "what to think!" Ideologues and their institutions have very specific agendas and perspectives that they want you to have. I want to get you outside of their little thought boxes, beyond their system of mind control and "talking point" logic. I want to build your immunity against manipulation and coercion.

The affect of the effect!

With the above considerations in mind, an important point to consider is "How does the negativity of ideology affect me personally." It's quite simple really: Uncertainty and confusion breeds anxiety and stress. Fear often breeds impulsive un-thought out reactions and responses. If they can get you worried and scared, then they can get you to vote or act without too much thought. It doesn't matter whether this vote is at the polls, at the conference table or at the kitchen counter. Their short talking points are designed to do their entire job in less than 10 seconds.

The repetition of negative messaging creates a negative view of the world. Anyone who has ever listened to continuous reports about a terrorist event or war can confirm how the barrage of negative information unsettled them. In today's media-driven world this production of anxiety is a HUGE problem because it is BIG business. They know that people can't

61

turn away from the train wreck. It's one thing when the call to action is obvious and outright, but it is harmful when the motive is covert and agenda driven. When we don't have answers to our problems, when we can't make sense of conflicting messages, we become worried on an emotional level and experience stress on a physical body level. We then want a solution; quick!

Some of the most radical ideologues and socialists like "Cloward and Piven" suggested that first you formulate a state or condition that you want to be in place then you create instability that brings down the current system. When the current system collapses, you have your solution available in the time of crisis. You destabilize the current structure and when it fails or when you can motivate enough people to act you offer your new state or condition as the only solution available.

Their evil plan works because the opposing ideologies weren't prepared for the chaos you created. The catastrophe you engineered then makes your ideology seems like the only reasonable and cohesive strategy to fix the problem. Since modern day humans want quick fixes they win the ideological argument and their train runs on down the track. Thanks to a perversion of what Democracy was meant for, the numbers win out over practicality and reality. The only real trick is to not let the system and the society know that you arranged the collapse. Scary right? This is another contagion that infects our society right now. This is modern day socialism and progressivism at work. PAY ATTENTION!!!! BE AWARE!!!

Trust the evil that men do

Have you ever had a great leader or boss? One of the major benefits of good leadership is an environment of confidence. Confidence breeds confidence. While that leader or boss may not have always been right, their confidence in themselves and your confidence in their confidence, left you less worried about outcomes because you believed that they could handle any of the problems that might arise. Much like the alpha dog does for his pack, a good leader allows the rest of the group's members to relax and tend to more personal needs. If your leader is incompetent or unpredictable, you worry about the future of the company and your own future financial survival.

These same insights work on the personal level as well. When we have confidence and believe that we can handle things we are less worried about possible outcomes. We don't even have to be capable; we just need to believe that we are. When we are unsure and lack confidence in our ability, we look to the people who seem to have it figured out.

If I can distract you and make you feel uncertain about a subject then you will look to me as the authority and then to me for the solution. This is one reason why people who are losing a "logic argument" often attack your personal character and credibility. That way they don't have to believe you because you suck, because you're a "sexist, racist, commie homophobe!"

Creating disequilibrium is how the above Cloward-Pivens strategy pays off. First they make you uncertain, then their ideologues and cultural bullies are there ready and waiting to "help" you find a solution. Since the majority of society can be fairly lazy, we are often too quick to let someone else fix things. This intellectual laziness is costing us dearly. I hope this makes sense to you. It needs to because these are the methods in place.

Another thing to be cautious of is when people provide dramatic changes and solutions for somewhat simple problems. Ideologues and progressives of all ilks usually have solutions that, under close scrutiny, seem overly dramatic. They offer big permanent solutions for small temporary problems. That's when you catch them.

For instance; raising taxes is a drastic solution to a deficit problem because cutting spending would be the first approach that most family homes and small businesses would use. Ideologues will frequently implement solutions but never fix the actual problems because they can still get more traction out of the problematic issue later. They got your support when they needed it and once they are in power you can't do anything for 4 to 6 years. By then you forget what you asked for or they simply blame the other side and remind you that you still want it. This may be why the government never seems to actually fix things. They will claim the issue to be much more vital than it is and suggest that desperate times call for desperate and drastic measures. This happened and is still happening with Healthcare. More people were actually better off, before the government fixed it. It was really a power grab over a large section of the economy and of human trust. The issue was just a way to get votes by getting people to the polls. Since people in modern society love that quick fix and don't want to have to do anything themselves, they are ripe for the manipulation. If you fall for these tactics it's OK, everyone does at some point. It works, that's why they do it. It's selfish but they don't care because they know what is right for you.

Progressives from both sides are people who determine your needs and wants without asking you. Why? Because they think that they think, better than you think. They actually believe that they know what you need, when you don't even know you need it. Their conscience is clear because they righteously believe that they are doing all of us stupid people a favor. They truly believe that we should be grateful they are acting on our behalf.

Do you remember the Reagan adage, "trust but verify?" Maybe it could have been; "consider it critically then investigate it." Never trust people with only one solution to a major problem. They have a biased agenda. Whichever side of an issue you do choose, remember that people with one solution are warning signs; they almost always have a personal gain connected to their solution. That is the setup. The purveyors of the solutions are trying to gain your allegiance and they are trying to put you in a very small thought box where dissention is not allowed. Be suspicious of quick solutions in times of trouble. Be aware of large permanent fixes to small temporary problems. When times are tough, you are most vulnerable to manipulation. A pacifistic society doesn't argue, challenge or debate. The progressive motto: "Never let a crisis go to waste!"

Laugh or cry

One of the problems with finding appropriate solutions to various different problems is that many valuable voices have been silenced by coercion and repression. Your quiet voice may have a valuable solution but if you don't speak up it can't be considered. How many times have we all seen the loudmouth in a group get their way? Their rants create avoidance from people of good conscience who just want the drama to end. This is their tactic. They know that the squeaky wheel gets the grease, not the quiet ones. When we allow ourselves to be silenced, we get short term relief in exchange for long-term unresolved problems.

The more civil and more reasonable solutions to a problem are usually offered by more civil and more reasonable people. Unfortunately pacification has trained us to remove ourselves from the debate or face the wrath and retaliation of the lunatics. People of good character have all been taught that being reserved is a form of politeness. This reality is not helping.

The people who usually avoid drama are not the type of people who demand to be heard. Sometimes arguments have their value but someone needs to object in order for the debate to begin. Just like on the playground, your unwillingness to speak out lets the bully remain in charge; this public silence is the result of pacification brought on by the cultural bullies.

Most of the time, "Pacification" is a social dynamic practiced by the majority who want to lend the minority a disproportionately louder voice. Pacification is, in essence, what made the Silent Majority silent. The majority will often sit back out of courtesy and give voice to the less heard ideas because they are confident in their ability to survive and overcome the minority if necessary. The problem is that the wise majority is no longer able to overcome the loud fanatic self-entitled minority who is rewarded for their faux victim status.

This passivity in the majority creates an underlying tone that misrepresents reality so that the minority opinion seems louder and more supported than it is. This is how small problems become big problems. For instance; "White cops are killing black kids and it is thus a racial issue." That is the tone that is set. The truth is that many more whites are killed by police and the numbers actually reflect the population at large making white cops killing black kids a non-bias phenomenon. The issue should be cops killing people but these numbers are way down.

While these victim voices are being heard the reality that 90% of black are being killed by blacks goes unspoken. According to the 2013 FBI Crime Report, the number of blacks killed by whites was at approximately 0.77 per 1,000,000 blacks, while the number of whites killed by blacks was at 9.83 per 1,000,000 whites. What is the real problem and why wasn't it discussed in the course of this public debate? The answer is simple; because reality wasn't serving the ideological and progressive agendas to sustain a victim. This is why you need to seek the truth: they won't give it to you.

The lesser problem with the larger solution ends up seeming more important simply because it is given more time and attention. It is given more of a voice. This occurs because people of good reason are not speaking out and challenging what is being fed to them. Unfortunately, progressive and ideological approaches do not facilitate the true pool of possible solutions because it already had its solution in mind when the crisis was created.

Once the minority voice is attended to then objections to it get labeled as antagonistic or racist. Anyone who would refute the tone of the discussion is then easily attacked and refuted as being one-sided and not willing to give the other side a chance when, in fact, it was their supposed courtesy that gave the overly represented voice to the minority in the first place.

This silencing of the majority may seem trivial on first blush but the true problem is not about who is being heard and who isn't; it's about not hearing all the possible solutions to a problem. It's about limiting positive outcomes because all aspects are not being considered. Only the agenda of the un-silent minority is heard. Meanwhile a solution to the problem that doesn't exist takes away energy from the valuable goals and solutions that might be tended to instead.

Sadly we often confuse public discourse with a form of entertainment. We spend more time entertaining the solutions offered than we do thinking critically. The people who wish to divide us win. Politicians have figured out something very important (to them). They know that if they can keep the people polarized, separated and mad at one another, then the people can't unite to be mad at them. This way the people don't realize that the politicians have not fixed the problem they got elected on 12 years earlier. You see, they know that if unity happens they'll be the ones out of work or maybe even in jail.

Follow or get out of the way

So what! Big deal! If people don't speak up and use their voice then it's their own damn fault right? Right! But what happens when voices go unnoticed and unheard for too long? Do they just disappear into oblivion? NOPE!!! The truth is they usually end up more resentful and angry. Even worse than that they usually become apathetic and stop engaging in the process all together. The person who doesn't speak up may even feel victimized by the un-accepting crowd and possibly angered if they were embarrassed or negatively labeled; they become passive-aggressive.

Some issues are obviously much more threatening than others. Some responses and reactions are much more dangerous than others. What if getting you to tune out was their goal in the first place? Is it ok if you were manipulated into tuning out? In fact the goal of any real opposition is to get you out of the fight any way they can. If it happens to a mature confident adult then you can be sure that younger people will struggle even more. Elders model behavior for the younger generations. This tactic of the ideologues has resulted in fewer and fewer people participating in the public discourse and election processes.

These same repression dynamics occur in college classrooms all around the world. Students are taught and conditioned to either support the professor's perspectives or withdraw from the debate. Students' views get validated by their grades which are merely the professor's approval of their thoughts and beliefs.

When coercion is applied to the more immature and irrational young mind their responses are either pro or con but they are always quite passionate and extreme. Fervor can build very quickly in the young mind where hormones outrank intellect 10 to 1. We see this all the time. A story that shows up in the news can turn into campus demonstration is mere minutes.

On college campuses the school yard bullies of grade school are often replaced by the progressively minded professors. Some teachers even give class credit for people who attend demonstrations. (No ideological reinforcement there.) Either they are offered credit to go or they are forced to write opinion papers in support of the issue. The progressive professors not only demand consideration of the issues, but they grade students on their written submission and support of his or her (the professor's) political and social views. Comply or fail the class. The young person thinks the professors must be right if the "trusted" school system is letting the professors do it.

Regardless of the setting, I believe this kind of coercion or repression of thoughts and ideas, coupled with the personally leveled criticism of the students who don't comply, increases the possibility of passive aggressiveness and extreme violent responses. Their internal dialogues get distorted and that eventually leads to an explosion of emotions in the form of violence, rebellion and acts of hate; with sometimes deadly consequences. Their retaliation may just be a harbinger of what's to come, as college campuses are merely a microcosm for our society at large. The sad part is that the college classroom was once one of the few places where discourse was supposedly allowed and encouraged. Could this repression be why high schools, college campuses and the so called "safe zones" are the primary locations for acts of extreme violence? YES!!!

PC is Repression

Political Correctness represses true expression and then magnifies narrow thinking by the personalization of negative attributes placed upon the PC offender. Political correctness supposedly champions diversity yet stifles different perspectives. Tending to politically correct words will never fix our ills. Political Correctness has never changed anyone or anything, it

69

only represses. Political correctness is actually the language of creating hate and division by setting unrealistic standards. Being PC has only increased our societal sensitivities and things have only gotten more uncomfortable for our society at large.

Chapter Four

BEING HUMAN

Profiling is human nature

Have you noticed the outcry to stop what the progressives call "profiling?" What genius came up with this idea? Answer, a defense lawyer in a criminal case. Basically what they are saying is; stop noticing certain attributes about people, things that "we" don't want you to recognize. Why would they tell us not to see things? What's the motive behind that and how realistic is it? Does it create a faux victim from a perpetrator?

Everyone profiles everyone else, all the time. Saying we shouldn't do it is foolish ideology. Asking police and safety officials not to do it is dangerous. In many major cities in America where most of the residents are not white, white people get stopped for being white all the time, but yet there is no outcry or complaint. They are pulled over and asked why they are in an area under the suspicion that since it is a not a "white neighborhood" that they must be trying to buy drugs. (They might be, but they may live there or have minority friends.) How racist is it to suggest that a white person shouldn't be there? It actually suggests that white people don't have minority friends.

Many large city police departments issue what they call "contact verifications" which are "ticket like" receipts (evidence) the police are stopping white people too. I know because I have one in my file cabinet. I guess we were mixing a little too much. It didn't bother me, but I was shocked to know that there was a thing called DWWiBN (Driving While White in Black Neighborhood). I was told by the officer that they do this because they were accused of only pulling over black people. IT'S A BLACK NEIGHBORHOOD!!! All this to appease the

71

PC police. The PC'ers thinking, demands that 3 types of racist acts be committed to prove that one wasn't. It seems to me that their pulling me over was more of a racist act since I was the minority in that neighborhood.

Labeling and profiling is an inborn survival technique, a necessary resolution to anxiousness and fear. It is a way to feel safe from harm, its natural and you can't (shouldn't) stop it from occurring. REPRESSING THESE PROCESSES CREATES ANXIETY. Unresolved anxiety eventually results in anger and resentment and sometimes even violence. Take away our ability to assess for safety and security and we end up with panic attacks and other anxiety related disorders. The process that has been labeled as "profiling" actually helps the individual create a sense of safety and security in their mind through awareness of their environment. The entire natural animal kingdom does this.

We "profile" all types of things, not just people. We can profile a storm cloud or a loud noise. If you were raped by a guy in a hoodie you will be mindful of guys in hoodies. It just makes common sense.

Remember, the cultural bullies use words, definitions and perspectives to achieve their ends. The most ridiculous part of this profiling mechanism is that you can't stop labeling no matter how PC you want to pretend you are. What ends up happening is that the people, who comply, stop following their intuition in order to make sure they are being just and fair.

Following the terrorist bombings in France a government official said "I would have retained that guy with the long beard after the bombing but I didn't want to be insensitive." So he got away! The neighbor of the terrorist shooters in San Bernardino CA said she saw some odd things but she chose not to call the police because she didn't want to be racist. What's more important? Death or hurt feelings? Hurt feelings are not illegal.

If an alarm is going off and you see a guy running the other way, what would think? One of two things; either he is guilty or he is scared. There isn't a wrong answer. If you say, "Hey stop" and he ignores you totally without saying, "Run!" suspicious at the very least. What if he had a face mask on? "Profiling" is a healthy and natural reaction. It is not "hate-based." What if it was hate-based? So what? Hate is not illegal. Hate is natural; it's a human emotion. The point here is simple; profiling is an aspect of human nature.

Being clear, if we are interviewing people for a new job we need to be aware of any bias we may have, but that does not preclude us from using a profile as a tool. Ever taken a pre-employment test/survey? If so, then they profiled you; legally.

Example: serial killers. Do you know the profile for one, ever heard it on TV? Most people know what that the "typical" profile is; a white male, mid 30's to early 40's, short hair, etc... Wait! Is that all you know about criminal profiles? How about black guy with a hooded jacket pulled down over his face? Live in LA, blue or red bandanas? What would you think? Think about the owner of the convenience store in a big city, what is his race? If I go into a Chinese Restaurant and its run by white or black people I'm leaving. If I go to a Sushi bar do I want to see Asians working there? Do I want to see Italians in an Italian restaurant? Is that hatred? No, but you have been conditioned to believe that it is wrong. It's not, it's natural: Maybe even wise.

Here is a more clinical view. If I see someone I love get beaten with a baseball bat, then I'm going to be hyper-aware of people with baseball bats. If a person with a Yankees baseball cap shoots a friend of mine, I may become cautious of people wearing Yankee caps. This is human nature and it is not wrong, its survival. It is a way to protect oneself from danger; it is an aspect of intuition. Profiling is a survival tool.

I am not a cop and I'm not hiring anyone at the moment, so profiling is not something that I need to avoid doing. While there are some circumstances where the process can be abused, it is not possible to eliminate the stimuli that create our concerns. You want to blame someone, blame Hollywood and the news media because they show you the images, (real or not) that create profiles in your mind. Better yet, blame 40 million years of evolution. Do you think that the first black man to see a non-black man in Africa freaked out? How about the first American Indians to see a white guy? How about a white toddler who sees an Asian for the first time? Are their reactions natural or not?

In psychological terms, these awareness's are called "cues or triggers." They are associations that we make based on both familiar and unfamiliar attributes. Ice cream has an association for you and so does a bottle of beer. It's just how our brains work. Just like the name implies, cues cue us to danger or pleasure. If I am mugged by a Chinese guy, I'm going to begin to look twice when I see an Asian person behind me. This is not prejudice, it is called discernment. If I get hit by a pickup truck while driving my motorcycle, I'll be twice as cautious of pickup trucks. Not surprisingly, and pretty ironically, "Political Correctness" is not correct on this issue. It is merely another means to create the victimization needed to polarize people.

"Not Profiling" is an agenda-driven concept that is not optional in regards to human health and well-being. Labeling or tagging things as helpful or hurtful is a part of the survival mechanism for all animals, including humans. Even a squirrel will label (profile) objects and other animals based on survival and threat criteria. Ever seen a squirrel run when it sees a dog? Is that prejudice against dogs or hatred of them? Certainly not; it is a matter of conditioning. It is nature. When a Chinese guy sees another Chinese person in a room full of Caucasian people, do you think it sends a message to his brain: Perhaps a message of comfort so that he doesn't have to feel so different?

With that being said, humans and all animals, for that matter, can be falsely programmed to react differently to different stimuli or cues. A Hispanic kid can be taught to fear white people merely by repetition; by being told over and over again that he should get away from them as fast as possible. Police are stereotyped all the time. In this same way, a soldier can be taught to fear a bump in a dirt road. It's not about people, or race, or anything other than survival. It's about tagging things as "safe" or "unsafe." (According to the FBI stats cited earlier, perhaps White people should be afraid of blacks; they're killing whites 10 times more often than whites are killing blacks and blacks are only about 1/3 of the population.)

For many people, religious figures such as nuns are seen as "safe havens of mercy" (I was going to use Priests, but many of you are now taught to profile them as not so safe for young boys). Is that OK? Are you profiling in that instance? Is it necessary? Would you feel safe telling your child that it's "OK" to stay over at the Priest's house for a while?

When I was child, people were happy that a kid showed interest in the priest. Is it wise? Are concerns about protection and survival for your child OK?

My point is that we all profile and we will continue profiling. Making you feel bad for doing what is natural is merely a method of throwing you off balance so one side of an ideology can rate themselves as superior to the other. It places them as the new credible source for your thinking and it has you question your own credibility for being so biased. It's a scheme!

Let me be real clear here. Don't be an ass. Everyone has the right to be happy and free from as much fear as possible. If you hate people for how they look, you're acting from fear and that is not healthy for either one of you. You need to be safe but you cannot be happy being paranoid about people who are different from you. If I enter your sushi bar and the sushi chef is white, I am going to look at you funny! Promise! (Right now there are some men reading this book thinking about what it means for a man to eat sushi. When they're done, they're going fishing.)

If you are a racially-centered person of any race, know this: You have been programmed by either people with agendas or by negative experiences; neither are healthy ways of reacting or living. You will be happier without the fear, anger and resentment; trust me, I know, I'm a professional.

Manipulated by a fear of labeling

Each of us must stand up and take the REAL world head-on. We must learn how to lighten up a little when ridiculous arguments are proffered; but we also need to confront them for their lunacy and keep them in adult perspective. We need to stop taking ourselves or others so serious that it breeds hate; remembering that we all fall short. By being and displaying who we really are we allow others to do the same. By allowing others to be "who" they really are, we allow ourselves to be who we are, just a little bit more often. If you operate from hatred, you will always see hatred. If you operate from fear, you will always see threats and you will always be angry. If you operate from acceptance, understanding and even love, you will experience more of it. You just need to be smart about who you trust. Use your brain, even if they tell you not to.

We change our world by changing how we operate; by not being more offended by truth than we are by lies. When people actually speak the truth, people freak out like "drama queens." People tell lies, get caught and no one really seems to care. It makes us all phonies. Rage against the lies and the liars, not against the honest or the frightened.

One thing that really scares me in a modern democracy is that people seem alright with letting dishonest and fake people represent them by voting FOR them. Societies used to be led by Higher Power based morality and by people of good moral fiber; now we are led by selfish, self-serving women and men who serve no one but themselves and their own beliefs. Why do we stand for it? Is it because we're fake too? Demand truth!

For real for real

Personally, I prefer the real you. The reason I prefer the real you is because I have incorporated this thing called acceptance into my consciousness. I once heard a black man say that he would rather be in a room with an outright bigoted Klan member than be surrounded by people who act like they aren't prejudiced when they really are; people who might placate him by speaking to him as if he was a dumb child unable to control his reactions. He said that he respects the first type of man more for being real; much more than the phony ones who pretend they like him so they can have a black friend.

He said the reason is because the bigoted man stood up for himself and what he believes in: He did not doubt his own ability to face the reality of the circumstance. He preferred the straight-forward man because at least he knew what he was dealing with. Hiding racist sentiments serves no one. Personally, I want to know if you don't like me. I respect that. Your truth might even help me to change.

Do you want respect for who you really are or do you want people to pretend to like you to your face because all they know is the fake you. Would you rather have people take off their masks or pretended to be someone they're not? You can't get everyone to like you; it's better to be liked a little for who we are, than to be liked a lot for who we are not.

77

Single faced

The problems with fake people go well beyond the scope of this book because when the truth is lost everyone loses. When people pretend to like one another, their false pretense eventually fails: They feel lonely in a crowd. We end up living in a world of two-faced phonies, where illusions are shattered in moments of extreme social embarrassment and discord.

Let the world see the real you. Most "real people" appreciate uniqueness much like an original work of art. If the world doesn't like what they see, that's their problem. Believe it or not, you can even still love people who don't like you; it's a choice.

Trying to make hatred illegal is about as possible as making emotions nonexistent. Trying to outlaw and stop hatred will only breed more of it. Trying to force love will only make less of it and make it harder to find. Control is an illusion that most often results in catastrophe. Letting people be, is harmony!

One of my motivations in writing this book speaks more directly to the observable struggles of many of my clinical patients and their families; people internally confused by unmanageable external variables and lies: People who have been tormented by both lying family members and lovers. People made anxious by the inconsistent, spoon-fed news-of-the-day, postulated on by unrealistic ideologues preaching discord.

In the modern world, no one wants to acknowledge the elephant in living room because they want to avoid some short-lived drama. They exchange this brief respite for what amounts to long-term discomfort and confusion. In the next section I will show you ways to be more genuine to yourself and to the world around you. Being authentic and genuine is the antidote for disharmony in this modern world of false prophets and fake solutions. We, my friends, are going to kick the elephant (and the donkey) in their cultish asses!

78

Chapter Five

THE FOUNDATION OF COMMUNICATION
Accuracy and authenticity

Have you ever been to couples, family or marriage counseling? If so, what was the first problem identified and the first solution offered? Most likely, it had something to do with how you communicate. Communication problems are at the core of almost every type of workplace, community or family relational struggle. Accurate and authentic intrapersonal communication (self-talk) is even more important, because it is the base of all of our emotional exchanges and perspectives.

Over the past several chapters, I have repeatedly mentioned the phrase; "words, definitions and perspectives." Let's take a deeper look at why our comprehension is important and how we can actually correct some of the missteps brought on by the popular culture's misguided big mouths.

At its core, a communication problem is about words, symbols, meanings/definitions and perspectives/interpretations. It seems to me that the majority of people in modern society today suffer more from what they are not being told and by what they are not hearing, than they are by "how" things are being said. People suffer more from what they don't know than from how harshly someone might speak. Not because of lies of omission, but because people are inhibited about and censored from, saying what is really on their minds. The repression brought on by the cultural bullies and their PC dictates are making America and the rest of the modern, world emotionally and mentally ill. We have been conditioned to speak more respectfully to strangers than to our own lovers, parents and children.

Remember the old saying; "We don't talk anymore." Notice I didn't say, "We don't interact anymore." We interact plenty; unfortunately the forms that we do it in are weak means of communicating. In fact, when it comes to communication, a day of text messaging can usually be outdone in 2 minutes of actual conversation. Instead of getting it all at once, we get tiny little bits of dumb-downed exchanges and WAY too much time in between to dissect and analyze them. This may be one reason why we are so sensitive these days. We over think these little 10 to 100 character messages, squeezing all the self-worth and validation we can get out of them; usually with negative results.

I don't want to spend much time on texting but I will say that when it comes to communicating, texting has hurt us a lot more than it has helped us. Maybe we should be suing the telecommunications companies for creating tension in our relationships. (Just kidding, that would be how the progressives would polarize us making someone a victim.) Just stop texting.

Personal responsibility

When it comes to communicating, it's our job to make sure that the person we are speaking to knows exactly what we mean. It is our job to make sure our point is clear and that they understood us as we intended; it is not their job to figure it out. The easiest way to get our point across is through actual face-to-face interactions where we can hear tone, observe body language or reactions, understand the environment and experience the real time pace between when they received a message and how they reacted physically. When we are face-to-face we can see if they were distracted or if they got the point.

Real communication takes place when there is sending, receiving and validation of what was said as well as the awareness of how it was received. Video communication would be a close second to actual face-to-face interactions with audio communications being third, emails fourth (because we usually speak our whole message,) snail mail fifth and at the very bottom just before smoke signals and Morse Code, is texting.

More is only better when there actually is more of an exchange of data. Data is not text characters. Data is words, tones, visual cues, body language and response time. The truth is, texting was a way for the big "communication companies" to reduce actual telephone line data usage (it knowingly reduced data exchange amounts, thus limiting communication data). It was designed to help the big cell providers save money and bandwidth when everyone first started using personal cell phones. They just told you (sold you) that it was cool, so you jumped right on it just like they hoped. Perception brought to you by a self-serving agenda and clever marketing.

A lack of communication, in its most simple form, is about not getting the entire point. Poor communication is inaccurate perception. For instance (male to female), "I'm not going to make the party tonight," text response, "I hate you." How many ways can that little exchange be perceived? How much can be misinterpreted and how many different presumptions can be created?

Good communication is determined by accurate perception. Perception is learning. Poor communication is the result of a lack of accurate information. Next text in the above exchange; "My car broke down I'm on the side of the road." Can you see how much discomfort is created in the relationship because of the lack of content, tone, environment and the duration of time between the exchanges? (It would be about the same time it took for you to get to this point in the reading.) Can you now imagine how a face to face or even voice exchange would have changed the context and perception?

81

Half the truth and nothing butt

Telling the truth is not just an issue of not lying. Giving someone the truth of a matter is about giving them the whole picture, all of the data. What are "white lies?" They are lies with ideology and propaganda! "White lies" are just lies. They don't tell the truth of the matter. There is no such thing as a "half truth;" it is merely a purposeful act of not giving someone the whole truth. When we deny someone the whole truth we are manipulating them; even controlling them. If you know what someone is asking you, know what they want to know, then not giving them the information they seek is deceptive.

This leaves us with a simple definition. Communication leading to a belief that is anything other than the reality of the situation is deception. Deception requires intent to mislead and the actual false belief being held by the receiver. If you purposely get someone to believe something that you know is not the whole truth, then you have created a lie; you have deceived them. Getting someone to think something as other than it is, is a lie!

Manipulating the truth is how perceptions are controlled. This is done by providing selective information be it from person, government or media outlet. When we control the truth we can control the person, because they can only act from what they think or know. They don't know what they don't know. Not giving someone the whole truth is denying them the right to make correct and accurate decisions for themselves. When you lie or manipulate the truth, you rob that person or group of the management of their lives and of their own right to determine their own future destiny; even if it is only their opinion of you. There is nothing innocent about withholding the truth!

It has been my clinical experience that people who suffer emotional torment are often operating on only half of the truth or half of the story that they needed to have in order to make decisions for their own lives and futures. This withholding of information is often justified as a way of being nicer; even sparing someone the truth. When people, institutions and governments withhold data, they deny autonomy and freedom.

If the adults around you "won't" (not can't) speak honestly or are unable to talk and respond like adults, then that might be a clue for you about your personal communication issues and your current emotional problems. While there is actually a chance they're just not accustomed to being honest or that they don't know how to be direct; that doesn't let them off the hook. The motive for a half truth is irrelevant. Learning how to tell the truth is their responsibility if they want to be in your life; not knowing any better or not being able to function better doesn't make them healthy people to be around.

Healthy communication requires disciplined commitment. Good communication requires honesty and accuracy; these are the result of practice. Real communication is concise, reflecting actual states and conditions or dynamics. Good communication is easier to do when we are not emotional or having an emotional reaction to what we are communicating about. Some people call this the "I" before the "E" to emotional well-being. It stands for the "Intellect" before "Emotions." The intellect allows us to be more factual than the emotional part of our brains. It sounds crazy, but the emotional part of our brains doesn't really care about facts; it just wants the annoyances to cease.

Thus, without accuracy and honesty, words become merely manipulations. Without these healthy conditions words become unplanned mistakes and sometimes even lifelong regrets. Some bells cannot be un-rung and sometimes, all though rarely, it can be too late for the truth to be effective. (This occurs when the trust has been lost or damaged beyond repair.)

83

For these vital reasons, I want to examine some problematic words, phrases and scenarios that you may find yourself involved in every day. We are going to discuss the traps that people speaking to us, often fallen into. We will also discuss how ill-conceived communication can negatively affect our own self-concept. The "Golden Rule" of treating others as we would like to be treated is a great regulator of healthy communication. Simply provide for others the information you would want to have about a situation if the roles were reversed. Just like us, our friends deserve straightforwardness.

Accidental censorship

As a society we have increasingly censored ourselves from speaking words that might more accurately describe our true thoughts, feelings and realities. We feel unknown and alone when we aren't able to be our authentic selves. It's easier to protect our feet with slippers than it is to carpet the world. The PC culture seeks to carpet the world in a hope of avoiding stubbed toes: Foolish ideology with an emotional cost to individual self-awareness and self-concept that is unfathomable.

Unfortunately, when it comes to self-esteem, self-worth and self-concept people tend to internalize the outside world's reflection of how they see themselves. Have you ever left a party thinking; "if they only knew what I was thinking?" By not speaking your perspective, you unwittingly censored yourself and internally deemed yourself a misfit for that group. (Costly)

The real tragedy is that you've embraced this isolation without even being certain that others at that party would not have supported your opposition. You are inhibited to speak your truth and have become pacifistic due to PC culture coercion. When events like this occur your self-concept suffers needlessly. Your awareness of your social position is distorted and hidden.

Is it any wonder that the rise of the PC culture has brought along with it an increase in social anxiety disorders, panic disorders and other social phobias? Could the PC culture be responsible for the increases we are seeing in social phobias or for issues related performance anxieties and approval issues?

Negative cultural pressures that cannot be endured lead to internal changes in perspective, desired or not. Most susceptible to these pressures are people from dysfunctional families of all types; especially those people from families that struggle with addiction and/or abuse. You see, this population is more vulnerable because they have learned at an early age how to "go along to get along." They either become chameleon-like and blend in or they rebel drastically responding in extreme ways.

Not being able to speak directly about truth is a form of dishonesty, but worse than that it is repression. Sigmund Freud, the father of modern psychology, believed that "repression" of thought and emotion caused many of the mental illnesses and mental health problems that we experience today. Repression is the result of pressure being placed on someone that inhibits their ability to act freely without retribution.

Since truth is the thing that supposedly sets us free, I recommend that we first find and live our own truth. If we want to be known and accepted for whom we really are, we need to speak our heart's perspectives clearly and without censorship. We must push back hard against repression because repression is most often experienced at the hands of some form of tyranny.

Modern faux freedoms

As many of you know the United States was settled and founded by English people who had a need and a desire to be FREE from repression. It meant so much to them that they were willing to leave their homes and risk their lives: To sail in a wind driven boat that could possibly have fallen off the end of the

85

Earth. Before they left, they knew that some people would die on that boat and that some would not survive the primal existence they would have to endure in the wild new world.

Imagine if you left your house today with what you can carry, to get on a boat without a motor, for a 2 month journey to then land in the woods, without any civilization to fall back on. You're with 40 people you might not even know. You won't ever see your other family members or friends again and there is no way to communicate with them. This is how important freedom was and that's how much they were willing to trade for it. After going through all they did to attain their individual rights and freedoms how dare anyone now suggest that you don't have the right to speak freely without coercion, manipulation or tyranny.

Modern people want the freedom to speak about what they like, to freely think what they want to think and to freely believe what they choose to believe. They want to practice their religious beliefs without encumbrances placed on them by a tyrannical government or its officials and they want to be heard.

The US was founded by people with a need to protect themselves from tyrant rule. The brave souls that founded the New World yearned for a place where they would be safe from government reprisal and control. When the English presence here grew too oppressive the people rebelled in the form of the first American Revolution. This happened because England broke the system by adding more and more rules and sanctions.

Our founders risked everything to escape the King's rules against free speech in matters of both state and church. (THIS TYRANNY AND OPRESSION IS OCCURING RIGHT NOW IN THE UNITED STATES OF AMERICA VIA THE PC CULT.) The pilgrims sought separation to keep the state out of the church's business. The separation of church and state does not mean that the two could never cross only that the state could

86

not be a part of the church. The people of the church however retain their right to influence the government. In God We Trust.

In a manner of speaking!

No matter where we are or who we are, we must learn how to communicate effectively without being intimidated by bullies. We will need to be brave and courageous. The road to the solution is not a one way street. We must also learn how to appreciate those persons who think and feel differently from ourselves without feeling threatened and without being intimidated or offended. Whether you are religious or not the Golden Rule is a wise practice: "Do unto others as you would have them do unto you." This means, quite simply; don't be the way you don't want other people to be; from driving your car to talking behind someone's back. In order to have freedom for ourselves we have to give freedom to others and fight for it. This equal balance and this fight, is the cost of freedom.

Open up and say duh!

If I want you to accept me, then I have to accept you. If I want you to hear me, then I have to hear you. If the even playing field doesn't exist, then neither of the exchanges can be had. This congruency is vital in healthy communication because it creates a balance of power. If I don't believe that it is possible to accept you, then in my heart and mind I can't believe that it is possible for you accept me. Acceptance exists or it doesn't.

Tolerance only exists when we disagree and never when we do agree. The balance of acceptance is essential to our emotional health and wellbeing. I have said for many decades now that a thief always has the most locks on their doors. Why? Because they know firsthand that "thieves" exist and that people steal. They subconsciously believe that if they are weak enough to steal, than so is everyone else. This works the same way for positive attributes. I know that forgiveness is possible because I have forgiven, thus I know it is possible for you to do it too. This is a form of Universality.

Accepting that balance must exist between ourselves and other people is the only way to let ourselves feel free because it opens up that same possibility for us. This is the only way you will learn how to be true to yourself without fear of retaliation. You must make it OK to be different so that the people around you can accept your differences just like you accept theirs. After you live this way for a while you will become more comfortable confronting the inconsistencies in others because you confront them in yourself. It's more important for you to leave the party feeling genuine then it is to beat yourself up all the way home for being phony or for selling yourself out. Being phony is what the PC police require you to be. Your personal welfare and happiness are not the concern of the cultural bully; they are only concerned about their agendas.

The expression of repression

Freedom of expression is a dying ideal. While it is the very core of the US's foundation, that foundation is eroding. It's only a "right" for as long you are allowed to have it and for only as long as you extend it to others. Freedom is no longer free. I doubt there is anyone over the age of 21 who hasn't had their speech restricted by regulation or by coercion. I bet there isn't anyone over 5 years old that hasn't been repressed in some way. I wager that very few people can make it through a week without having to SHUT UP or hold their tongue. Repression is in effect.

Repression occurs when some type of force is used to control someone or something. Repression is the state of being controlled by force and the act of not allowing a feeling, thought or desire to be expressed. Doesn't that sound pleasant?

Repression of expression has a far worse impact on the individual than harsh words of rejection will ever have on society. This was realized during the times of the ancient Greeks and Romans. Even back then they knew that prolonged repression could lead to acts of violence. It has been well known that if a person is repressed long enough they eventually lose their composure and do something extreme. Supposedly, even the Greek gods reacted to repression.

It is this author's theory that this same type of repression by the academic cultural bullies may be playing a role in the college campus violence we see today. When counter arguments or insights are not allowed (repressed) and when people don't think they can speak or believe freely they eventually retaliate and explode with extreme violence. When a person is not heard they eventually begin to believe that their existence does not matter. A hopeless person is dangerous.

When humans feel irrelevant they become toxic and ill. Much like a toxic spill, anyone in the area can be contaminated by the contagion of their repression. "If you won't listen to me I'll make you listen to me." "You'll hear me and see how serious I am when you're all dying and running for your lives." This is why many perpetrators want their faces seen and why they leave messages behind for investigators to find. It's because they were making a loud and emphatic point! Dying to be heard.

Temperament

As mentioned earlier, this book is also about how we are being made weak and ill by efforts to temper and repress our self expression; efforts that find us placing others frailties and fears before our own emotional self-expression and truth. It's not my job to insulate you from reality. It's your job to learn acceptance and tolerance or else be uncomfortable. It's not your job to insulate me from reality; I strongly prefer that you don't.

Efforts to stifle human creativity and individuality eventually limit our personal ingenuity, creativity and innovation. Hearing tough truths will make us both stronger and smarter. Being emotionally and intellectually protected makes people emotionally and intellectually weaker. Words won't kill you and they won't even hurt you. If words hurt you, then the rest of life is going to destroy you. With that being said; words can make you emotionally ill, but only if you allow yourself to be exposed to them for an extended period of time. GOT FEET?

As you have already noticed, I have used words and discussed issues in this book that you have been cautioned not to speak about or even think about (think about that). Have you ever heard someone say: You shouldn't think that way? How scary is that? You're being told not to think. Why? Maybe the reason is not so innocent. The motivation seems to be to protect you from retaliation but in reality it is to protect the person's belief who is suggesting you not bring the issue up.

There are currently no thought crimes in any legal code anywhere in the modern world. (Isn't it interesting that you had to question that statement for a minute?) Thinking is not doing. Thinking is not verbally threatening. While expressing your opinions may result in retaliation of some kind, thinking something cannot: Probably because no one can prove you thought it unless you communicate it or write it down. Regardless, there are people who, as mentioned before, will tell you how to think and that "you should not think that way."

Without expressing a thought, there is no way to get caught. As questionable as that may seem to you, the real truth is that it is not illegal to express yourself either. (Not yet) While you do have to take into account the reaction people will have and the actions people will take, it is still legal to speak freely. There are some situations where you are not allowed to use language to

90

instill fear or terror, but the truth is that a good lawyer can get you out of those pretty easily. You may, however, go on a government watch list.

Since thinking isn't illegal, the issue then becomes about expressing your thoughts. As far as I know "the freedom of expression" in the US Bill of Rights in the 1st Amendment in the US Constitution is still the actual law. Sharing your theories and insights in both word and art are still protected. Just because most of the people in a room say something is unacceptable, it doesn't mean that they are right or just. Chances are they'll just think they're better than you if you disagree.

The law in the US exists as follows: "Congress shall make no law respecting an establishment of religion, or prohibiting the free exercise thereof; or abridging the freedom of speech, or of the press; or the right of the people to peaceably assemble, and to petition the government for a redress of grievances. (That last part says that not only can you say it, but that the government has to hear you.)

Abridge means: "to shorten; (a book, a play, etc.) leaving out some parts; to lessen the strength or effect of," (something, such as a human right). Not abridging free speech is pretty clear. What one needs to remembered though is that private property is still supposedly the caveat to where you can do it. This is only because the owner has the right to have you removed from their property for creating a "disturbance" or because you are "unwelcome." That's why it's called "private" property.

You shouldn't think

Preventing yourself from thinking is a form of repression; self-repression is perhaps the unhealthiest of all the forms of repression. It is, in essence, self-abridgement: The shrinking of oneself down for the benefit of others. It is often the case that self-repression is an issue of self-confidence and self-esteem;

91

usually centered on the belief that one's opinions are not valid, valued or important enough.

Obviously all forms of childhood abuse and domestic violence can greatly impact one's self-concept and their willingness to voice their views. This is very sad, but it can be overcome. This recovery can only take place if people who have experienced these atrocities speak up and speak out. Finding your voice is one of the few methods of reversing the pacification and repression brought on by abuse and neglect.

What if I told you that cultural and governmental abuse due to repression was almost as detrimental to the human psyche as living with a violent abuser? Abused people often fantasize about retaliation. They often think about covert ways to "get even." What if people living under an oppressive regime thought the same way? Not so hard to imagine, right?

Well, let's say you were physically abused, had become a little passive-aggressive and were then ridiculed and bullied in a school or office setting. It's not so hard to see how a bullied individual could fantasize about ways to get even. Since the abused person was already taught the "value" of violence, they would see this avenue for revenge as the primary method to achieve their goal. Their method would be irrelevant; be it knife, gun, bomb, pissing in food, running you down with a car or even cyber revenge. The point here is simple; prolonged repression leads to violent and extreme expression.

If the government and the "powers that be" can get you to abridge yourself or can convince you to limit yourself based on shame and the mere false threat of reprisal, then they don't have to respond to you. By being silent you take yourself out. This silencing is the role of the cultural bully; to make you self-censor. Self-censorship is your option, but why would you? Fear, perhaps? Don't let them win the war before the battle starts.

Not thinking

You don't need to think; the government will do that for you. When it comes to not thinking enough or not considering issues thoroughly, we are at fault for our own ignorance. Not taking the time to consider proposed notions or ideas denies us the ability to have a thoughtful response to our own real life dynamics. It makes perfect sense then that the PC cults and their bullies want you to think less. The cult just wants your allegiance to their ideas; they really don't want any new ideas unless those ideas build on their agendas. They want you to believe that certain words are wrong and shameful so that there is no way for you to voice objection. Propaganda and indoctrination limit your thoughts to a narrow view point. They use intimidation to limit your speech and emotional reactions to limit your behavior. (The drama Queens are in power!)

It is for these reasons that I must speak freely, that we must all speak freely. I take special effort to use words accurately and with their true/original meaning, in their original context. I do not subscribe to revisionist history, which includes the redefining of words, for the simple reason that these things are always revised as a part of an agenda or as a conspiracy to manipulate thoughts. Old sayings and insights that have evolved over thousands of years can be altered by changing the intent of the original thought or by changing the meaning of a word. This can happen in a mere year and all without you knowing it.

If words offend you, then you needed this book more than anyone else. When you can grasp the idea that words, data and even contradiction are healthy, then you will begin to grow and heal emotionally. Embrace people who think outside your box but don't be gullible. The real reason why some people don't get confronted is because no one really cares enough to set them straight. As Ralph Waldo Emerson said; "Let me never fall into the vulgar mistake of dreaming that I am persecuted whenever I am contradicted." Confrontation and even healthy criticism, helps us refine our beliefs and our understanding.

My notions, arguments and ideas have become stronger because they have faced the light of contradiction. Contradiction has helped me refine my perspectives and the input of others has helped to expand them. Hiding thoughts in the dark only makes them weaker and of less use.

Don't be passive or aggressive, be assertive

Despite popular pop-psychology misconceptions, words can't actually hurt you but they can make you emotionally ill. I stated this above, but it is worth repeating: If you are an adult and you remain around people who use hurtful words then you are not being abused; you are, instead, subjecting yourself to sickness. If you do remain around these types of people their toxic words will act like a contagion that will eventually engulf you and you will become emotionally sick too. You will begin to think like they do because they will repeat their words, definitions and perspectives over and over again. No matter what you believe, if someone tells you something enough times eventually you will believe what they are telling you.

If you are experiencing verbal abuse, then it's time to take responsibility and make a move to assert yourself. Get away! Toughen UP! You have a choice and telling yourself you don't is a lie! You may have to ask for help or even live in a shelter but you have options. If you are being repressed or oppressed and you are not able to share your thoughts, run like hell. Get away as fast as you can. Create a plan. The longer you stay, the weaker you will become. It is true that some people are victimized, but playing the victim role is a futile endeavor! Some people stay because they like being the victim. Playing

94

the victim role is a self-fulfilling prophecy that will only make you more of a victim, more often.

The victim role is a self-imposed impotence over our environments! Victimization and the victim role will render you powerless over your environment and it will have you accepting unacceptable behavior and circumstances much like a martyr. Victimization breeds a sense of entitlement. Entitled people have to constantly find a way to paint themselves as the victim as needy. Once we are adults, victimization usually has more to do with the environment we subject ourselves to, then it does to some unfortunate twist of fate that we are doomed to experience.

Despite what you think, it's easier to change your environment than you know! Evolution gifted us with FEET for this very reason; to flee from threats and danger. If you don't use them, then you are a volunteer and not a victim. Start making your move today. There is help. I am not saying it will be easy but it will be worth it. It is impossible to both change the world and join in with what everyone else is doing. Create a small goal with a larger one attached. Toxic is called toxic for a reason. If you stand too close to toxic people you will get sick too.

Chapter Six

UNLOCKING THE ECHO CHAMBER

Hello! Hello! Hello!

Echoing my point from earlier, my goal in writing this book is not to provide you with a perspective. My goal is to provide you with insights that will help you to clarify and validate your own perspective/s based on what is important to YOU. I don't want you to retain the perspectives that someone else gave you or a perspective that you have held onto for years based on fear and misinformation. Instead you should attain perspectives based on clarity, reality, true data and actual facts. I would not presume to suggest that I can give you all the facts without bias, but I'm trying. My goal is help you figure out HOW to think, not tell you WHAT to think. I will, however, make you think. That is why I ask so many questions. I want you to see that there are other perspectives that are outside of the echo chamber (box) you live in. You might want to highlight or circle the questions and come back later for more serious consideration of these issues.

Due to the confusion of the political haze cast upon us and due to the personal self-serving agendas of people in the modern world, we often find ourselves feeling lost and confused about the state of the nation and the world. Sometimes we end up struggling to see how we fit in. People are struggling to make sense of what they see because what they are "shown" is not based on reality or cognition but on emotion and ideology.

What we operate on is "data," which has been filtered through opinion and ideology; often from people who don't understand the issues themselves. Mostly because they are just

97

echoing forth or repeating what they have been told. Modern humanity struggles to resolve what it hears with what it sees. So we tune out and surrender to the big mouths and the bullies, often telling ourselves that the hassle just isn't worth it.

When we give up they win and we lose, because that is their goal; submission. Trust me when I say that avoidance and cowardice are much more destructive and uncomfortable than actual conflict will ever be. Mostly because conflict always has an end; avoidance and cowardice do not.

While I have already explained some of the external mechanisms that have created the Echo Chamber problem, I am also going to explain to you how some of the internal mechanisms come into play for us individually. There are some very simple reasons why these mechanisms of repression have been able to be put into place. Sometimes it is the result of other people's agendas and sometimes it is the result of our own intellectual laziness.

People say WORDS matter: I suggest that words don't matter as much as they once did, mostly because people don't use them correctly. We have become so lazy with our use of language that we are now more susceptible to subtle alterations that occur without our awareness. We too often see words as an art form of expression, but we forget that they are symbols and agreements that structure our core beliefs and the foundation of our society.

I suggest to you that what really matters are the definitions and perspectives and not the words themselves. I say this because people seem to have their own definitions of what words mean and that most people do not take the time to verify these meanings with the people they are communicating with. This is the reason why I define so many mischaracterized words and concepts. By not seeking clarity and congruency in language we become a prime candidate for being duped, tricked, and fooled.

The deformity of conformity

When it comes to our own distorted view of the world around us, what seems to be more important than the words we say are the definitions we use: In this regard we have become very lazy. You see, it is impossible to make sense of concepts based on wrongly-defined words or words we don't fully comprehend. Currently, in the modern world, the majority of our definitions are not attained from actual dictionaries or credible sources. When it comes to the meaning of words we seem to be suffering from a form of "cultural drift." This cultural drift usually presents as a slight change in meaning or an accepted misuse of a word which later becomes the norm. This drift can lead to new meanings and perspectives in our subconscious without our conscious knowledge of that drift.

The word "Marriage" has experienced the latest major drift in societal understanding of a word. Remember; words, definitions and perspectives. Has your understanding of the word marriage changed in the past 10 years? Even for those who didn't want it to change, it still has. But does it have to? Is it still OK for someone to believe that marriage is between a man and a woman or are they now suggesting that there are "thought laws." (Take a minute on that one because this is vital.) Does the Supreme Court now tell us what we believe? Sorry, but to me they just aren't that supreme; they hold no divine insight.

Tolerance of beliefs and ideas goes both ways. The process of stopping someone from thinking and believing what they want can be easily defined as a human rights violation. No matter what side of the ideological argument you are on, telling the other person "how" and what they have to believe is a human rights atrocity. This doesn't mean that any one of us is more "right" about marriage. The truth is that marriage is/was a religious practice first. The marriage issue is an example of government overreach, because the government has gotten involved in a religious practice. Anything not religious would be a civil union. If a person has the right to believe one way, then the other person has just as much right to believe the other way. Remember at the beginning of the book when I suggested that ideology created conflict, well here is a perfect example.

When the new marriage ideology came into play it took something away from someone else. This is where the real tension was created. It's not that gay people shouldn't be able to get married, if that is what they believe, but those voices who scream for rights are forcing someone else to redefine their words without their consent or the power to do so. By law, they can keep their beliefs without being targeted as haters.

Suggesting that a devout Christian, Jew or Muslim cannot maintain the belief that marriage is between a man and a woman is a violation of the First Amendment. (Congress shall make no law respecting an establishment of religion, or prohibiting the free exercise thereof.) If you suggest it is not OK for them to have their belief without being hateful, then you are "prohibiting the free exercise thereof." This is hard for non-believers to understand because they don't have that much of a commitment to anything "set in stone." They can't grasp the importance of the belief in "traditional" marriage. If you are changing their beliefs then it is you that is wrong and doing harm. Just a reminder that tolerance goes both ways and that it only exists when we disagree and never when we agree. You can't demand tolerance while not having any. It's not that Christians, Jews and Muslims have reacted negatively towards the cause of gay marriage. Instead, they reacted negatively towards people who were trying to change their beliefs (ideologies) about what marriage is to them.

This polarization was created and very slanted in the media by ideologues who sought to demonize the opposition; it worked. Gay people felt hated and religious people felt as if their religion was being taken over by the government. The real truth is that the topic was only used to get liberals to the voting booth as they were made to feel threatened (emotions,) that they would not have the same rights as others. (Feelings aren't facts.)

Words, definitions and perspectives are the cultural bully's tools of division. Remember I'm using these as issue points and I am not suggesting perspectives for either side. I am showing how division and polarization are created to co-opt public momentum. As a couples' therapist, I sometimes question the whole institution of marriage due to the romantic laziness and relational inattention it often fosters. It's great for families but it is a strain on relationships without children (it changes everything).

Let's move on past that one word and all the confusion around it. Most people operate with definitions they have never investigated or tried to validate. Many of the definitions that we use we have attained from someone else, who got them from someone else, who got them from someone else.

One problem is that even the dictionary definitions don't match because authors and publishers have ideological stances, too. If our definitions don't match then our symbols don't match and we can't help but disagree. I promise you that if you were to stop right now and chose five dictionaries and one word to look up that they will not define the word from the exact same perspectives. One of the five may even be significantly different. (Don't use the net, most sites just copy the larger sites; use actual physical books so that you can be sure the definitions weren't altered.)

It's all in your head

As a therapist, I can tell you that many people carry the answers to their major life problems in their own words, definitions and perspectives. Inaccurate understanding of their own lives and of their environments is a major reason why many people end up in therapy. They come into therapy because they need someone to help them make sense of things that don't make sense. They need an objective view to help them put things back in order.

While it can be hard to make sense of things in our lives when we have inconsistent perspectives, it is still possible to open our minds and learn without professional help: It will require due diligence. Therapy is just a faster way of achieving this goal (provided you have an accomplished and ethical therapist).

For instance; there are many people reading this book right now who have already been forced to seriously reconsider some of their arguments and perspectives on marriage. Others in regards to the right of people to believe what they want to believe without infringement or coercion. Some have changed their perspective because of what they have read in the prior sections. Their perspective didn't change because the other side is right or wrong but instead, because they believe in real freedom and because they value truth and clarity. You either believe in freedom or you don't. You can't have yours and not give them theirs. Freedom is universal; no one should have to pay for it with allegiance to anything other than the source of it. If someone threatens your freedom, you owe them your defiance.

Need more insight? The phrase "Merry Christmas" has been subjected to intolerance much like the gay marriage debate. People have become afraid to say "Merry Christmas" as if it were somehow mean and thoughtless. Personally, I got tired of trying to figure out what people were so I just say happy holidays most of the time, but also because it covers New Years too (a personal favorite).

People are afraid to speak their mind or challenge the perspectives of others even when it means it might diminish some of their most valued customs. This is pacification. Allowing someone else to "remain wrong" in order to avoid conflict is not doing them any favors and it is certainly not preserving truth or freedom. If you don't stand for something you'll fall for anything (Mark Twain).

We are all too willing to allow the people around us to operate with notions about us that are in accurate. People are afraid they will be labeled, bullied or attacked if they challenge the status quo. This is self-repression and self-censorship.

There will be fallout if you speak your truth, but the price of not doing so will take a greater toll on you personally. If you speak out or challenge the mainstream in the modern world you will most likely get labeled with unfathomable names which could injure your public standing and even color the perception that other people have of you. The cost of not doing so is greater to your personal self-concept and your community at large.

Regardless of the outcome, being real and genuine will mean much much more when you lay your head down on your pillow at the end of the night. Shakespeare suggested in Hamlet; "To thine own self be true." This is the wisdom of the ages and possibly a warning from a beautiful mind; one that routinely challenged the status quo.

Intent means everything

They say the pathway to hell is paved with good intentions. Difficulties with intentions usually occur when intentions are not truly understood or when the intent is not fully conveyed. The truth is that the more languages and cultures we put together in

103

one community (Diversity,) the greater the struggle to communicate clearly. There is no escaping this reality.

This struggle to communicate is happening all around the world today. In our modern information age it is easy to get 5 different perspectives and interpretations of an event in less than 2 minutes. That means 5 different ideologies in play at the same time all trying to get recognized and trying to gain support. If you prefer, you can even get an interpretation of events that fit your personal perspectives and mindset, right from your own little echo chamber, be it; MSNBC, PBS, CNN, CBS, ABC, BBC or FOX. This can be done remotely on your channel selector or by logging into the media outlet of your choice; perhaps even via notifications on your cell phone to make sure you are in with the party chatter. Today it's easier than ever to listen to the talking head of your choice and hear what you want to hear, from wherever you are. The result is very little unanimity of thought between people and stronger ideological reinforcement from the echo chamber you choose.

Some of you can remember back to a more innocent simpler time, when the daily news programs would lead with; "And now the news!" or "In the news!" Now they say; "With the "STORY" here's Billy Youngblood on the scene" (usually with some official looking building behind him to lend his "story" creditability.) Personally I don't want news "stories," I want the news: "Just the facts Ma'am" and preferably all of them.

We can't have healthy perspectives without the whole truth. Abraham Maslow said; "Full knowledge leads to right action. Right action is impossible without full knowledge." Without all of the facts we can stumble into the right decision or act rightly, but having full knowledge has to result in the right act.

Ideally

In a better world we would all demand the straight NEWS and ALL THE FACTS; not stories presented through partisan filters. The "free press" is supposed to be our watchdog against government corruption and the abuse of power. Now the "Media" outlets are simply perpetuators of the myths and distractions of those in power; the nanny of the political elite. They deliver the pabulum of government and special interest.

We need facts to live in reality, not opinion. Ideology is not factually based. Ideology is instead often the opposite of how things currently are. Ideology is emotionally based. Ideology is how someone wants something to be seen and not how something currently exists. Why are we trusting Billy Youngblood? Because he's on TV? We all know that little Billy Youngblood wouldn't lie or blindly follow his paycheck dispensing boss's direction; you know, the boss that offers him fame and fortune. We need to think more critically. (I guess at some level they are at least warning us that it's not all true by calling it a news "STORY." Words, definitions and perspectives.

Communication breakdown

One of the major reasons we have communication struggles in modern society is because we often assume we know what a speaker means when they use a certain word. We often assume that we know their perspective before they have even finished expressing it. When we cut someone off in mid sentence, or cut them short when they are speaking, we are presumptuously implying that we know what they mean to say and that they don't need to finish saying it. We turn off our listening device. We make most of our perceptual mistakes or misinterpretations when we are not willing to give real communication the time and attention it requires. Words, definitions and perspectives matter; not just our version of them.

If we were to look a little deeper into the above behavior of assuming someone's perspective, we might see that the act is actually a sign of disrespect and arrogance on our part. As if they were wasting our time by continuing to talk. These lost nuances in communication get more severe if we are communicating with people from different socio-economic or cultural groups. There are even perspective differences between people from different cities in the same country; sometimes even in the same city. Let's see exactly how different some peoples' views can actually be. (Brace yourself)

Do we all see; gay, race, marriage, liberal, career, rightwing, freedom, oppression, guns, honesty, war, progressive, peace, rights, fairness, citizenship, patriotism, responsibility, life, parenting, truth, God etc... all the same way? Of course not, yet these are often some of the major issues that we have to cope with; issues that we will always struggle to resolve in a diverse community.

Stop for a minute and consider who defined the above list for you? How have you attained your perspectives and how sure are you about them? Can your views stand the scrutiny of facts and contradiction or do you avoid talking about certain issues because you don't want your beliefs to fail by challenge. The only way you can learn about these issues is to talk about them with people who maintain opposing views. Talking only to people who agree with us is living in the echo chamber we discussed earlier. Thinking that everyone who disagrees with us is stupid is pure arrogance and ignorance.

Good communication is not simply about hearing someone speak; it is about understanding what is being said from their perspective, not ours. Communication is understanding what the person speaking means when they use certain words. In our current fast-paced society almost no one gives personal verbal exchanges the time they require. When we start talking while someone else still is, we fail. Good communication requires an understanding of the speaker's intent and perspective.

Intent is the thing most often lost or diminished when we use modern communication methods like texting and emails. These methods are the modern day emotional equivalent to smoke signals. Even the flag signaler can display energy. Emoticons are a futile attempt to save these forms of communication from epic failure. THEY ARE NOT WORKING!

Just the facts

Another major aspect of understanding what someone is saying is the use and misuse of facts. Truth no longer retains the importance or priority it once did; mostly because people, politicians and organizations of all types (including media) are not being held accountable for their purposeful lies and misrepresentations of facts. People seem unconcerned with real credibility. Lies are often justified in the personal conscience under the notion that the withholder of information is somehow sparing the recipient from otherwise uncomfortable data they can't handle. This is pure ARROGANCE! Unscrupulous sales people hide their greed under the pretense that "it's sales" or "it's business." No, it's still lying and maybe even fraud.

The fix is in

There is a fix for our perspective problems: We have to clarify the words we hear, confirm the definitions we assume and then get validation on the perspectives that are presented. These tasks are ESSENTIAL since the human animal operates from perspectives they gain through their knowledge and experiences. Perspectives are formed by how we interpret and process things and events deep within our psyches.

A quick example; White people have been "told" that they can't discuss or understand racial issues because they're white.

That is absolute nonsense yet it is suggested all the time. What this false notion has done is remove "white people" from the equation of the issue of race. As if white people don't have feelings and empathy or as if they are not a race, too. The truth is that the "white race" is not the majority race on Earth, so it is a minority race. It makes up only about 20% of the Earth population, down from 25% in 1950 (UN Populations Division).

Hey White Boy!

First off, I don't see myself as white any more than an Asian sees themselves as yellow or American Indians see themselves as red. I grew up spending half my life in a place called Greek Town in Baltimore City. I heard what people called us. My name is Emmanuel; when I was a kid there weren't many people with that name who weren't Greek and there weren't many Greeks around when we moved to the suburbs. It was my Grandfather's name. Our last name was stripped away at the legal immigration gate so that we could become Americans and melt into the melting pot. Before my ancestors came to America our last name was Diakogianis (Can I sue someone because they stole my heritage). My father's house was outside the back window of the Greek Orthodox church and it wasn't English that the people in the area spoke. Yet you call me "white." What do you call a white person from Africa who migrates to the United States? An African American! Since all of humanity supposedly came out of Africa, that term makes no sense at all when it comes to race. Should we call blacks Early Human Americans? Just curious!

So what makes a person White? If white is defined simply as not being Black or Hispanic then white people truly have been stripped of their culture and identity. If you're not "white," do you see that as fair? Would you want that done to you? I see myself as Mediterranean not as a Caucasian; check the route of that word out. Cauc-Asian. Are we a version of Asians?

If white people were really as racist as they are labeled, then they would just call everyone else, NOT WHITE! If white is simply not being black, then that is the biggest piece of bigotry we have going. I say this from the perspective of having been stripped of my heritage and thrown into a group of people who are not really like me or my family. We were put there and are now even blamed for slavery. (FYI, poor people didn't own slaves.) My family has only been here for about 100 years.

Do you think White people should be able to have a white pride parade in America? A white history month? Do you think it would be possible without someone from a different cultural group belittling them and telling them that they can't? That the celebrating of the white race is bigotry, stereotyping and racist? You bet-cha! Blaming all white people for slavery makes as much sense as blaming all the Japanese people on the planet today for Pearl Harbor, all Muslims for terrorism, all middle easterners and Asian peoples for opiate addiction, all the German people for Hitler, all the Irish for famines and all the black people for the current crime in the big cities. ALL WHITE PEOPLE DIDN'T OWN SLAVES!!! The reality is that there weren't even enough slave owners to fill a small stadium.

Since black people have been involved in riots I guess that from now on we should blame them whenever a riot happens! Right? One more, how about all of America's Indians for the attacks on the settlers? It's all ridiculous ideological nonsense!

No one else can tell you what is in your heart. I'm not a racist but there are cultural bullies right now who are reading this trying to figure out how to turn me in and force my silence. Not happening. I'm willing to die first. Why, because I know what is in my heart. I rarely see race through my eyes with the exception of the Asian culture of which I am very fond. I've studied Chinese for about 20 years now and have been blessed to train WuShu with real Shaolin Monks. I am an Ashtanga Yogi and I embrace differences because I know the value in them.

Don't let the cultural bullies tell you what's in your heart. White privilege is a cultural bully echo chamber LIE, an ideological polarization technique! The truth is that being white in America today has somehow become equated to a lower emotional-compassion IQ based on what some other group of black and white people did or didn't do many years ago. The blaming of the entire "White Race" (Northern Europeans) for slavery makes as much sense as blaming black people for suntans.

There are more poor white people in the USA than poor black people. (Pay attention; I said more, not percentage but more.) This eliminates the possibility of there being any type of white privilege unless you suggest they just didn't want the perks of being white and wanted to be poor. To label all white people as being any one way is the epitome of bigotry, stereotyping and racism. It's using racism to stop racism. That should work great! In a clarified world that notion is absurd. ALL WHITE PEOPLE WHAT????? (Wait, don't stereotype me yet Ms. Bigot. I will clarify this issue much more in the following chapters.)

Don't join the echo chambers or you will end up looking as clueless as they do. The cultural bullies need numbers; they believe that they can bully enough people into silence. I think it's going to blow up in their face, if it hasn't already. They failed because they hypocritically suggest that "WHITE PEOPLE" are all..... They are the ones that keep the race issue alive and only for selfish reasons; mostly so they can have a victim and a transgressor in order to manipulate at the voting booth. You can't have hero if you don't have villain.

110

Chapter Seven

REDEFINING THE MIND

A universal perspective

Before we can solve macro (large) community issues, we must first understand the micro (small) systems at play in any community; that being individual mindsets and person- to-person communication. One of the biggest emotional missteps in modern communication is one that is often unintentional but can sometimes be the tool of deceptive and manipulative people. Since I know that I have stirred up a lot of thought and emotion, I want to take some time and discuss how we process and communicate our emotions to one another and how our emotions evolve from our personal perspectives. "We feel the way we feel because we think the way we think." If our thinking is confused then our emotions will be too.

Before we talk about actual feelings I want to talk with you about the things you THINK are your feelings. I want you to know right now that I care about your REAL FEELINGS but not about those things you mistake for your feelings. Your thoughts are not your feelings.

Let's get real right here and now! If all that ever gets hurt in this world are your "feelings" then you're really lucky. Count that as a "win."

We have to straighten this "feelings" thing out because too many people seem to get too easily offended these days; mostly because someone else says they should be. So let's start by getting this; "you hurt my feelings" statement straightened out once and for all. Pay attention because this is huge and it will begin to change your emotional life by improving both your emotional IQ and your communication skills at the same time. It will change the way the world impacts you. Sounds big right?

Have you ever said, "You hurt my feelings" to anyone? I know you have. Think about the last time your feelings supposedly got hurt and how you responded. (Seriously, stop and put that event in your mind before you continue.) Was it at work or at home with your family? Driving down the road maybe? Which feeling was it? Did you name it when it happened? Can you name it now? Name the emotion that you claimed you felt was affected during that event?

I'll help you to name it now. Complete this statement. "When the above event happened, I felt ____." (Fill in the blank with one word.) When that happened, I felt ...... (scared, happy, rejected, excited, unappreciated, important, etc..) The word you put in the blank is the feeling you had about the incident. Identifying an emotional response is a one word process. I felt worried. I felt joyful. I felt angry. Feelings are not sentences. Much like different colors, feelings are one word or compound words.

Most of the time when we "feel" that someone has hurt our feelings, we are not actually getting our "feelings" hurt. We usually make statements like this: I feel that you..... I feel that we should..... I feel that the government....... Just because you use the word "feel" it does not mean that you are talking about a feeling. The majority of the time what is actually getting disturbed (hurt) is our "thinking-s." (Feel free to reread that again because, like I said, this is huge.) If you want more clarity in your life and relationships then what I am going to teach you is vital for you to understand.

You see you can't hurt feelings because feelings don't have feelings! You can't "hurt" a feeling. Why do we say "feelings hurt" plural? Which of these unidentified feelings are getting

112

hurt? Why wouldn't you have told us which feeling got hurt or how what happened made you feel emotionally? Why wouldn't we just tell the person what the feeling was? Instead we create a freakish guessing game about what is actually going on. Why don't we just say, "I feel unappreciated?"

The reason is simple. First, we haven't personally processed the event in our own minds enough to know what is actually going wrong. When we don't take the time to understand it, we simply take on a victim role before we are even clear about what has occurred. I believe that this is the result of the cultural shift ✗ toward constant victimization and polarization.

The confusion we experience is actually an effect of divisive ideological polarization projected onto the individual. This confusion is the result of our failed modern methods of relating to one another and societal divisiveness. It is an un-thought-out victim-first mentality resulting from a default, "emotion first" response to the world. It has become our culture to be wounded. "I am disturbed by what has occurred around me so I must be being victimized."

Pacification resulting from PC culture repression creates a state where people spend more time defending themselves and attacking others behaviors than they do to process their own real "feelings." Personal responsibility has been lost. If I'm uncomfortable it must be due to something on the outside and not something on the inside because I wouldn't do this to myself on purpose.

Secondly, we sometimes take the victim status as a way to create disequilibrium in the person or thing we want to control. A way to CONTROL the behavior of others is by using the other person's supposed rudeness via the hurting of "feelings," to make them change or to get their attention. If we are successful, we actually get them to owe us for their atrocity. They feel wrong (shame) so we are, by default, right. This is a popular tactic spread by the cultural bullies.

All this happens while the person we are talking to is still unaware of which supposed "feeling," if any, got hurt. Isn't identifying the feeling that we felt more vital than a pronouncement that we've been wounded at someone else's hand? Isn't saying, "you hurt my feelings" really just proclaiming loud and clear to the world that I AM THE VICTIM and YOU ARE AT FAULT? What does that accomplish?

Have you ever heard of an "I" statement? It's perhaps the single most productive tool in human communication. Instead of making judgment calls about how the world is functioning, why not just focus on the one thing we can actually do something about, ourselves.

We have become confused and I believe that phrases like "You hurt my feelings" reflect our own loss of identity and self-awareness as we become part of a social collective instead of the individuals we are. We become dependent on the outside world being right in order for ourselves to be OK. We have been so manipulated to guard against offending others that we now use being offended as a means to create change in our world. This is a contagion of the political correct virus infecting us now.

As a therapist, it is my impression that people are just using the "hurting of feelings" to create a change in someone else's behavior. It is an attempt to control the environment and to avoid conflict and conversation about what is really going on inside: A way to not have to change our "thinking-s."

Are we really so afraid of being rejected that we don't just ask for the change we want? Is it really easier to bring everyone else down than to lift ourselves up. If our request goes unmet, don't we actually learn something about the person we are interacting with? Why not just say: "Please act differently" or "could you call me next time you can't make it?" Maybe what we are really afraid of is finding out that the people around us are not who we think they are and that we are not who we think we are. This confusion can be a form of denial and self-deception; a mental defense against difficult information.

Me first

The next time you're in urban traffic, see if the "me first" mindset exists in the driving habits of those around you. See if you think that the people driving on the road are being selfish and self-centered (maybe check yourself). Me me me works great off the grid in the woods when you are trying to survive, but it can be the downfall of any civilized society. No matter how brilliant we are or how well intentioned we are, when it comes to fixing our world we must look inside first. Over the last 20 years modern society seems to look outside of themselves in an attempt to adjust their environment to fit their wants and needs rather than to try to fit themselves into their environment. People seek to change the outside first, sometimes never even considering the real avenue to contentment. Big misstep!

We must understand our feelings before we can understand anyone else's. Understanding how emotions and feelings process within ourselves first is crucial to CONTENTment. Learning how our thoughts form our perspectives on things is the key to managing ourselves emotionally and to maintaining our emotional composure. Knowing what a feeling is and what is not a feeling, is vital to our mental and social wellness.

Need some more examples; Gratitude is a feeling I often have and it has never been hurt. Frustrated is a feeling I experience from time to time and it hasn't been hurt either. "You hurt my frustrated." Seems a little irrational right? On the other hand "you make me frustrated" is sort of the same thing because it's jumping to the victim role and putting the other person on the

115

defensive. It makes them responsible for our emotional well being. "You" statements have the opposite effect of "I" statements. When we say "you," we instantly put up a wall between ourselves and the other person. The same thing happens when we say they or them. (External) It's an inside job.

Let's say that something happened that did result in my feeling frustrated. What is it about the event that frustrates me? Is it really just about this one event? If not, then it is not about the person who triggered this frustrated feeling inside me. If I'm black and I see or experience a person being racist is that one event really the problem or is it my outrage related to what I perceive of as a long history of similar problems? More times than not, the reaction to an event is only minimally related to that event, especially if I have an ideology about the whole race thing already in place. If I am a female who hears a male cheating on his wife, am I really mad about that or is it because it happened to me or someone close to me; perhaps my parents did it to one another. That other person has the right to live any way they want as long as both parties are consenting adults. It's their problem.

In popular culture we call these leftover feelings "emotional baggage." These are leftover emotions because they have not been processed or resolved. So "you make me frustrated" is not a factual statement. Perhaps; "you trigger my feelings of frustration" is more accurate. Perhaps; "when you do that it reminds me of how I was treated when ......" (Still victim centered.) Resolving the underlying cause or healing that wound would prevent this person from eliciting that emotion in me in the future. In essence, we can prevent being offended by letting go of past hurts and by letting old wounds heal. Let the past go!

Could it be that some of us are just walking around waiting to get our "feelings hurt, expecting to be offended?" Are we waiting to confront people for being offensive and insensitive as if we were Justice incarnate? If so, how did we get that way, it seems a little unnatural doesn't it? Why do we feel entitled to be free of negative feelings? Who created that fallacy? True balance in life would be a 50/50 mix of fortunate and unfortunate events. We might actually accept the sucky things in life more easily if we could keep that in mind. When I ask a client what the mix of fortunate and unfortunate should be they usually tell me around 70/30. Unrealistic expectations are the death of serenity and they breed resentment and victimization. (Lots of questions for you to ponder, I know. I told you I was going to make you think.) For the younger readers, it's important to know that the world wasn't always this sensitive. It's really only become this way over the past 20 years.

So how did we get to this place of hyper-defensiveness and hyper-sensitivity? How did we become so sensitive, weak and vulnerable that we need everyone around us to watch what they say and how they say it? How is it that we can no longer communicate and resolve our conflicts in a productive way like we used to? Why aren't we using our logic to overcome these problems so that we can move past the supposed injury or slight?

The only major phenomenon that has been added to the stream of social consciousness in the past 30 years is political correctness and the speed with which we react and respond. The notion that our solutions rest in some ideological safe zone is immature and unrealistic; it's weak. Looking to the outside for comfort is immature at best.

Despite popular left-wing news media agendas, most of the major racial issues in the US were overcome in the 1960's with Martin Luther King and the 1970's "hippie-love movement." Everybody loved Mr. Hendrix, Sidney Poitier and Richard Pryor. It seems they'd have a tougher go of it today than when they were here: In case you don't know, they were embraced by white culture and the only people who redrew these lines are the race-baiters we hear on TV who are always pointing out the division.

This 60's and 70's era of racial interaction transcended the many generations of racial divide that existed before. How do I know this? Because I was there; sometimes even being rescued from white people by my black friends. While there were still many pockets of hate, those boundaries quickly became morally inconsistent with rational thinking. As a "semi-white" young teen I knew that people with long hair didn't go into certain rural areas either. This was not an issue of race but of difference.

Despite all the laws to end hatred and the first "bi-racial" president of the US (Who was not the first black president on Earth), we are in worse shape today racially, than any time since my early childhood in the 60's. Thanks to the progressive ideologues, using their politics of division and their "divide and conquer" strategies, we are more fragmented and uncertain now than at any time in the last 40 years.

What I am convinced of is that political agendas, polarization and bullied ideologies are at the root of this regression. These groups spend all their energy pointing out and creating discord in the form of race-baiters who stand to benefit personally from the divide. These are groups of people from all races who use your emotions to overcome their own logic deficits. Why, because they want you to get passionate and outraged so that you act first and think last. They want you to go out protesting and raising hell and to push others to do the same. They want you pissed off!!

Is it possible to circumvent their lunacy? Couldn't you be, shouldn't you be, thicker skinned than you are? We all need to grow up and grow out of this ridiculous idealism that there is a world where people don't feel negative emotions: A grownup

118

world where we don't need to be protected from each other and where we care for one another because it's natural to do so. If you're over 21 and you want to be treated like an adult, great, GROW UP! Stop whining like a spoiled little brat who isn't getting their needs met by someone else's efforts. Stop playing the martyr as if you are going to save the world from a problem that didn't really exist until it was created to serve an agenda. Stop trying to carpet the world so that you don't stub your toe; it can't be done.

Feel this way

Connected to the above scenarios ("You hurt my feelings") are usually the explanations that soon follow. First, a defensive response on the part of the accused: "What do you mean I hurt your feelings?" After a couple of you, you, and you statements we throw in an "I feel that..." or "I feel that you...." Quick quiz! Are these statements feelings? Does "I feel that you...." Actually reference a feeling? NOPE!! Let me outline what I'm about to teach you.

Remember these little nuances in language are huge! Simply stated; if the word "that" follows the word feel (as in "I feel that,") you are not talking about a feeling at all. Example; "I feel that you should call me when you're going to be late." What is the feeling word in that statement? There isn't one, because once you use the word "that" you begin to discuss your thoughts and not your feelings; you hypothesize. Remember accuracy and authenticity is our goal and clarity is our destination.

What you are saying in these scenarios is, "I think you should call me when you are going to be late." Perhaps even more productive would be; "I would like you to call me when you're going to be late." In the latter statement there is no victim, there is a solution and it is very clearly expressed.

119

You may think this is just semantics, but not if you believe that there is a distinction between your thoughts and your feelings. It might not matter to you when you're talking, but it better start mattering to you when you are listening. The modern day belief that these things don't matter is how we have allowed ourselves to wander so far off the rational path. If what you are trying to do is to have a serious discussion about needs and fears or thought and feelings, then you need to get honest with yourself and put forth some intellectual effort of your own. These things can't be given to you no matter how entitled you are.

While it is possible that this verbal inaccuracy is a subconscious attempt to make ourselves less uncomfortable at someone else's expense, all blame really does is create distance from the people we want to be closer to. "I feel that you,,,," is a way to not have our thinking challenged; not even by ourselves. It's a way of saying, "you hurt me, you owe me, now change this thing about you to prove you care so that I think less negatively."

Not sold yet? Don't take my word for it; try to identify the feeling in the above statement. That person certainly has emotions but nothing is actually being said to identify them. Go ahead, take a minute and figure out what I just said because there is no way you've been this inaccurate; this off-track for this long without realizing it. I'll wait here.....................

Did my tone above hurt your feelings? If you said "yeah" you might be missing the point. Are you sure it's a feeling? Is it really me that is causing the discomfort or is it something from your past? Let's use this current dynamic as a teaching moment. "Mr. John, when you write like that I feel......?

What is your answer? Something to consider is that you could have inserted stupid, dumb, talked down to, belittled or something similar. If you used one of these, then ask yourself if

120

you are really talking about a specific feeling. Aren't these responses and statements actually referencing an intellectual concept; a type of thinking issue (stupid, dumb, talked down to, belittled). Our words evolve into our feelings and perspectives.

I know that 99% of the English speaking world does the above speaking misstep and if your therapist has not discussed similar word usage with you, then they are probably to blame for your ignorance as well as some of your continued suffering. ("Ignorance" that is the correct word, did that hurt your "feelings" too? Which one? Quick!) I hurt your thinking! I made you question your awareness, accuracy and ability to communicate clearly. Don't use your emotions right now use your intellect.

I don't want you to think you're "stupid." I want you to get smarter and to increase your awareness because clarity will take you further in this lifetime then your feelings ever will. Keep your intellect before your emotions (I before e). People who operate from emotional mindsets always find themselves in more emotional conflicts than those who don't.

Let's continue with the phrase. If you say, for instance; "I feel that you should have called me." What you are really saying is "I think that you should have called me" or "I think it would have been considerate if you had called me." There is no feeling called "should have called." What I think you really mean to say is; "I can't figure out why you didn't call me, so please help me understand. Help me make "logical sense" out of why someone who claims to care about me could disregard me in this way." Doesn't that really speak to what is going on more accurately? Why are we afraid to express ourselves in this way? Perhaps because speaking more accurately, in this way, is a risk and you may even get rejected. If you want to have that clarity and realness in your relationships, then this is vital. This simple little

121

tool is one that you'll beat up for a couple of years until you agree completely. Trust me, I didn't buy it at first either.

It has puzzled me for years now that so many people claim to be so offended. I believe it is because they are getting their "thinking-s" hurt; possibly because they don't have all the facts, but most likely because they have become intellectually lazy. Perhaps the real problem is that someone confronted their thought processes and they felt odd because they were operating on faulty assumptions. Perhaps it was an emotional experience because they have low self-esteem or a big ego. Their self-concept is challenged because they are experiencing the possibility that they were thinking incorrectly about a person with whom they are in a relationship. It's much easier to remain blind.

Having our thinking challenged should not be threatening because that is how we learn. The only real problem is making sure that the person, or source that is educating us is ethical. Challenging our thinking is how we clarify our thinking. It is only threatening when our beliefs are ill-founded or when we don't have confidence in how they were contrived. If you take your beliefs from a 15-second talking point, you will not have much confidence in your beliefs and you may feel slighted by a person with more information. It helps if we don't take a knowledge knife to a fact finding gun fight.

Assert this

Do you need more information on this subject before you change your whole emotional world for the better? Good! Before you begin to assert yourself in your relationships, before you improve your ability to really think clearly, let me give you some more positive direction for emotional well-being.

A feeling is simply stated with one feeling word following "I feel ____ ." Insert; scared, lonely, frustrated, excited, ignored,

122

worried, happy, thankful, angry, loved, irrelevant etc... Take a minute and lock that one in. It could save your relationship/s. I feel_____. This little tool will improve your relationships because it improves your communication. Going into your boss's office and saying "I feel that you should give me a raise" is a bad idea. Saying "I have been doing some thinking and here are the reasons I believe (not feel) that I deserve a raise" is a much more effective means of communicating. (Most bosses want you to be effective.)

By correcting these missteps you will become better understood by others, more self-aware and even raise your emotional IQ. Learning to listen to these variances will even keep you from being BS'd by confused or devious people. I promise that because you have considered this issue, you will now start to hear the confusion others present between their thoughts and their feelings. Hopefully you now see that there is a huge difference between our thinking-s and our feelings.

Over the next week I want you to pay attention to the world around you. Whenever you hear someone say "I feel that" listen, see for yourself if what they are actually talking about is what they are thinking and not what they are feeling. You will be amazed at how frequently and flagrantly this occurs. Again, this may seem like semantics but it is a vitally important distinction. The things we say out loud are stored in our self-conscious minds to be sorted out while we're asleep. Words, definitions and perspectives.

It's on you

If what I suggest is true, that words are everything, then weak communication spreads weakness everywhere and strong communication builds strength all around. Perhaps most concerning is that weak communication creates weakness of the mind; a lack of mental discipline. People who feel out-of-

123

control and confused by life often lack emotional self-discipline. Confusing your thinking-s with your feelings creates dramatic disharmony in your relationships; especially new ones or those where high levels of pressure already exist. A great example is the communication in Emergency Rooms where there are very few vague terms. Commands are clear and understood by all; this clarity creates the environment necessary to deal with dire circumstances in a positive way, accuracy limits mistakes.

I have become convinced that most of our struggles in the modern world are born out of failed communication; both sending and receiving. The results is people misunderstanding one another and increased levels of anxiety due to the participants not comprehending what is actually transpiring. Eventually, they get emotional and stop thinking intellectually.

Confusing our thoughts with our feelings is one reason why we are so emotionally and intellectually confused. People argue and feud because they make simple semantic mistakes in their exchanges and because divisive language puts them in opposition or on different sides of an issue: when, in reality, they actually have the same ultimate goals. This is polarization caused by the unintentional misuse of language.

Ever had an argument with someone you cared about over something seemingly stupid and trivial. How much energy was wasted and how much damage occurs during that type of confused exchange? That's my point. These seemingly small things can be HUGE!

Feelings matter

While these little communication missteps are often an innocent error, they can also be a maligned way to get others to accept what is being said without it being challenged. It can be an attempt to foster sympathy and attain agreement without debate, based on the ideal that everyone is allowed to have their feelings. The speaker is saying; "you can't argue with me about this issue because these are my feelings on the matter. I have a right to my feelings." We do have a right to our feelings but not to our "thinking-s." Having a right to our "Thinking-s" would suggest that we have a right to our own truth and that reality is somehow based on what we feel. The truth is static, it just is.

You are certainly allowed to have your own feelings and you will; no one can stop that. Yes, you can believe what you want to believe, but that does not mean that what you believe is any more true because you believe it. Reality, truth and facts are rigid and not subject to different interpretations. Ideology paints a future picture, not a current state. Unique and unproven ideas are called beliefs, not facts. Just like feelings, thinking can be highly inaccurate and even dead wrong.

Let's review what we have learned so far. Interpret this statement: "I feel that you don't care about me." Is this a feeling? No. The actual statement is "I think that you don't care about me." One could even say; I believe that you don't care about me." Both are thoughts generated from a person's mind that are most likely based on a recent event or exchange that the speaker did not like. The speaker can think that way all they like, but it doesn't mean that you don't care. Perhaps you don't care enough to meet their standard, but you still care. Their logic upon which they have an emotional reaction can be wrong. "FEEL THAT" should become a warning for you that this is just a person's thoughts and not actual feelings. Propagandists, politicians and their spin masters use this tactic all the time.

Unfortunately, people who accidently make this misstep create a credibility issue for themselves in regard to what they say. Being aware of this misstep may be valuable insight to have if you are going to trust what the speaker says in the future. You don't have to fix them or set them straight, but knowing this can

125

improve your own insight and clarity. If you chose to assert yourself and confront them, then you might try the following. You can say clearly; "You mean you think I don't care about you." (That they don't have enough evidence.) If they acquiesce to your clarification, you can than say, "You are wrong because I do, maybe not enough for you but I do." Do you think this is important stuff or just semantics?

If you are the first speaker above why not use the stronger language; "I don't think you care about how this affects me" Better yet, "I felt irrelevant when you didn't call." When someone communicates with you in this way you can respond to their emotional reaction to the event less defensively and decide if you want that person to feel irrelevant or not. This is only important if you want to have more productive and accurate communication. It's not just semantics if it can change your relationship. This tool is a way to forge strong, healthy, more intimate relationships with others and to guard against BS.

One further amplification: If I say, "I feel that 2+2 is really 5," I am trying to add weight to my point by classifying it as a feeling that I have a "right" to have. It will certainly make the person hearing me stop to consider what I am saying. They may think I'm crazy but they will hear the statement differently.

Confusing thinking and feeling is a major reason people struggle to have productive discussions in the modern world: Especially when we talk about emotionally-charged issues. If there were 10% less arguing, fighting and disagreement in the world, the world would be a better place, right? If so, then this little change is worth considering. Stating our truth is a form of self-actualization and assertiveness that will most certainly communicate who we really are to the people who genuinely matter. Not letting people draw us into their faux emotional-dramas is emancipating.

More dynamics of human perception

I'll give you another little insight because I know some of you are interested. If I walk into a room with ten people in it I can feel very welcomed and appreciated; hell, I might even feel magnanimous or generous for showing up! The truth may be that no one in that room wants me there and that without knowing it I may have sucked all the happiness right out the door when I opened it. I still feel the way I feel; no truth or reality required. I am feeling what I'm feeling, but it is not based on any facts, only perception.

The opposite of the above may also occur: I may feel unwanted and ignored but in reality the group may feel relieved that I am there. No reality needed. What I feel is not reliant upon reality. "I feel the way I feel because I think the way I think." And, scary to say, my thinking could be dead wrong. If it isn't reality, then I am feeling negative feelings that aren't even necessary. I'm sure you will agree with me when I say that I think we have enough drama in our world today without having to seek out fake things to feel. Perhaps this creating of faux feelings is a big part of our current social confusion.

So, feelings aren't facts! They are real and they do happen but they are not contingent on any reality as much as they are a product of our past experiences and personal baggage. When we adjust, "I feel that....." to "I think that ....." we improve our accuracy to others and in our own minds at the same time. If I say; "I think you should be more considerate," then you can hear me better and either become more considerate or inform me that you will not be changing. Both are alright! If I simply say, "I feel frustrated," then you can respond more genuinely and perhaps even speak to the actual problem of concern; my frustration. Much more effective than, "I feel that you..."

As mentioned above, this psychotherapist believes that inaccuracy in communication is one of the major struggles currently faced in human relationships from our bedrooms to our board rooms to our election boards. It is the incorrect use of language that has led to people's justification of their own faux outrage. Their personal victimization demands and perpetuates their "right" to be offended over the rights of free speech and freedom of expression. The echo chamber is one of the reasons why people often feel threatened if everyone around them doesn't agree with them. This is because their weak notions are untested by confrontation and debate.

Redefining your village

Upscale your own communication skills and the standard will rise for everyone around you. Let's take language to the public square for a moment. Once upon a time the largest voice in any community was spiritual in nature. Back then it was the voice of "spirit" as interpreted by the elders of a community that guided us. (Elders are the ones with life experience.) These elders evolved into a form of governance usually determined by age (wisdom) or familial relationship. The chief often chose their sons to replace them just like the medicine men trained their offspring to follow them etc... Eventually many tribes formed a council of elders who choose their leaders by consensus, but usually only when one passed away. They often believed that spiritual forces would work through the chosen person to make the right decisions and lead the village toward prosperity.

These elders and leaders made management decisions for their tribes for everything from determining roles people would play, to when they would relocate the village to access better resources. No one objected to their leadership choices because they had confidence in them, because they were trust-worthy.

128

In essence, these governing bodies/councils helped shape how the tribe would exist. Nearly all of these leaders were guided by their emotional connection to their spiritual beliefs and traditions; not by their opinion, ideology, intellect or selfish motives. It should also be clear to you that sometimes tribes would restrict other tribe's movements with the threat of war; most often as a means of self-preservation, to protect resources and not exclusively for reasons of possessiveness or ownership.

Nonetheless, these leaders of both tribe and village began to rely on agriculture and this began to dominate the decision-making that was once based on spiritual tradition. People tend to do what they've always done. Just as you will tend to do what you've always done!

During that time period progressive change and liberal thought was very limited. Progressive ideas (new ideas) about how things should or could be done (ideology) were quickly frowned on and tossed aside as ideological speculation. They were tossed out, because the elders knew these types of changes were a threat to harmony, peace, tradition and social stability.

During those times, the most progressive of thoughts often resulted in war and murder because change meant altering what was, taking something that wasn't yours or moving to a place inhabited by another group or even animals. People resisted change and progressive thought because by its nature it required change; change creates conflict: The need to change creates conflict where none previously existed. Conflict is the precursor to disagreement and war (Recall the ideology train referenced earlier.) Therefore, progressivism equals conflict. It could easily be concluded that progressivism is at the root of all conflict and war. Forced change will always be met by resistance.

While many of these tribes and villages had open discussions about options, the chief usually made the final decision.

129

Eventually larger groups developed tribal committees or groups of elders. Those groups had a pseudo-democratic method which was ultimately left up to the chieftain, or chief elder, to make the final decision. (Much like a president can veto a bill.) Many of these groups lived in harmony for eons without major conflict over anything but land and other resources. (Hopefully you see how these dynamics relate to today's social struggles?)

Eventually, albeit occasionally, change did occur but these changes all began with the (I hate the term) "lobbying" of those in a position to vote for or approve an outcome. They used words, meanings, and perspectives to shape change. This is IMPORTANT: Shaping perspectives is essential to any social change, be it good or bad. Shaping perspective is the goal of all politically-minded cults and media outlets in the world today.

Then, like now, the truth was not as important to these change agents as was getting the numbers needed to "believe" in the argued-for concepts. This is why the antidote of truth is vital; not half-truths but whole truths. As was suggested by Abraham Maslow, you cannot make a truly right decision without ALL of the facts of a matter; both pro and con. In fact, deception usually requires a select number of chosen truths to support the false belief and the purposeful withholding of other truths that would argue against it. This is how you create a void for the new agenda to fill. This is how revisionist history serves ideology.

People can't be convinced to commit terrorist acts with all of the truth, only with selected truths. If you can control the information you can control the perspective. Imagine how much BS we would be told if we did not have the "Information Super Highway" to look things up. Access to information is the "Achilles heel" to those who seek to control and rule. (I caution the world to keep the flow of internet information ungoverned

130

and unregulated. They know it's in their way.) If you need proof just look to those countries that do not have unfettered access to the internet, like South Korea, China, Venezuela, Iran, etc... Controlling data is the first step toward totalitarian rule. Being able to shut it down is tyranny.

You've got played

Over the course of your lifetime you have been programmed with half-truths that were purposefully presented as whole truths, so that you would adopt a chosen perspective. The reality of it probably makes you a little mad, but all you can do now is to try to learn the rest of what they didn't tell you. Not as easy as it might seem, but you are halfway there.

There are three ways to influence or control a person's perspective. The first has been mentioned above; the control of information both given and hidden. The second is by repetition. Guns kill people. Guns kill people, Guns kill people. (If you would have said that anywhere on the planet 100 years ago you'd be thought a fool; then probably shot for being stupid. Most likely followed by the statement; "yep, wasn't me, must have been that gun's idea.")

The third way to control perspective is to make the target of your agenda complicit by telling them what they want to hear and by shaping how they see things. Example; "The liberals are all clueless; here's what they're up to now." You gain the targets agreement first, then tell them the idea you want them to believe. "Gun owners are all fearful people; why wouldn't they want background checks. They must want criminals to have guns. Since blacks get shot most often, it must be racist." Manipulations of reality like this often lead to the targets belief without any type of investigation on their part. It works because they play on your ego and sense of racial self-righteousness. They rely on you being lazy.

131

These manipulations of facts are not merely ignored truths but are actually a conscious decision to spin the information given; it is purposefully ignoring of insights that might negate the desired perspective. The receiver is complicit because they are intellectually lazy and because they are not willing to give the issue critical thought. They are too willing to act emotionally. This is also a form of personal revisionist history. If history argues against your ideology, you simple avoid the historical accounting. "The KKK were all democrats, etc..." In this same way many socialists avoid investigating past socialist governments that have failed because they want you to embrace the ideology behind everyone being prosperous.

This author recently examined a text book that discussed the fall of the Berlin wall with six graders. The accounting did not mention Ronald Reagan or his historical call; "Mr. Gorbachev, tear down this wall." Why wouldn't that be in there? It was a major shift in modern society. The most obvious reason would be that they don't like Republican presidents, or maybe because it was the weight of the Free-market economy over government-regulated industry that countered the socialist agenda. A similar revision was committed by withholding that it was a Republican named Abe Lincoln that freed the slaves. That during slavery the South was mostly Democrat; that Lincoln's assassin was a Southern Democrat.

Hopefully my simple examples have allowed you to see how words and definitions build the structure for how we feel: How our feelings evolve from our perspectives. This is not a history book, but since I choose facts over ideology, I am forced to use real accounts to make my points. Maybe some of you are not yet convinced that your thinking can be programmed and reprogrammed by simple changes in language. Maybe you doubt that mere repetition can change the very definition of the

132

words you use. If you doubt it, take a minute to investigate to see if there is another possibility for what I suggest.

Can anyone reading this deny that GREEN is a color? There used to be an old adage where someone would proclaim "he's really green" and that meant inexperienced, like a new plant. Twenty-five years ago no one believed that "green" referenced being kind to nature or the planet yet everyone seems to use that term now as the default definition; often even forgoing the obvious color reference or the lack of a person's experience.

Try not to get lost in the following example: I don't care what you think about the following statement politically; just pay attention to the example's content.

Forty years ago the word marriage was something that a man and a woman did when they wanted to start a family and have kids. (They got married because they didn't want their kids to be bastards and they wanted to be able to legally and morally have sexual relations.) That's reality, whether you like it or not; whether it hurt your "thinking-s" or not.

At one point marriage meant that you wanted to have sex because fornication was frowned upon and even illegal in some places. Yes, having sex without being married was considered illegal, it was called fornication. People would actually shoot you for sleeping with their daughters and usually not go to jail. "Take" a woman's virginity or "get" her pregnant and you'd have a shotgun wedding where the male was forced at gunpoint to marry the female. If you wanted to "hook-up" back in the day you would have to get married first. Originally you got married with the church's permission, not the states. There was no such thing as a marriage license when the church and state were separate. There wasn't any type of legal standard; all that mattered was that the church validated the union. Hence the church created and regulated marriage. There was a real separation of church business and state business; the separation of moral and legal. The above was the defined perspective on marriage and it was created by the church. That was the definition and it was defined by the church; not by the Supreme Court which is now somehow involved in religious practices. If the separation of church and state is legitimate, then there isn't any foundation for the state (Court) to dictate what marriage means to anyone?

In the late 60's and 70's (with Alfred Kinsley and The Kinsey Reports) the perception and meaning of the word gay began to change from a state of happiness to males having same sex relations. At that time, most homosexual people were not even considering "gay marriage" or why anyone who was homosexual would even want to get married; certainly not in the era of free sex when marriage was for "squares" and considered a sellout to the establishment that was trying to tell you who to love.

You can argue that homosexuality has been going on for thousands of years, but you will struggle to find any evidence of social interest in marriage within the Gay community until some ideologues made it a point of polarization for an election wedge issue. Originally the homosexual community just wanted the same rights of parenthood, survivorship/next of kin, medical benefits and certain credit and taxation perks given to married couples. Being able to visit partners in medical settings during the AIDS crisis, was the first real line of division because only married people and family were allowed to visit the critically ill.

Obviously the term "marriage" has been changed for many people. Some people preach tolerance but refuse to allow other people to continue to define the word as it has been for thousands of years; not without calling them names. They will even attack those who have traditional (original) values and who lead traditional religious lifestyles by labeling them with terms

134

like bigot and homophobe just because they have their beliefs; beliefs which the "Bill of Rights" guarantees them. It is the progressive change in perspective and their agenda to perpetuate the politics of division and polarization that have made the issue a conflict where people must choose sides: An argument about definitions and semantics like Gay Union or Gay marriage.

To reiterate, the definition of "Gay" first meant happy and excited, at least until the 1960's. Later in most of the homosexual world the word Gay was a reference to man-to-man sexual relations. If we are actually going to be gender-sensitive the term for women was/is Lesbian as in the gay and lesbian culture. I hear heterosexuals who claim to be supportive of homosexuality say "she's Gay" all the time but for some reason they don't see this as insensitive. Words, definitions and perspectives. The term "gay" has been used inaccurately for so long and so frequently that now many lesbian women have even adopted the "Gay" generalization. Why the changes in meaning? Because Gay and Lesbian together as a group are a larger voting block for the left; they have united with the "Bi," transgender and the poly-amorous communities to create a larger more powerful alliance. (I caution this population because the creation of your own community is actually creating separation while you are arguing to be included or treated as equals.)

Finally, one more change in meaning; the term "guys" and now "you guys" means any group of people male or female. Not just males. Words and definitions; "they are a changin."

So, does changing a word change the perception for everyone? No! If you are being honest about it, trying to make people redefine their understanding of a word is a little fascist. This is a demand for "pacification." This is intolerance. This is a demand that traditional groups change their core beliefs and perspectives held for thousands of years because others don't like

135

it. It isn't OK to insult them because they think and feel differently. That is intolerance. Ironically, people fighting for tolerance are being more intolerant by demanding that others be a certain way and accept certain standards. They are attacking people for supposedly doing what they're doing. That is pure arrogance in every aspect of the word. This is lunacy!

Despite popular misconceptions, most straight people could care less about what others do. Most healthy people are just not that focused on sex because sex doesn't define their lives. Abstinence is actually cherished and respected by many people no matter what their gender or sexual preference is.

For most of the people on the planet, procreation and starting a family are the ultimate purpose for having sexual relations. This is why birth control is sometimes frowned upon by many religions, including the Catholic Church. In nature it is what animals do to perpetuate their species. Many people view the natural act of sex to be for having offspring. No matter who you are, or what you believe, the mixing of the genders is essential for mankind's continued existence. (I can hear the haters now.)

As a therapist, I have had many gay clients who have felt railroaded by the media because they were not in favor of gay marriage for a multitude of reasons. They were happy the way their lives were; living without the added emotional and legal pressures of marriage. Many people know and agree with the phrase "marriage changes everything." The truth is that the government financially benefits from the marriage license fees. Lawyers seem to be the biggest benefactors of the marriage laws; their support is not altruistic.

Since the "legalization" of "unions/gay marriage" by the Supreme Court (who can't write laws,) many long term gay and lesbian relationships have begun to struggle with the pressures of permanency now placed upon their relationships. Marriage

136

changes a relationship. You probably won't hear the cultural bullies, TV pundits and pop psychologists warning the Gay and Lesbian population about those facets of the issue because it doesn't serve their agendas. You've been played! The man is now in your bedroom too!

My caution to the progressives: Before you provide a solution you should first determine what problems that solution will create. You should then, in the spirit of full disclosure, let the population know the whole truth. Many homosexual couples now face legal problems they never had before; monetary problems, property problems, divorce and alimony costs, etc…

Groupies

No group is homogeneous in thought; meaning that no group of people all believe the same way. In fact, the numbers show that many "gays" voted against gay marriage in California; evidenced by the referendum voting percentages which suggested that many gays could not have supported the legalization. (Did they tell you that the exit polls didn't match the vote? That upon exiting more people said they voted for it than the actual votes that were counted. It means the privacy of the booth worked.) The vote was actually overruled by a judge who robbed the people of their voice; some of which had to be Gay and Lesbian. A judge went against the people and reversed the referendum. This is called "legislating from the bench." It only became legal when that judge (a progressive who thinks he knows better than the people) went against the vote of the people. The people spoke via their vote several times and then the state's judge went against it. Is some of this news to you? Why didn't you know about it? There are only two sources to blame; yourself for not researching it and your willingness to believe 10 second sound bites from the main stream media.

I could give a thousand such references, but I would get bored. I just want you to understand that words do change in meaning. I'm sure that if you tried, you could come up with more than the examples that I have given you. For those people who like to curse, the word BITCH used to be a female dog and was not a negative curse word. Then it described an angry woman (sexist) and now it has even jumped genders and is often used to refer to a wimpy male. So not only did the word change but it has also changed in a very negative way. It has become a more hateful word when it originally wasn't. The word "bitch" was changed merely by pop culture repetitive use.

The change in definitions and agreements about what words mean is a major contributor to why emails and texting are so often misinterpreted. Marriage is now merely a legal contract and if people want to enter into a contract because they need it to be together, then who cares. In my opinion a good relationship doesn't require an income tax designation. Personally, I think legal marriage was never about people but about governments, taxes and a governmental attempt to have control over religious practice. Redefining a word like marriage falls under what is known as "cultural moral relativism" (suggesting that different cultures retain very different perspectives).

Ponder this: Thou shall not covet another man's wife. Marry her and she becomes property that another man can't have without defying God. Long ago, state sanctioned marriage was a way to organize society, property rights and inheritances for the aristocracy as women could not own property. Before that marriage was only considered valid when a cleric attested to it. This was, essentially a religious dude who lived in the same house/castle and who was seen as the religious part of the family. It's like; "Uncle Joe says you're married so, yeah! Have at it!" "Make non-bastard babies" because of a legal word/state called "married." In modern society you have to get a government license to make your relationship and your baby production legitimate, it is no longer an act of nature or God. The marriage process is now merely government approval of your choices.

Over isn't easy

It's not easy to change people and it is even harder to change entire groups. Some of you will continue to struggle with the issue of believing that you can be easily programmed, but here are the facts; many of which you probably already agree with.

Repetition always wins no matter how intelligent you are. Through repetition you can convince an ugly person they're pretty, a pretty person they're ugly, a smart person they are stupid, a dumb person that they are smart and even a generous person that they are selfish. All you have to do is repeat something enough times and people will eventually believe it.

"Conservatives are against gay marriage." "All liberals are socialists." Trust me, most conservatives don't care what you do and in fact they would rather everyone mind their own business, this includes the government. The truth is that most Southerners think people should mind their own business and let others be. Want to guess who created all this faux outrage: People with agendas and a need to demonize their opponents.

Many liberals don't know what socialism is yet they supported one. There are as many wealthy liberals as there are conservatives; possibly more as much of the South is very poor.

Repetition is how we learn everything. Repetition, is in fact, how many emotionally abusive people stay in control of their victims. The repeated negativity affects both their spouses and their children's self-concept. (If you don't agree that you can program a child, please throw this book away. I can't reach you.)

The processes suggested above for using words and their definitions to program and reprogram the human mind works

139

because of the separation between the conscious and pre/subconscious mind. A person can even program their own mind by the use of positive affirmations or with negative self talk like, "I'm so stupid," "I'm a perfectionist" and "I can't do it."

Eventually the target of any verbal programming will begin to refer to themselves with the label they hear most frequently. It doesn't matter who or what is saying it. The effectiveness of positive affirmations proves the point of repetition. Need proof? Try this daily for two weeks: "I'm a good person and I deserve good things." I promise it will change your outlook on the world. You will begin to reprogram yourself just by repetition.

This repetitious messaging is how battered significant others can believe that their abusers still love them. "I love you but you need to leave me alone when I'm tired. You make me hit you when you keep talking to me and when you don't listen to me!" "No one else will love you like I do, you should thank me!" Yeah, words and definitions followed by a perspective brought on by repetition. Somehow they end up believing that the person who violates them actually loves them. Ever ask them why they keep going back? Programming! It's easier then you think and you have probably been a victim of it more times than you want to admit or perhaps even realize. Advertising works in just this same way, ever wonder why they pay so much to bombard you with the same commercial over and over again in the same commercial break? Repetition works!

These seemingly semantic distinctions are important on two levels; one for healthy social communication and two, for the subconscious processing of who we really are. Correcting these issues is about creating clarity of mind. The inaccurate and lazy processing of language and our failure to be conscious of these missteps has made us weak and vulnerable to manipulation; that has made us hesitant to act when action is required.

140

Chapter Eight

IT'S A CONSPIRACY

What was I thinking

Like the old saying goes "just because you're paranoid it doesn't mean they ain't out to get cha." Maybe it's not an accident that you believe some of the odd things you believe.

Perhaps you are one of the fortunate people who were offered a class in school called "Critical Thinking." Critical Thinking used to be a required part of a good high school education. Now most colleges don't even offer it. Maybe that's why critical thinking seems to be a lost art. You often hear people say; "people are stupid." Stupid is usually seen as having information and still doing the opposite of what it suggests. Stupid is about people who have a healthy intellect, but who just don't seem to use it. The truth is that the critical thinking skill set has been deemphasized. Ever wonder why such an important tool has gone missing from human learning? Maybe they really are "out to get you!"

If you have ever wondered why people don't think more than they do, then you will really enjoy our next communication faux pas (French for "false Step"). I want you to critically analyze the following statement before you continue reading; "I don't want to hurt your feelings, but the following insight is going to upset you." What is being said in this statement and why?

What did you come up with after analyzing it? Did you notice the word "BUT" in that phrase or were you waiting to see what I was going to go on about this time? How about in the earlier referenced statements made by the abuser? "I love you but you have to..." Is my statement or the statement of the

141

abuser, a factual statement? Are they cohesive or are there any inconsistencies? Do you see how we tricked you? Go back and look at mine again. I actually lied to you. Where's the BS?

Have you ever heard or made that statement; "I don't want to hurt your feelings, but you ,,," This is perhaps one of the most frequently practiced uses of inaccurate language. This is a tragic "faux pa" that we exchange in our personal one-on-one relationships in the modern world nearly every day.

The word "but" is a negation in the English language. When it is used in a sentence it splits the sentence in half and only one part of that sentence is actually true or supported by the speaker. The prior half of the statement is usually false because it is negated by the word "but." Either "I don't want to hurt your feelings" or "I don't care if I hurt your feelings because I'm going to do it now by saying what I'm about to say, I know will, in fact, hurt your feelings." Read the prior statement again? "I don't want to hurt your feelings but the following insight is going to upset you." If I am going to say what upsets you then I must not be that interested in sparing your feelings because I could have just remained quiet. I might have said "I'm sorry this is going to hurt your feelings; I have some bad news."

If the person making the prior statement didn't want to hurt the targets feelings, then they could simply remain quiet! In fact, the person who makes this type of statement has already decided they are in fact OK with hurting the targets "feelings" and that the targets feelings are not really as important as the statement about to be made. They are either lying to themselves or to you. Most often it's both, perhaps more importantly, to themselves. It is just an inaccurate statement and therefore not the truth. They are saying things that are not true, sometimes without knowing that they are double talking.

142

In fact, they are telling you that they are going to hurt your feelings and have decided that their wanting to say what they are going to say is more important than your feelings. The statement actually suggests how you are going to feel as a result of what they are about to say. You feelings don't matter because their needs come first. Hence, "but" negates the "I don't want to," because now I am going to, hurt your feelings.

Example; "I do believe that Bob is a good candidate but he is not honest." See the problem. If being a liar makes him a bad candidate then he isn't a good candidate as suggested in the first half of the sentence. I want you to watch a group of TV news pundits over the next several weeks and see how often they talk out of both sides of their mouths. That's what but-ers do! Watch a politician or a roundtable discussion on a news program and see how many "buts" you hear! You'll be shocked by the double-speak once you learn to listen for it.

Let's talk about your "buts!" Americans use the above phrase all the time. Using the word BUT is a very common communication misstep. Very similar to someone saying: "Ah, yeah, no." That little inconsistency is the effect of pacification on our language because people have become afraid to just say "no" or "I disagree!" They try to soften it and they sacrifice accuracy to do so. They are not being straightforward.

There is something gravely wrong when we have to pay a penalty for simply expressing ourselves in a society that has supposedly been built around the freedom of speech (Remember the Amendment says - Unabridged). This is proof that the overly sensitized world we now live in makes us inhibited to speak freely. It makes it necessary to apologize before we speak our minds and it makes it seem mean to confront someone or to put up resistance when we disagree. First it became wrong to be aggressive and now they are attacking assertiveness. This is the

143

result of the progressive ideologues and of the contagion spread by Cultural Bullying.

Are you Pacifistic? YEAH - NO!

Have you noticed people are now saying "yeah/no" before they respond to a statement? The practice seems to be growing at an alarming rate. If you had made a statement like that 35 years ago, you would have been thought a lunatic. If you worry about dishonest people, then pay attention because people who struggle with forthrightness do this misstep all the time. If you have noticed this occurring, then you are probably a critical thinker. If you are doing it, then you are probably not very sure of yourself or you struggle with the truth no being good enough.

This trend is more proof of "The Pacification of Humanity" and the existence of pacifistic thoughts and pacifistic thinking. Pacifistic thought suggests a need for things to be resolved in a peaceful and non-confrontational manner, without anyone becoming upset. The progressive belief is that we can say what we want just as long as others peoples' feelings are put before our free speech and before honest and accurate communication. They have devised reasons why "not telling the truth" is OK.

People who live with the mindset that other peoples' feelings need to be considered first, are not interested in reality; they are overindulged ideologues who do not comprehend the importance of self-expression, truth, reality or free speech. These people don't see things as real or not real; they see things as nice or not nice. They don't really care about the truth or reality because they live on emotions. In their eyes, the individual ranks second or even third to their ideals about how the world "should" be and how things affect the collective. They live in a socialistic ideological dream world where Fairies and Unicorns have baby butts and their human rights too. (In full disclosure I don't have any proof that Unicorns and Fairies aren't real.)

Pacifistic people are usually people who have faced negative social difficulties and interactions in the past when they were outwitted or outnumbered by the cultural bullies. Since this has happened to them, they have adopted the strategy of "lying low" and "not making waves." Just what the bullies wanted.

The cultural bullies frequently run into trouble themselves in a discussion where they are confronted with facts and asked for details or proof of their beliefs. Like "global warming is caused by man;" oh wait, it's changed since they got hit with some science. Next it became Global Climate Change and now, since it is not happening everywhere on the globe, it's just called Climate Change. (Do you think the emotionality that has been connected to the weather makes you see major weather fronts and major weather changes differently? Programmed!)

Like all bullies, when their logic fails they make you the problem. They will claim that you are unreasonable and narrow-minded when you require them to be factual or logical. They will quickly try to ally with others in the room who support their ideology or methods. (Don't worry "little hippie wanna be", no one is watching, open your mind.) Like all bullies, they operate best when they have an audience of known supporters. (If you feel like running out and showing one of your cult members how stupid this book is, then you have been baited and caught.)

The bullies see the "confronter" as being a mean or unreasonable person. When intellectually cornered, this once supposedly peaceful person suddenly becomes aggressive by personally attacking the confronter's values. (Suddenly, being aggressive is OK!) Since they operate from an emotional place, they experience everything from an emotional perspective. That is why they attack your emotional self. This is one of the ideological contagions this book exposes. Now that you have learned some of these insights it will be harder for them to beat

145

you up or beat you down with emotional attacks. You now know they are emotionally-centered and scared. Healthy feelings and opinions evolve out of the accurate use of words, definitions and perspectives. If your personal perspectives are well formed then their tactics will not work.

Finally, people who speak out of both sides of their mouths by using the rapid "yeah-no" are sending a subtle warning (like a "tell" in poker) that they are not confident in what they are saying. They are either uncertain or they know what they are about to say is an untruth or unfounded. Often this yeah-no is an attempt to make you think they agree with you, then they try to adjust your thinking instead of confronting it. They have drunk the pacifistic punch and are now championing the cause of the PC bullies by not being direct. Good communication is as much about accurate listening as it is about accurate speaking.

Is saying "NO, I disagree with you" really that hard for people today? Is it too hard to stand up for what we believe in without having to make the other person feel OK first? Do we always need people to back us up? That is immature. Using "Yeah-no" is like saying; "yeah, you poor thing, with your little mind, let me placate you then enlighten you without you noticing that I am trying to do it."

The two examples above, "but" and "yeah-no," suggest that the speaker feels pressured to talk before they've figured out what they actually want to say. This happens more often in fast-paced environments like urban settings, where exchanges are often rushed in a faster-paced society. The pace is not the problem. If the truth be told, this is less about confusion and more about self-confidence. It seems that societal pressures to fit in have made it hard for people to be emphatic! Current progressive social "norms" try to convince you that creating disagreement is wrong or somehow harmful. (Convenient if they

146

don't want any opposition.) All this does is make everyone more sensitive and hyper-aware of feelings. Apparently they have pretty large segments of society already trained. How about you?

People only become stronger by overcoming obstacles and managing conflicts. You do not become stronger by avoiding difficulties, you become less capable. Lack of practice has never made anyone better at anything. Want to make someone dependent? Do everything for them and protect them from conflict. Not confronting people when they are wrong is an injustice to both parties. Letting people be wrong and letting people do dumb things is not doing them any favors. At some level we are enabling weakness by protecting one another from reality and growth.

Members of modern society currently struggle with just allowing their real thoughts, feelings and opinions to float out there in silence after they have said what they wanted to say. This is sometimes referred to as the "pregnant pause" (the stretching of time when a girl tells a guy she's pregnant). That moment of quiet that waits for a response is important and should not be reduced in the name of fear or discomfort.

People seem so worried about how they will be perceived in the PC culture that they try to cover all the bases with double-talk. These behaviors actually create more anxiety, not less. People have become so henpecked by the scrutiny of the cultural bullies that they have to presume how they will be taken before they finish speaking. The only reason they do this is to prevent themselves from being labeled as "insensitive" or worse. This creates anxious discomfort for everyone and it is the machination of coercion. It's an over-sensitization to others at the cost of truth, clarity and individuality. These practices may quite possibly be the cause of the increase in social phobias and

147

anxieties disorders over the past 20 years. They believe it's the chemicals in the food (victimhood over personal responsibility).

Is the truth expendable?

Here's a great example of where truth takes a backseat to protecting "feelings:" Dude, you're getting fat! Is it the truth? I live in the United States, where fat cats aren't fat, the only place on Earth where the poor people are fatter than the rich people. Where poor has little to do with staring or even going without. Most of the poor people in the world are skinny with distended bellies; many are dying from malnutrition. BUT NOT HERE IN THE U.S.!! Travel the world and see. When was the last time you heard of anyone starving to death in the US; that is unless, someone else did it to them intentionally.

OK, it might not be appropriate to say that to a stranger because what another person does is none of our business. My friend/spouse/sibling/child may actually need to be confronted about the problem in order to save their life not their feelings. Maybe by confronted my friend I could help save his life. If I think it and don't say it, I become complicit to it in my own mind, especially if I never say anything and he dies from it.

I have treated morbidly obese people who were well over 500 pounds and the first thing they talk about as an obstacle to losing weight are the people around them; both avoiders and enablers. Most obese people have an accomplice that they sometimes call "feeders." Very few obese people have anyone around them who will tell them NO. Instead of having people who set boundaries and confront the truth, they have people around them who will even prepare their food for them. Would you make drinks for an alcoholic? Maybe the reason no one says anything is because they are afraid to have the person mad at them. Is that selfish?

How about; "I want to lose weight BUT….. (excuse here)." Reducing eating is the solution to all weight loss. Overeating is the cause of 99% of the overweight problem in America. Why is it that everyone tries to tell each other "what to eat" to lose weight when the real solution is not eating something. I'm not making a point here about weight I'm making a point about speech. Get real and the people around you become more real; everyone is better off for it. I know what you are thinking; I don't want to hurt their feelings. If you're fat too then maybe you think you don't have any room to talk. Convenient!

To be honest, I would personally rather step on your feelings than walk to your grave. People don't have a problem telling skinny people to eat more. Why? Shame is why and shame grows in the dark. Overeating is a behavioral issue and ignoring it only makes it worse. Ever heard anyone say; either lose weight or I'm leaving you? Maybe not out-rightly but there are people who would just leave the relationship because that's easier than talking about it. Is that better?

Just to be clear. There are medical reasons for being overweight, but most fat people (is that PC) are fat because they are gluttonous. Do you know how much eating effort is required for a person to remain more than 50 pounds over their suggested weight? If an overweight person eats only 2000 calories a day (the norm) they would immediately start losing lots of weight. A fisherman on the Bearing Sea in Alaska only needs about 4000-5000 calories a day for energy. Many obese people eat over 10,000 calories a day with no exercise or work. Start counting calories and stop BS-ing yourself that you need more than 2000 calories a day, because you don't. What you need to do is face the truth head on and get honest about reality. You're gonna die!

Some of you are getting mad right now. Remember the old saying "The truth will set you free." Is not confronting them helping them or is it hiding the truth in the dark where things go to die. Do you really think that not talking about something could save someone's life or help them in any way?

You can bet that the progressives have a solution to your weaknesses. They, the progressives who run most governments think you are so weak-minded and incapable that they have to step in to stop you from eating too much. You can't even buy an extra large soda in NYC and in many government buildings you can't buy a soda/pop/cola because you aren't strong enough or smart enough to take care of yourself; this is the nanny state. Recall my earlier point about the government's ability to gain substantial power when they use health as a justification. There are restaurants in this country that aren't allowed to cook with butter or certain oils because you aren't wise enough to choose.

We are not trying to shame people when we are confronting them. We are not insulting people by disagreeing with them. What we are actually doing when we publicly disagree is use our personal capital to reach someone we care about. An example of shaming would be giving someone a hard time about their weight when they are actually eating 2000 calories a day, but have not yet lost the weight. Don't use sensitivity to argue against it because that is the very reason things aren't working.

We can't make someone feel guilty; guilt is an internal mechanism that we either have or we don't. If we are not guilty we don't feel guilty. In those instances, the person is feeling shame about their own lack of success or failure to try. One caution; don't confront them unless you're willing to help them solve the problem.

I promise you can't make me feel like a "hater" or feel guilty about hating because I know what is in my heart. You can try, but I may remind you of the three fingers pointing back at you. I may inquire as to why you are so focused on that issue of hate and why you see it everywhere you look. "Eye of the beholder" maybe? I can tell you that I worked for 10 (low-paying) years of my life helping young black people in the hardest areas of Baltimore City. I was often the only white guy in the building, taking personal risks every time that I went to work; because I was "white." I eventually left because I thought that what was really needed was for successful black men and women to be the ones to come back to the hood and prove that success and overcoming these obstacles was possible. My best efforts were still met with racist insinuations that because I was white I couldn't understand. I left because I felt like I was filling the gap that needed to be filled by a young black man. I loved my work.

I promise you that anyone who is overweight will, at some point, admit they are fat because they won't stop eating, not can't stop eating, won't! What if an alcoholic said; "My body handles alcohol differently, it's not my fault I drink and drive."

Can't means won't! It's OK to won't, just know that you are won't-ing and don't try to convince me otherwise so that you "feel" better about it. The fact is that most obese people do have major enablers who actually help them remain obese. Not confronting them is enabling them. Feeding them is killing them. Ignoring self-deception is feeding their denial. Get honest!

The self expressed

How big is your but! No, not that butt, this "but." As in "It's none of my business but I think you are too overweight and I'm worried about you." This is another good example of how a BUT can get in the way.

When I work with people who have damaged self esteem I have them exclude the word BUT (or can't) from their messaging and separate their statements with periods. Sometimes I have them practice a dialogue where they actually say "period" at the end of each point or part of a statement.

Here is an example. "There is something I want to say" (no but, period.) "I'm worried it's going to hurt you." (Period) "I do wish there was a way of telling you this without hurting your feelings. (Period) I'm concerned about your health. (Period) You need to lose weight, like now."

You might try; "I need to tell you what I've been thinking." When teaching assertiveness, I simply have them remove the first part of the sentence that would have been negated by the word "BUT." As in; "I need to tell you something that is going to be hard for you to hear because it is hard for me to say."

Referring back to the earlier examples, "I think you're a selfish person" or "You don't seem to take my needs into consideration" or "When you don't call me I feel irrelevant." Starting a sentence with "I know you love me but…" speaks to the speaker's lack of confidence more than anything else.

As a society we struggle with clearly communicating because the PC Culture has made it too costly. It has made us all vague, weak and pacifistic. Is it any wonder we have trouble communicating when we are double-talking all the time? "Say what you mean and mean what you say, just don't say it mean." People who don't speak the truth are dishonest.

There are times when the word "but" is accurately used, BUT only when the prior statement is meant to be negated. Example; "I have loved you for a long a time, but I need to move on for my own sanity." Or perhaps; "You've been a good employee here for a long time, but I have to lay you off." In these examples the BUT makes the first part of the statement irrelevant as intended.

Use your intellect on the following statement and see if you can recognize what happens here psychologically. If someone says; "I know I shouldn't drink and drive but all my friends drink too." Take a minute before you continue reading to develop your own analysis of what is going on here.

Yes, they are making an excuse in the above statement. Does this person know they shouldn't drink and drive? Do they believe their statement makes sense? Are they deflecting the focus away from the issue of what they shouldn't do by trying to intellectualize some other point? Did you hear them say they plan to keep drinking and driving?

If the person is forced to stop the statement before the -but-as in "I know I shouldn't drink and drive." (Period) What happens? They are forced to hear their own truth before they rationalize that truth away with the word BUT. The period stops their train of thought before it gets negated by their own rationalization. This is how people confuse themselves. In this case, it can even get them killed or in jail.

I will often stop them; "I know I shouldn't drink and drive but".... "STOP" I say. Do you believe that or not? Let's sit with that statement for a minute. If you believe it, what are you going to do about it? I might even say, "It's OK if you choose not to believe it, let's just be clear here about what you mean to say." What you are really saying then is, "I'm going to drink and drive because everybody does it."

Should they be allowed to continue with verbal misstep their rationalization is essentially suggesting that what comes after the word but is important and nothing before it. "...But here's what I tell myself and you should believe it too." What they said was "I'm going to keep drinking and driving because I have rationalized it to my own satisfaction and for my own convenience." Sublimely or subconsciously; "If you don't confront me, it will be even easier for me to keep believing it."

I know I shouldn't drink and drive. (period) Do they know it? They are now forced to answer for their own refusal to heed their

153

own awareness. I might say, "BUT you're going to keep doing it anyway, even though you are aware that on some level it is wrong or dangerous." I continue "So when something bad happens later on you are just going to accept the responsibility of the action and plead guilty, right? Because you knew it was wrong?"

We are making these types of missteps regularly and we wonder why the world doesn't make sense. It's because we don't make sense to ourselves and we believe things in our heads that just aren't true or accurate. Our "friends" let us get away with it!

Further, there is a major difference between knowing something and being aware of something. Here is a simple distinction that may work for you, too. If you know it, you show it, by your actions. I can be aware that I need to exercise, but I know I need to exercise when I actually do it. I stop drinking and driving when I KNOW that it is wrong. I am on a diet when I KNOW I need to be. Simple "awareness" only, allows me to continue the act, but knowing suggests change in order to adjust to that truth; to act accordingly.

What I am doing here is asking you to get real, stay real and stop operating on some confused verbal placations to others and yourself. It's double talk and it's unhealthy. When you stop doing it you'll start noticing it. It is my belief that letting these nuances continue in our daily lives is how we have become susceptible to being railroaded by nefarious people and institutions that use these nuances purposefully. You see, if we allow ourselves to do these things then we let other people do these things, because it's apparently ok to do it. If they do it, then it must be OK for us to do it too. Right? Wrong! Two wrongs don't make a right. Believing half truths is dangerous. Living an emotionally rationalized version of reality only leads to heartache, anxiety, confusion or even death. These are the games of the ideologues that live in the land of Platitudes.

More authentic and more genuine

Change takes practice. If you want to become a better athlete you practice, a better musician you practice and a better therapist/doctor you practice. If you want to become a stronger more intelligent person, you practice. You weren't weakened overnight and positive change takes time.

It is important to realize that if the people around you cannot allow you to be you, then what you both end up with is a relationship with someone other than who you thought you knew. I hear my couples say this all the time; "S/he's not who I thought s/he was." Critically analyze that one and remember that it is our responsibility to collect information and data from what we hear.

Hopefully you noticed that the statement "I don't even know who s/he is" does not even imply that the person has ever actually been the way we thought they were. The speaker has apparently gotten themselves into trouble by believing their own half-truths. Believing what they wanted to believe about their partner. I then often hear; "I'm the same person I've always been." (That one I never doubt.)

It is not possible to be in a real relationship with someone who is not genuine and authentic. It is not possible to know ourselves if we are not genuine and authentic with others because we believe our own press. Women often cite "he's good husband material." What they are saying is that they knew he wasn't what they wanted in the first place; they just told themselves they could fix him later. Got Clarity?

When we are not authentic we essentially alter our vision of who we are and the world around us never sees the real us. When we do not speak truth we believe lies. We become an altered, edited and stifled version of who we are. We end up feeling lost and confused because we settled for inaccuracy. When you settle for less than you deserve you get less than you deserve every time.

Let me show you: If I meet someone and she likes orchestra music and I say I do too because, well, she's attractive, then I shift the whole basis of the relationship with that one little fabrication. I become someone I'm not and she believes I am someone different because I did not present the genuine me who has never listened to an entire CD of orchestra music on purpose. Personally I could take it or leave it. In the above exchange I have manipulated/tricked both her and myself. This is what I mean by communication is manipulation. Did I trick her? Mislead her? Lie to her? The end result is that there is no difference. I did not speak the truth; even if I was planning to like her music later.

Many people play this little game of letting someone think they are different than who they are. Later, when relational conflicts present, it's our own fault. Especially if we end up arguing over topics like which radio station to listen to in the car, which music to play in the house or which concert to go to. This gets more convoluted because after she asked me about orchestra music I probably didn't ask her if she liked Metal or Country. If they don't know who you really are because you didn't make yourself clear, then they don't know how you really think or feel: These behaviors make it easy to feel disconnected and alone.

Perhaps you don't want them to know the real you because you are trying to achieve some selfish goal. That's another issue. Are you afraid of being alone? Do you think you're too weak to handle the possible disapproval or rejection? The Universe/God can't put the right person in your life if you're busy settling for whatever is easy. Mr. Right is not going to settle for Ms. OK.

156

Being real is risky but (the "but" here is a purposeful negation example) you have to decide; do you want a real relationship or do you want to be engaged in shallow interactions with other people who are possibly being fake too? If you want real, you have to be real. Honestly being who you are means being strong enough to face the consequences of being you in the real world; warts and all. This takes practice too.

FYI: A stark reality for many is that learning how to be alone actually transcends the fear of being alone, because then, you no longer have to live out of the fear that you may be alone. When you are OK being alone you will not settle for less than what you want. If you think you can be alone. try it. Being alone is much harder than you think. Just ask the people who want to be left alone. (Feeling lonely is much different; that usually results from not being known for who we really are!)

Here is the catch: If you don't accept and allow others to be real with you, then you will not allow yourself to be real either. You will be alone in a crowd. Allow people to say things that speak truth to who they are and you will feel more comfortable doing the same. Embrace differences; don't fear them. Despite the current generation's lock-step mob mentality, unique is cool; consider it a form of art and appreciate it. Don't hide who you are like a pacifist. You are stronger than you think and you are not going to fall apart if the people you want near you become uncertain. You see, they have to be uncertain before they can become certain. Otherwise, we're all pawns living a delusion.

If we do not provide the truth then the person we misrepresent ourselves to becomes dependent on our revision of reality; a picture that must be constantly repainted. This is how people get caught in lies. One lie leads to another and now we have to act like we like their music again and again. We could find ourselves sitting at the opera when our favorite band is

157

playing its final gig down the street. We then begin to resent them for "making us" miss our preferred event, as if we did them some type of favor. (OUR FAULT) By not giving others the truth we also manipulate their choices and they are not given the RIGHT to choose for themselves the kind of person they want to be with. We steal their freedom to decide truthfully for themselves. The failure becomes all ours.

If your life is full of fake, shallow people there will be no room for real people. If the people in your life don't fit your REAL self, then change the people around you. People will eventually respect you more for having standards. Being alone makes you stronger and being alone never lasts.

Being afraid to do or say something and giving into that fear does not strengthen you for your next challenge, it only reinforces avoidance. If we are accurate with our words, thoughts and feeling then we are more confident and thereby less inhibited to be genuine. Ultimately, what others think about us doesn't change us. I don't have to adjust who I am if the people around me already know me. It is not your job to protect anyone from reality; protecting them often does them a disservice because it makes them too weak to handle reality. Humanity is on a train quickly heading in the WRONG direction, while self-righteously claiming to be mannerly and nice (PC). Manipulation is NOT nice, it's theft; be it committed by a person, a school, a community or a government institution.

Chapter Nine

DISTORTION

More people more problems

Many people struggle with the use of language and almost as many people struggle with the constructs of race. There may be a connection. We have become increasingly more intolerant of one another regardless of our viewpoints. People are carrying around more anger than at any point in human history. They are quicker to find differences than they are similarities.

What if I told you that "stereotyping" is a natural occurrence in the human animal? That it is impossible for the human animal not to profile or stereotype? Some of you are doing it right now. Probably stuffing me into a little box labeled he's in "the ____ group!"

Does my claim that we can't stop it surprise you? Would you automatically think I was going to justify hatred? No, you wouldn't dare suggest that stereotyping is unnatural while at the same time stereotyping me. That would be crazy!

Relax, talking about it will not make us racist or make things worse for the whole world even though that is what the cultural bullies have been programmed you to believe. What I am suggesting is that you've been tricked by something or someone for no other reason than to acquire your emotional support or allegiance to an ideology; maybe to distract you from some other issue of the day that they didn't want you focusing on.

Stereotyping at its core is a natural occurrence that is seldom about race. It's about a little, forgotten phenomena called "in-grouping and out-grouping." This Out-grouping occurs all the

159

time. It occurs every second in nature and for this reason it is natural; it's an ancient survival tool that all animals use. Monkey tribes do it all the time. Antelope and other animals like zebras rarely pack together unless they're all at the watering hole. Some behaviorists even suggest that similar looking horses will group together. Ever heard "like attracts like" or "birds of a feather flock together?" How come it is natural for animals but not for humans, who said so? Are we just that much more advanced?

It is a natural aspect of human nature and humanity to in-group and out-group. How come they don't mention this stuff in school or on the evening news? Ask yourself why they don't educate young people about this very human trait? The answer is simple; they are using our emotions about race to polarize us. It's not an honest mistake either. We have purposefully been given half the story in order to fulfill an agenda; to win our allegiance and to gain our support on an issue.

In Grouping & Out-Grouping

If we put 10 people who are exact copies of one another in the same room they will still eventually sub-group according to personal preferences. If I had 10 black men born in Africa, into the same tribe, same IQ's, who ate all the same foods every day, with no media or favorite stores or music they will still sub-group. Some would be better hunters, some leaders, some farmers, some followers; some will like the color red while others will like the color blue. Many would argue together over all the above. Do you see my point? Hopefully that's simple enough. People naturally group together; social animals do it even more often. That is what social animals do because, like attracts like.

Man cannot separate himself from or intellectualize himself out of his limbic system functioning (the part of his brain where fight and flight reside, the survival mechanisms). Grouping is a

160

part of nature. It is left over from the herd and pack mentalities we once had as cave dwellers just trying to survive. You can't outthink this part of the brain and you can't legislate it away.

No matter how alike a group may start out, eventually some of the above tribe members will get together and plan the hunt and call themselves the hunters and others will manage the farming and call themselves farmers. The farmers may even start to criticize the hunters when they come back empty-handed etc. Then there is gender grouping; we all know that women and men group themselves up at parties. This is in-grouping and out-grouping and it is not a gender issue either.

Racism does not begin with race; it's about in-grouping and out-grouping as a survival strategy; as a way to assess safety issues and limit threats. This part of the brain does not use logic, rationale or memory; only conditioning. Any suggestion that we have evolved past this would suggest that grouping is a product of logic, which it is not; it's instinctual.

It is possible to be conditioned to hate or fear a particular group, but that only lasts as long as the conditioning continues: As long as people are still being reminded of their conditioning. A black kid taught to hate whites will eventually change his mind after some exposure to good white people and less exposure to haters. He is actually more likely to group up with people from the same socio-economic class before deciding on race; why, because this group will survive in a familiar way.

Hence, sub-grouping is natural and perhaps even necessary. The more obvious the differences, the more quickly grouping or separation occurs. "Grouping" occurs with age, gender, height and race, but it's still only about grouping and not about hate.

If I brought 4 men in from another tribe (same race) it could even start a war. War is a major sub-grouping event usually

161

created by more obvious differences, but often only over competing ideologies and perspectives.

The point here is not about racism. No matter how hard we try, it is impossible for any society that embraces different cultures into its ranks to not have cultural (group) separations. Unfortunately, there are people who ignore this simple truth. They believe that you can change and control your instincts. They are called ideologues. They make ideology reality and then demand that because they can think something is real that it must be real and that out-thinking nature is possible. We have to adapt to nature because we can't out-think it. Nature is not wrong it is natural. In the long run Nature always wins!

Trying to ignore nature is a form of an ideological contagion that suggests out-grouping is wrong; an ideology most commonly spread by institutions of "higher" learning. These self-described intellectuals are the owners of the biggest echo chamber on Earth. Most of the really farfetched lunacies in society come from our college campuses where academics (People who don't usually have real jobs or live in the real world) live in their little bubbles of bad ideas that have been handed down and passed around from the prior generation of academic elitists and ideologues. They're protected from reality and nature.

Academia is one of the most strictly regulated and controlled echo chambers in modern society. A place where is has become common practice to only hire other people to work in the system who pledge themselves to progressive liberal thought. Living in these ideological echo chambers makes them delusional (a form of mental illness) because they don't operate on reality or facts. They are very self-deluded people who believe that if enough people feel (Think) the way they feel (think) then it must be real. The ideologues are the people who literally wrote the books on "I feel that..." and "yeah, but no,,," Their numbers and their influence are so vast that they lend a faux credibility to their unproven ideals. These people are responsible for keeping hate and division alive because they bully everyone around them. No one is allowed to object out loud so their self-deceptions fester and grow. Their echo chamber even provides sustenance for the cultural bully. They perpetuate division by choice, so they believe that division is a choice and not an aspect of nature.

The Polarization Clique

The polarization clique is the Gestapo elite of the cultural bullies. They are the gatekeepers of information and they are aware of how orchestrated and slanted the information they contrive and disseminate is towards their own secret ideological agendas. Their primary agenda is to gain your allegiance through the manipulation of information; known as propaganda! Just like the greatest propagandists in history, their primary tool is using your emotional reactions to issues, to cloud your intellect, which is then overridden by emotional outrage.

The first step towards the achievement of polarization is creating various sides of an issue; sometimes where sides and issues don't even exist. They create these various divisions on somewhat important or popular emotional topics; like abortion and health care then they add other smaller less concerning issues to the supposed "right side" of the split. Since you have already chosen a side based on the information you were given on the more dramatic issue, you are covertly coerced to support their newest issue by proxy; often without realizing it or being informed of it. If you don't support their new "little" causes, they'll argue that you don't support their bigger causes. They often use false choices such as; "you are either one of us or one of them;" "you're either with us or against us."

This polarization technique is how both the Democratic and Republican parties function. For instance, if you support gay rights you must also support abortion rights or else you have no side to vote with. If you vote for this person, then you are forced to support issues you may not support such as reducing gun ownership. You're forced to choose. (FYI Not all conservatives support gun ownership; many just support the right to own the gun for those who want to. All Democrats do not support Gay marriage because some are very Christian, etc…). These are false "all or nothing choices" and that is polarization.

Coercion requires that a group of people be split into segments. This is the only way to create the pressure to act. You can't be a victim if the other side isn't trying to do something wrong, so they make sure you know what the other side is doing wrong. Evidence of this polarization is occurring now and can be easily seen in modern life. There are no practical reasons for our society to be arguing more than ever before. Modern society has not been this clearly segmented in many decades. Perhaps the speed of information is increasing these divisions but only because the Clique wants it that way. The truth is that most Republicans could care less about what you do in your bedroom and most liberals see the value of gun ownership. It is systematically impossible to find the middle ground in a two party set up. This is polarization and we have all been getting played for far too long.

Perhaps this is why so many people try to call themselves "Independents." They have realized that they are in the middle and not "all or nothing" voters. There is however no Independent Party. The simple reason being that triangulation would take place, thus canceling out the straight polarizations of; DEM and REP, North and South, Black and White etc… Three parties would break the Electoral College; a system designed to keep only two parties in place forever.

When it comes to polarization, the best hoped-for outcome is to have a majority in one group and as few others as possible in the opposing group; but you still need an opposing group. This necessity is what makes the process so ugly, hateful and bitter; because the emotional connection to a side of the issue is vital to the bully progressive agendas on both sides. It becomes a necessary tug-of-war with you in the middle. We can view this as forced in-grouping and forced out-grouping; it is manipulation using the control of information. That is propaganda.

This forced grouping is actually very easy to do; just figure out one thing that may have nothing to do with your goal but that will create division. If you look behind the curtain, you can easily see how this might be working today in our culture. There are many issues being used to achieve this goal; gay/straight, black/white (notice this is never black/brown or white/red or yellow/black etc..) REP/DEM, prolife/prochoice, women/men, guns/no guns, and, oh yes, the most popular and the port of last resort for progressives over the last 2000 years, rich/poor.

Are you in-grouped yet? Are you on one side of these issues? Do you see the clear lines between left and right on all of them? Are you allowed to be a prochoice Republican or a prolife/gun Democrat? Out loud, in public, without retaliation from the cultural bullies?

Once the sides have been polarized, it is quite simple to just throw in another issue or group other issues with them. You either support our side or you don't. This is how the Civil War started. Slavery was the WEDGE issue, but not the real reason it started. It was actually about state's rights to decide on slavery, but because everyone believed in State's rights the progressive ideologues had to make it about something more emotionally divisive so they used slavery as the wedge issue.

165

As mentioned briefly above, once you are forced to one side for any issue you are then required to be one of us or one of them (polarization). You can't be pro-gun and prochoice; or so they say. This is how fascism was given birth. Polarization is how the Nazis attained power and control.

Not buying it yet because of the "overused" Nazi reference? (Psst,, they want you to think it's overused because then the historical evidence can be negated.) Just read the words of Herman Goering at the Nuremberg trials when he was asked how they got all the people to follow them and die for their sick cause. He answered; "Of course the people don't want war. But after all, it's the leaders of the country who determine the policy and it's always a simple matter to drag the people along whether it's a democracy, a fascist dictatorship, or a parliament, or a communist dictatorship. Voice or no voice, the people can always be brought to the bidding of the leaders. That is easy. <u>All you have to do is tell them they are being attacked</u>, and denounce the pacifists (The people who don't want to fight for the cause) for lack of patriotism and exposing the country to greater danger." This is coercion by the use of propaganda.

I don't want you to denounce the pacifists; I want you to see how they are forcing you to be one. I want you to speak out and speak out no matter what side you are supposed to support. Stand in the middle and scream with the rest of us.

Want a modern day example of propaganda? "Guantanamo Bay prison creates terrorists. You must support us in the closing of the facility so that you will be safer." The under-informed individual declares to themselves that they want to be safer so they voice their desire to close GTMO. Remember, they do this with no proof or evidence of what they are saying; only your emotional response blended with repetitious messaging and the hiding of anything that would counter their point. Suggesting

166

that GTMO creates terrorists would also suggest that the existence of jails creates more criminals because they are mad that the jails exist.

The Nazis tugged on the emotional heartstrings of the majority; made them fear the Jewish people with propaganda cartoons. They coerced the German people into protecting themselves from the Jewish people who, they were told, wanted to steal the bread from the mouths of their children and to erase their God Jesus. This was "us or them" polarization.

During this same time, the same tactic of polarization was being used by Joseph McCarthy (the anti-communism guy). Sen. Joseph McCarthy (R-WI) June 02, 1950 *"Is it because we are less intelligent than the Communists? Is it because we can't match them in courage?* (Denoucing the pacifists*) Is it because their devotion to atheism is greater than our devotion to God?* (Threaten your God) *Is it because we are less willing to stand up and fight for what we think is right? Ladies and gentlemen, the answer to all those questions is "No."* (See how he grouped them together? See how McCarthy did exactly what Herman Goering did, a man supposedly so different?) He continued *"Then what is the answer? Is it in our leadership? To that my answer is "Yes," and I challenge anyone to find another answer. (Polarization and Bullying) I have been naming and presenting evidence against those leaders who have been responsible for selling into Communist slavery 400,000,000 people-those leaders responsible for the creation of Communist steppingstones to the American shores."*

McCarthy's use of polarization gave him immense power to violate civil rights with the support of the American people. He used the fear of being labeled a communist as coercion. He was a "Cultural Bully." You either support our efforts or we will investigate you too. (Threat)

Isn't it interesting how people supposedly so different from one another (Nazi and McCarthy) were doing the exact same thing? They were merely serving different agendas in the same way; not serving the people. They were simply manipulating information and using emotions to gain allegiance and power. During their time it was even easier because the access to truth was limited to what you heard on TV or read in the Newspapers (if you could read.) If the newspapers didn't report what McCarthy wanted, he would start looking into them too. So they did exactly what he demanded. Did you notice that McCarthy asked lots of questions, generated fear, and then suggested that you could trust him, that he would save you? He shouted; "JUST GIVE ME POWER," to solve the crisis he created!

The need to polarize the populous is why people are often pressured to be on either the left or the right. Large groups in lock-step are easier to control than individual aspects or numbers of smaller voting blocks. This girl is Red and this guy is Blue; if you are red trust her to represent you and if you are blue trust him to make the changes that you want. Just give them power.

They want large groups because when groups are too segmented it becomes much harder to get everyone to drink the cult's punch at the same time. It's easier to provide two flavors of punch at the party and let people pick one or the other. (FYI, color coding is subliminal in-grouping for the lower functioning citizens. You don't have to listen or know just follow the colors.)

Despite popular belief, there are Conservative gay & lesbian people, black conservatives, conservative who don't care if you have an abortion, (most don't). There are liberals and socialists who support the right to carry a gun and even liberals who are pro life, etc... There are tons of poor people who believe in the free market economy (this means no government interference) and there are even liberals who believe the government is way

168

too big and that entitlements are out of hand; yet it is impossible to vote that way in a presidential election.

I hope you understand how you have been (and are being) managed, molded and manipulated. It is time for the people to run the government as representatives of all the people in their individual districts, no matter how many different views there are. It's time to return the power to people where they live, in the states. Not to people siding up in National Government Parties.

Un-revising history

Once upon a time it was known to all that Abe Lincoln was a Republican and that it was the Republicans who actually ended slavery. Once upon a time people knew that the KKK was and still is a Democrat invention. Few people in the US today know that when the Civil War was fought that the North was Conservative/Rep and that the Southern/DEM slave owners called themselves liberals. Ask yourself why most people don't know these simple realities today. The reason is simple; it doesn't serve the agendas of the power-hungry people who want you to think and do things their way.

It's obvious there are sides and that theses sides have been manufactured: Created by back room deal-making and by what is known as revisionist history. History is revised by teaching people about those events and realities that preserve and serve a specific agenda. If we want kids to vote Blue we can't let them know about the good things the Reds have done and vice versa.

So who keeps these groups separate and battling with each other? Basically anyone who has an agenda they want to perpetuate. Did you know that Google is a liberal-run organization? That they track key phrases and limit exposure to certain types of information? That FACEBOOK does the same thing by reducing the visibility of posts that don't support their liberal ideological beliefs or corporate needs? Have you ever

169

seen an ad for another social media page on Facebook? How about a Republican banner on the top of your "FREE" yahoo email? (All these are possible FCC violations). Have you ever noticed that Facebook assigns a number to your image name? That way they can tell if it is reposted. They can blacklist the number they assign so if someone saves and reposts it their filters will find it and keep it from being shown if it is not within their corporate or ideological interests. (Rename them when you save them.)

Remember when you used to see every post that everyone put up in a social media platform? When your "top ten" search results in Google were not a bunch of ads paid for by one company or the top five companies paying the most for you to see their messaging. Once upon a time you saw everything in the news feed and no spontaneous page suggestions. This is both manipulation and control; according to some standards these organizations are monopolies.

Speaking of bias, information, data and news; how about the bias of mainstream news agencies of all types and colors? We used to get all the news in 30 minutes now they can't seem to give us half of it in 24 hours.

Here is some real history for you. Those old rich liberal plantation owners have all moved up North and they took their money with them. They left their factory workers down South where many real Conservatives still work cheap and where operating costs (taxes) are lower. Let's not forget that money buys allegiance, money buys exposure and, contrary to the programmed beliefs of many, the Right does not have all the money. In fact Democrats hold the richest districts in the US, which means that the people in the richest districts vote mostly Democrat. The truth is that all in all, wealth is a pretty even split, but that is not what they'd have you believe. (Remember that class and money are the oldest of polarization techniques and they seem to be working just fine.)

Let's not forget the great paying jobs of the liberal academics where almost every job in an entire field is 100k or more. Then there is the tons of Hollyweird money in all parts of the media machine. Bill Gates, Zuckerberg, Soros, and many of the richest people on the planet complain about the imbalance of power yet they all perpetuate their own liberal political preferences from the dark shadows.

Basically there is no real division when it comes to $$$$. When we talk about the political process, not all the money in play comes from US citizens either. It is now possible for rich people around the world to influence voters by ad campaigns and the disclosure of favorable information about their governments and the creation of polices there that can influence elections here. Despite all the money in politics, the real data is controlled by the colleges who program the "youth vote" by training the young mind on "what to think" and not "how to think."

Let's not forget the congressional hearing that found the IRS guilty of favoritism when their bias was used to pick winners by controlling who could spend money to provide information to the public in the 2008 and 2012 election cycles. They did this by not approving 401-c3's for conservative organizations. That is the foundation that the current propaganda machine rests on; the proof of the manipulation of information by a government.

Educational Indoctrination

Language isn't something, it's everything. This is where your "feelings" "thinking-s" and "buts" come into play. The educational system is the origin of most of the progressive political sentiments in mainstream society. This is where the foundations of our words, definitions and perspectives get co-

171

opted, corrupted and redefined in order to serve the collective. Academia is where individuality is lost.

As discussed earlier in this book, it is impossible for us to process an emotion without language. It is impossible for us to share or communicate anything without an agreement on symbols and words. (Words are merely agreed-upon sounds and symbols (letters) that represent an image or a concept.) It is our logical left brains that processes and stores these agreements. Perhaps you may already understand the importance of not confusing our right side (creative/feeling) brains with our left side (logic/organizational) brain hemispheres. Nature seemed to think it was important to separate these two processing centers and we should pay attention to that.

Trying to make sense of a feeling can be confusing enough without confusing thoughts for feelings which, in their own right can be quite overwhelming. Trust me; it is vitally important for your own emotional wellbeing to keep these distinctions between thoughts and feelings better organized. If you can't separate your thoughts and emotions on your own now, you will end up paying a professional to help you do it later. You might just miss out on many of the joys life has to offer. If you do seek a professional's help, please don't enter the process already knowing what the therapist needs to know to solve your problem. You got there because your thinking was flawed. (You wouldn't hold information about your cars dysfunction back from your car's mechanic would you?)

These agreed upon symbols only exist because someone told us they did; probably a family member or a childhood acquaintance who was taught these agreements by their caregivers. At some point we were told what they were and we agreed to use someone else's sound and term to represent that concept or thing (a teacher perhaps). Due to the fact that young

172

people are so easily programmed, the people who program our children need to be trustworthy. The information that they relay to our young minds needs to be verified and validated. Ideology should not be taught to children (unless that is what you are paying for). You have a right to teach your child your vision.

We have to be very careful that we are in fact, trusting the right sources of information; that the information is accurate. That if theories and ideologies are to be taught, that they be well-balanced. As an educational designer I can tell you with full certainty, that this means that the people designing the curriculum, writing the text books and disseminating the content, need to be credible and nonpartisan (not having a side).

Obviously, if you wanted your child to be an atheist you wouldn't send him to parochial school and if you wanted your child to be a "believer" you might want to reconsider sending them somewhere that demands separation from God. It sounds simple. Have you double checked?

Children who are purposefully taught differently from their parents cannot be expected to agree with their parents. If the family members see things differently, discord will be present. Our adolescents are usually taught by people in their twenties who are not always capable of giving our children opposing ideologies. (Ever met a twenty-something who knew it all?) If we don't pay closer attention, we can't be surprised later when our teens values are different than our own or when there is intellectual discord at the family dinner table about right and wrong. The dinner table (without phones) was once used to balance these perspectives of media, school, church and home.

Certain media and social networks are often given more credibility and are often more trusted then they should be. Government curriculums, textbook writers and the government's teachers must be vetted well before we blindly turn our children and the future of our society, over to the agendas of people we don't agree with. A government-controlled school is more than just an education, it is indoctrination. We need to take an active role in the development of our children's world view by monitoring what they are being taught. Letting the government tell us what "we need to know" is pacifistic, lazy and negligent.

When it comes to harmony and good communication we need to be in concert with our symbolic agreements (definitions) or we will certainly be in disagreement later. It is easy to see how a nefarious programmer or the designer of educational information could interfere with family unity and generational congruency.

With that being said, there must be agreements for healthy communication to develop. If there are no agreements on what the words mean, then they mean nothing and the word becomes merely a useless sound. The lack of these agreements would be much like the experience of hearing someone speaking a language we do not know: Just odd sounds with no reference. Different languages are merely different sounds and agreements for the same things. We are completely lost when these agreements are not known and understood.

Here is an example: Do you know the definition of "capractic?" Can we discuss the concept if you don't? The word means nothing to you, right? It's a lost sound in your mind. You may be trying to sound it out or break it down to gain some insight because of the agreements we have for parts of their Latin or Greek roots. The reason you don't know what it means is because we have no agreement on its meaning (but mostly because I just made it up while typing). If we agreed that it was the practice of sizing a ball cap, then the next time I use it you know what I'm referencing. It's really that simple; just like you know that "PC" stands for political correctness. (Agreements)

174

Wait! Did you trust my definition? What if I was just trying to falsely program you? It's that easy. There is a reason why everyone used to have a dictionary from a single source called Webster (even though that single source thing is a little scary too). We trusted Webster and his daughter too, but we only trusted her because we trusted him, a man we never saw.

Without agreement the word "chair" would present no image to our minds; someone had to instruct us on its meaning. Perception regarding the type of chair, actually changes from person to person and culture to culture. I may see a kitchen chair, you may see a living room chair and someone else may see a wheelchair. Language only works because of these agreements about what the sound or written word/symbol represents. Letters are agreements too. These allow us to read and write. Like the name "Royce" which in Brazil is spoken as "Hoyce." But how would I know that if I wasn't told it. In China Tao is pronounced "Dow." You get my point; words, definitions and perspectives are variable and are most often only agreements in our memories.

Consider the recent struggles brought on by the redefining of marriage. These changes are slippery slopes and will always create conflict because changes are often met with resistance.

Selfishness and greed

One of the problems with language in a modern society is that if people, social groups or governments choose to, they can actually reprogram people by merely changing the meaning of the words the populous uses. They do it for purely selfish reasons. These acts are often extremely destructive and actually harm their "supposed" causes.

This will be a simple one since it is so obvious; let's use Racism. How are race relations going right now? I grew up, worked and lived in Baltimore most of my life; race relations have never been this bad and the division never more violent. I moved away because even though Baltimore has a history of violence, it was becoming increasingly more dangerous to be the wrong race in the wrong place, at the wrong time; at least if you're white-ish.

See if you agree with the current definition I use for Racism. While the word is not that old this is the historic legal definition of record for the "charge" of Racism. The original meaning went something like this: "Racism is the withholding of goods and services, or access to goods and services by one race that is in power from another race that is not in power, with that denial of such things being exclusively based on race."

How did we do? Sounds pretty good right? It should, because without one race being in power you have no negative outcome; it would just be dislike, distain, bigotry or hatred but not Racism. (Psst,, Right now there are some really freaked out people, freaked out about a word being clearly defined. They're getting really anxious because they have been programmed to have an emotional reaction to the word and its meaning.)

Real Racism

The real definition of racism is of no interest to the Ideologues. In truth "Racism" only exists when a good, service or opportunity is denied because of race. Thinking about denying someone a job based on race is not illegal or considered to be committing an act of racism. For racism to exist the job must actually be denied for the reason of race; regardless of the rationale. Simple test; "Am I denying this person something because of race." If you deny him the job for punctuality issues in the past it's not racism, no matter how many white people work for you.

Speaking about another race in a negative manner is not Racism, that's why they came up with the term "hate speech."

The problem with the term "hate speech" is that speech is supposed to be free and that is guaranteed by the 1st Amendment. They have resorted back to the word racism because it still has a lot of emotion attached to it.

The race baiters use race to coerce you into silence. They would like you to think that speaking about race is just as bad as committing racism. Many northern black voters have never been in the South, yet most of them are sure that everyone "down there" is filled with hate for them. (Recall the emotional aspect of polarization and how the Nazis used unrealistic fear to motivate support.) The left-leaning ideologues would be in major trouble if the religious Northern black vote unified with the Black and White religious Southern voters. It would end the Democratic Party. For this reason they are desperate to Keep Hate Alive! Their real motive is to engulf you in their argument and to get you to join them in their redefining of the word. The less you think, the more power and control they have; in a perverse ironic way, this assimilation of blacks as democrats is a form of ownership and slavery to their cause. (But I digress.)

The origins of the word Racism is not as old as you might think (which should give you pause). Its evolution had nothing to do with people of African descent. Leon Trotsky's 1930 work, "The History of the Russian Revolution" was the first time that the term was coined. The word came from a Latin transliteration of the word he used in that book. "Racistov" essentially meaning "racists." Trotsky was the cofounder and first leader of the infamous Red Army. Interesting enough, he was a Jewish man in a pre-WWII Russian State. He co-led the 1917 revolution alongside Vladimir Lenin as Commissar of War in the new Soviet government. He helped defeat forces opposed to Bolshevik control.

177

As the Soviet government developed, he engaged in a power struggle against none other than Joseph Stalin who had had him exiled earlier. It had nothing to do with people of African descent and in fact, it was a reference to a notion that Jewish people were not Caucasian. That is the original meaning of the term. Trotsky was arguing that Jews were Caucasians; just like Russians. Jews were being denied equal opportunity and access.

In 1960's America the term shifted to "Denying the access to a job, to food, to shelter, to opportunity; or to equal treatment based on race alone." The co-opting of the word was initiated because it was the same thing that was happening to the Jewish people in Russia. That is the original and still the modern, standard for defining racism. Did they teach you that in school? Of course not, it wouldn't serve their agenda so they are trying to expand it to mean more than it does. (Words equal Perspectives!)

Every other non-racial factor entered into the decision to deny someone access to something diminishes the impact of racism. The race that is "in power" is not relevant; it does not require the racist to be white. Slavery is not necessarily racism either. There have been many cultures that have enslaved their own race. People in the Middle East were the first to hold slaves and usually of the same race. The Muslims were the first outsiders to enter Africa and enslave black Africans. Black Africans (not all Africans are black, but you knew that too right) learned that if they converted to the Muslim faith they could not be held as slaves. According to Mohamed, one Muslim is not allowed to enslave another Muslim; hence the birth of the Black Muslims. (The Black American Muslim is actually celebrating a heritage of slavery by being Muslim.) While the faith freed them from slavery, it mandated or enslaved them into the religion/ideology. All this occurred long before the US was even conceived of. This information is not hard to find.

178

SHOCKER ALERT!!!

The first person in the US to legally own another person was a black man named Anthony Johnson in 1654. He sued and won when a North Hampton court allowed him to indefinitely retain and keep a black indentured servant named John Casor. Casor had left Johnson's keeping to be a paid servant/employee of a white man. Johnson sued in court for the return of his possession, Mr. Casor. His victory created the landmark case for ownership of a human being in the US colonies in 1655. Mr. Casor and those who followed, were the first property that a black man could actually own; yep, another black man. You can be certain that social order deemed that if a black man could own a black man, then a white man could own one too.

Why didn't they teach us this in school? I'll tell you why, because it doesn't fit their narrative or their agenda. Leaving out important facts like this is evidence that agendas are at work in the US public education system. This is revisionist history. Remember, polarization requires an emotional reaction with a solution in place for you to choose. It requires a victim. The black race can't be the victim of the white race if a black man fought for it and set the precedent.

Ideology is not routed in facts, but instead in the fantasy of how things "should" be, not how things actually are or where. In the worlds of the ideologues, "the means to the end" are not relative to the greater good of serving an agenda. If I get you FALSELY outraged, you then turn to me for more information. Bam!!! I then have control, power and trust; I own your insight.

Many of the cities struggling in America today are actually run by black people yet they use racism as an emotional bone of contention or as an original cause for the problem. A black-run city can commit racism by denying Caucasians, Asians or Hispanic peoples certain jobs in that city government by simply

179

favoring the black candidate over any others. That's real racism and it happens all the time, but no one says a thing and there is no law enforcement to stop it. If it's just their friend that they hire, then that is called Cronyism (no matter the race). Add a dose of racism on top of some cronyism and you will not be getting the best person for the job. Cronyism is a major problem in many of America's largest cities and institutions, including the Federal Government. Additionally, not advertising a job because you don't want another race to apply is racism (denial of access) and that is why many jobs in the form of government grants are required to be advertised for a set period of time. This, however, does not affect the hiring preferences.

Ask yourself the following: Why are these major black run cities not required to hire based on population percentages to prove their fair treatment in regards to race and to guard against racism? White-run cities are required to maintain certain equivalents based on race. Why should cities like Baltimore, Detroit, LA, Chicago and even New York (and others) not reflect their populations in their hiring practices? If the candidate chosen is similarly qualified to the rest of the applicants and then race determines the choice that is Institutionalized Racism. The ideologues believe that if they can keep the populace convinced that racism is a White/Black thing, then no one will even look behind the ugly curtain of what real racism in America looks like. FYI - Choosing by religion is bigotry or anti-Semitism

The person selected because of race suffers subconsciously regarding their own self-worth because they will always have to question whether their position was earned, deserved or instead token. While people being chosen for an affirmative-action position may like the money, they will always question their real qualifications; their own sense of accomplishment will always be personally suspect. Affirmative action robs each and every candidate of their real sense of capability, regardless of how qualified they are. In much the same way as when we elect a president who is black, he will always question whether he got the votes because he was the right person or because he was black; or even a little black. Any person chosen by race will still wonder if s/he could have attained the position if the playing field was truly level.

More than ninety percent of blacks voted for Obama, many came out to vote for that reason alone. They said it out loud; that was racist. Sure, they wanted to help elect the first black president but that is racist too, because they chose by race. Many said they didn't care; that they were voting for him because he was black and it was justice for them; rational to commit a racist act. He was chosen by race; quite openly I might add. Many white people also voted for him because he was black. They chose by race. Is that racism? Is there a difference to you? What if I voted for the white guy; not because I dislike blacks but because I favor the white guy? Suddenly something changes doesn't it? That is racism and this is critical thinking.

It's all an act

I chose the topic of race because it is a good example of how modern media and certain segments of society, including the educational system, seem invested in your belief that racism is only white to black, that is alive and well. They want you to think that it somehow rests in people's hearts and not in their actions. The fact is that racism was decreasing so dramatically that it became necessary to expand the definition in order to keep the emotional reactivity and victimization alive. Now, if you even "think" about race you're a racist. Convenient, but not true!

While some of this confusion is ignorance-based the majority of it is intentional and usually brought on by people in the background who you never see. Spurred on and given life by

181

people who work in safe zones and live in gated communities; the same people who grab their purses tighter and lock their car doors when they see a person of another race walking down the street toward them. Their often "faux outrage" about race is usually an overcompensation and an attempt to mask their real perspectives about equality. In fact, one might question their supposed need to represent the black race, as if the black race can't take care of or represent itself; that it needs them.

Unfortunately, many people in power in modern society have been affected by revisionist history. Proof of Revisionist history is in the mere truth that you were not aware of some vital facts in the history of human ownership in America, in slavery or of the real origins and meanings of the word racism. Words, definitions and perspectives.

I encourage you to become attentive to current efforts to revise history by entities that only provide examples of events that support only their agendas. What many people call "Racism" is actually bigotry and prejudice; not illegal. Hatred is not illegal. If it were we'd all have a record or be in jail!

As stated previously: "Trying to make hatred illegal makes about as much sense as trying to make love mandatory." Trying to stop hatred with legislation will only make more hatred as it breeds resentment. Trying to force love will only make it harder to find, because love is supposedly unconditional. Control is an illusion that most often results in catastrophe. Allowing people to be themselves always results in more Harmony!

One more brief consideration: If a white man hates a black man he is called a racist, yet ask that same black man if he hates any black men and like any other race, he will confirm that he currently does or has in the past. I don't like all white people, so I don't expect people of other races to like all white people. I can dislike a Chinese man and not be racist. Just like Martin Luther

182

King, I judge a man based on the content of his character. I judge character without pause and without caving into hateful labels and coercion. If you said, I hate that white guy; I certainly wouldn't suggest you are racist because you hate one white guy. I would not call you racist because you used the identifier of white. It's no different than that tall guy, it's descriptive not racist. I wouldn't think you hate all tall people, only that one. My point is that you have been duped!!! Played!!! You have been co-opted into serving an agenda you don't support or even understand fully. Are you mad yet? Yes/No? At me or at your school system? Good! In the next chapter I will explain how they did it to you and how to avoid it in the future.

Chapter Ten

MIND CONTROL

Dumb and dumber

You hear it all the time; "kids today are so stupid." The truth is that young people only know what you teach them. Children are blank canvases. It is probably more accurate to say, that "children are gullible." They will trust the people whose care we put them under, but only because they trust our judgment. We seem to trust the school system just because we paid for it or because we had a good experience 30 years ago.

The truth is that if kids are stupid, it is because they have stupid parents who don't pay attention to what their children are being taught. (Ouch!) If we don't pay attention, then we really can't blame the school system for teaching them whatever they choose to. We can't be shocked because they're teaching them what they want them to believe. Ap-"parent"-ly, we don't care enough about the content of what they are learning; simply proven by the fact that we don't know what they are learning.

"Not-caring" is over!!! It has to end. The educational SYSTEM has been co-opted by people with long-term agendas who want your children to believe certain things, be they sexual, gender, race, economic, religious, historical, etc... We can no longer TRUST an educational institution that does not seek balance. This includes all of the institutions that are funded by ideology. School systems are less and less concerned with data and more and more concerned about fanciful ideology, motivated by victimization and entitlement; often guised as fairness. The concept of "fairness" is an illusion created by someone who felt victimized, cheated or entitled. Fairness does

185

not exist in the universe; only in the hearts of ideologues who want it to be real or who want to use "lack of fairness" as a polarization and wedge issue.

"Have you ever heard the saying: The meek shall inherit the Earth?" Maybe what the gospel of Mathew was really suggesting is that the meek will be all that's left when the ideologues and the power hungry governments of the world have their way; perhaps it was more prophecy than conjecture. I wouldn't worry though; you can trust a self-serving one-sided academia and a selfless government not to manipulate their educational curriculum to gain your child's allegiance. (Cough)

Consider this; having a populace that is meek, passive, unarmed and dependent on the government to meet its needs is certainly a lot easier to control. Saying "the cops will take care of you" is the same tactic as giving them the same power to guard your health. They tell us we don't need guns, the cops will protect us then they attack the cops for abuse of power. "Sheeple" are the desired cash crop herd for governments of all types. Religion may be the opiate of the masses but the minds of the people are the opiate of those who desire to hold power.

I am not sure if I wholeheartedly believe that people are stupid, but I am 100% certain that people are under-educated, uninformed and ill-informed. The uninformed citizen is a new lemming being led to slaughter; a modern slave to the machine. In this context, "stupidity" is not an inability to reason or an issue of function. Stupidity is knowing what you should do, but not doing it. We can all be stupid at times but few of us can afford it or desire the end result.

If we truly are all equal, then why is it that some segments of our society chose not to self-educate? I find it astounding that there are people in our society who say "I don't follow politics." What they're really admitting to is that they don't really pay

186

attention to the people who control their lives. This trend should bother us all, especially in a society that rants for and craves individual freedom.

Intellectually retarded

Ah, the PC police are freaking out over the legitimate use of the "retarded" word. There are many wealthy people without college degrees, but none of them are intellectually lazy. They have all self-educated on some level. They have all demanded more from their lives than just accepting the information that was being spoon fed to them by the system.

There is a direct connection between self-educating and success. All successful people push their intellectual limits. It is my belief that successful people are the exception to the rule; they have navigated around the agendas of those in charge of information and they have refused to go along to get along. It has literally paid them dividends.

Why is it that some people never seek their own information or truth? Why do some kids who have intellectual ability grow up to be stupid people? The answer is simple; their parents are too lazy, uniformed and unmotivated to better themselves so their children just model that behavior. Either that or they were so enabled by their parents that they became entitled, whinny brats that can barely do their own laundry.

How do young innocent minds come to believe some of the crazy things that they believe? Stop for a minute and seriously think about that. Who could have possibly made your teenage child think the way they think? If it wasn't you, it was someone or something else. They didn't come up with their beliefs on their own. If they seem clueless, they're not. They were just given a different set of clues than you were. Due to the high level of media saturation today, it is safe to say that it came to them electronically; from a friend, in a 10 second headline, meme or sound bite talking point. NOT TRUSTED SOURCES.

Parents are supposed to be the providers and influencers of their children's perspectives about life. The school system is a self-serving entity of the government. They say they'll serve you, but they can't if you are not informing them of what you want your children to be taught. Remember the "Pledge of Allegiance?" It was a pledge to follow and trust. The government is the only service provider that we pay for that isn't held accountable for the quality of service they provide. We don't hold them accountable so they do what they want. We can't blame the school system for doing what they want if we don't show an interest in issues beyond lunch menus, bathroom labels and sports teams.

Getting schooled

The biggest influences on modern learning today are more obvious when you take the time to think about them consciously. Who holds all the power when it comes to the dissemination of information? The largest shareholders of data and information about important life issues are the government, the school system, the media, the family system and religion. It doesn't take much consideration to realize which one of these entities is most prevalent in your life, your child's life or in the lives of your neighbors.

One of these power brokers has constant contact with you, one is always in your ear, one regulates you, one waits for you to turn to it and the other is there from birth to death without a change in role. It's hard to tell which one is which. We could also argue that peer groups also influence the thinking/learning process but the truth is that peer groups are merely a reflection of the larger system; an echo. What if the peers are bullies?

I want you to use your critical thinking brain again. Why is it so easy to get an education today? Who else benefits from the education that people receive? This will sound a little "conspiracy theory-ish" but the most obvious answer is often the right one. The government! Dismissing this truth by saying "it is too simple" doesn't mean it isn't true. The very system that provides you with information also gains from what you learn and believe. The people who lend you money for school gain from your education. While there may be a handful of good teachers, there is no longer any real systemic altruism in the public education system as a whole.

Consider for a second the fact that the government makes you pay for a "free" school system for every kid; even if you don't have kids. It gives loans to anyone who wants one without qualifying and there are colleges everywhere. Now the growing trend is to forgive most of those loans. Why do they make it so easy? Is it possible that they want you (need you) to have the information they've prepared so badly that they are willing to do whatever it takes to see that you get it? Is it really because they want you to be happy or because they want you to earn more money so they can collect more taxes? How about both!

The truth is that everyone doesn't need a college degree to make a great living and not everyone with an education has a great income. Why are so many people directed toward psychology and feeling-oriented fields like social work? (Full disclosure I have a SW degree too.) Is it possible that they funnel people into these fields because being in touch with your emotional side feeds their emotion-based ideological agendas? Are emotion-centered citizens more easily manipulated?

A true student-centered educational system would teach you vocational skills without requiring the arts and humanities courses. Guess why they're required. The government expresses

189

concerns that not everyone is able to get an education even though information has never been more free or accessible.

Economies are fueled by production, not by ideology or intellectualization. Anyone can draw a picture of a million dollars or of a large building but not everyone can make it real. Is it possible that we've trained too many people to feel and not enough people to "do?" Is it possible Rand and Orwell were right about the problems of power? Who made all this access to education possible and why was it really so important?

As referenced above, many people argue that the government merely wants people to get better paying jobs, so that they can increase their incomes in order to pay more taxes. While this is true, we never-the-less have a tremendous number of educated people who can't find jobs. Notice that the above argument does not deny the government's role in the educational process, only that the reason for their control is just. The government has convinced you that learning their information is going to help YOU in life. Help you or help them? Many people are now arguing that public education has not helped them at all and that they are now indebted to the government to repay the only loans that can't be written off in a bankruptcy. The government collects interest on these loans for 20 and more years. Education is a long term government revenue stream.

Thirty years ago half of the populous who are attending college now, would have entered into manufacturing instead of pursuing white-collar jobs. Some people in the blue-collar trades are earning between $60,000 and $100,000 a year while working only a forty hour, five day work week. The factory workers of the 70's, 80's and 90's actually had more parity with white collar workers then they do now. I can remember counseling auto and steel workers who made 2 and 3 times more than I did. Failed ideology has shipped these jobs overseas. Did the government push society towards the white-collar service professions because they knew that their free-trade deals would destroy our manufacturing sector or did the lobbyists, paid for by foreign countries, just trick them?

An interesting example is the computer tech industry and its current share/role in modern education. The government didn't start integrating computer technologies into the educational system because they foresaw the coming tech boom; that industry was actually a surprise to everyone. The real computer tech boom was an accidental discovery that occurred in the garage of a college dropout named Bill Gates. The education system only added computer technology after they found out it was a great revenue generator. Before that, most computer training courses were privately conducted in self-pay trade schools and the military. (Recall the certifications of the 90's?)

Their designs on your children

Did you teach your kids to think the way they do? If not, which of the entities on the above list did? Was it a government, a school, a religious figure, or the media? (To be honest, when most kids were getting a religious education we had a whole lot less negativity and a whole lot more human kindness, caring, compassion and love.) If you or your church didn't teach your kids the values they now hold, who did, did anyone? YouTube?

I want you to think hard about your children's views on the world and how they match up with your own views. Who programmed your children with such a different viewpoint than your own? Hopefully, you gave them between 5-10 hours of attention a week; probably helping them with their school work. You were actually helping them learn the government's data. Even if you did correct the inconsistencies the system still demanded that you hand them over for about 40 hours of indoctrination a week. Sometimes they even instructed your kids

191

to teach you the "new thinking" the "New Math" and the "Common Core" (that sounds socialist doesn't it). It's quite possible that you too learned their ideologies without realizing it when you helped them with their homework; just like the school directed. How many of us passively read their textbooks and thought; that doesn't seem right. Or that's not how I remembered it, hmmm? But we trusted the system anyway.

If you are under 30, I want you to use your brain here. I'm an educational designer and the word "curriculum" is defined as a course of study. It does not suggest any type of balance in learning; in fact it is a focused group of classes or lessons designed with an end goal in mind. Education is designed to give you a mindset about a particular issue. In order to design a curriculum, we determine where the target group currently stands in regard to their knowledge base. We then determine what we want them to know and how we want them to operate; we then design instruction from there.

There is no standard in curriculum design that suggests contrary or oppositional methods and concepts need to be taught. Educational design is most often done for a gain, usually financial but that is not the only reason that educational curriculums are designed. Ever heard of public health education? It teaches you what the healthcare system wants you to know and sometimes purposefully withholds information to avoid unmanageable responses to outbreaks and bio-hazards; even to protect the government from lawsuits.

Despite what some people want to believe, schools and colleges design curriculum around what classes they can sell and sometimes around local societal needs regarding workforce training for specific fields in their geographic locations. Since the government controls the loan process and the accreditation of the schools themselves, the government officials get to say what materials and subjects are required.

Schools are profit-generating businesses, for the school itself, for professors and for administrators. The educational system in the US earns on average, around $60+ Billion a year. The school systems in place today teach what is profitable and beneficial to the school system at the direction of the federal government. The government controls the student loans (the revenue stream) so the schools need to provide specific learning criteria outlined by government agencies. If they don't meet the government's standards they lose the right to grant government loans. If the schools can't write the students loans, they're out of business. (Look up lost accreditation.) They have to create and regulate curriculum based on what the powers-that-be deem prudent and necessary. They do this or they lose 90% of their consumer base and funding.

Hypercritical

Let's go back to the critical thinking skills we used above. If you're an adult you are undoubtedly aware that there have been periods in your life during which major learning insights and awareness's have occurred. Some might say these periods are divided into formative years, pre-teen years, teenage years, college years, young adult/parenting years, 2nd careers, post-children years, pre-retirement, retirement/leisure years and elder years. If we think about our complete lifespan, the skills we learn in school are only a very small part of the life skills we will have to master. The experience of school (discipline, deadlines, researching) is much more valuable than the information we learned which we usually forget after a test. Writing term papers gives one the experience to write reports, books, to organize data and proposals. Most of our real knowledge comes from living, from process and from experience: On the job training.

Interestingly enough, the majority of our population fails to continue their personal educational and intellectual advancement once they leave the government school system. In essence, most people only acquire the information that their learning institution or government thought they needed to have. There are times when your bosses or your employers want to train you but that is because they want you to learn a specific method or skill-set; this learning is not personal, it's professional. People under 30 rarely read data or historical accounts for their own enrichment.

The majority of adult education in the modern world is rarely designed for the individual or by the individual, but is instead designed to make the learner a part of a society. Most adult education is pursued as a means of compliance. This motivation rarely fulfills our creative sides. It will never provide for you an accounting of all necessary facts and perspectives.

The school-fool

What I am saying here is that there is no way that the school system could have taught you all you need to know; especially in only one civics or sociology class. There is no way that the school system can determine what your internal self requires; nor do they care about individualized learning. That is not the goal of institutional education. Their goal is to give you a mindset, a matrix or ideology from which to operate. They give you a perspective and a framework.

The chances are that you were actually taught by people who you really didn't even like; people you knew almost nothing about and people you could not really identify with. Chances are you were taught by people you would not choose to associate with on a personal level yet; more often than not, their views were received by you as the gospel. Their views are required to be your views by the end of the semester. A successful teacher is good at getting you to buy into their perspectives.

194

While we all have one or two teachers in our past who made a significant impact on us, most of the people who taught us what to think were not people we would have chosen to be like. We were forced to echo their views back to them or face the penalty of a failing grade. Ironically or sadly, their only credibility came from their having echoed the voices of their teachers from 10 years earlier. This process is like the game of telephone where one person tells a story to another person, then to another person; the story gets more and more distorted and biased toward certain aspects of the story. This is the evolutionary cycle of revisionist history.

As previously mentioned, there is a nefarious aspect to the educational process. That being that you must complete your assignments with answers that reflect your allegiance to their views if you want the good grade. Noncompliance is penalized with a poor grade and perhaps even ridicule. This means that you are being conditioned and rewarded by the letter "A" to perpetuate their views (at least in word). This is behavioral conditioning but it should be seen for what it really is; coercion and mind control. Strong words, I know. There is rarely any opportunity to freely express your perspectives in modern education; only those views that fit the agenda. It's really demanded compliance that you pay large sums of money for.

Having personally attained what amounts to about 275 college credits during the accumulation of 5 college degrees, the only teachers that I can really remember are the teachers who taught me my 1st several classes in a subject. It is not about what they taught me as much as it is about how they encouraged me to learn and explore. I believe that I got lucky because I started at a community college. That is where I found these teachers. Teachers at that level are usually people who currently work in the real world and only teach part-time; they are not

195

academic elitists who control the data or curriculum: They share their actual real-world experience.

In all honesty, I remember those teachers because they highlighted my abilities. Later, in the larger schools, the truth is that the majority of the teachers there, the ones that I paid thousands of dollars to learn from, were for the most part, quite eccentric academics who had never had to survive in the real world. If they did it was during their internships. To be honest, most of the University teachers seemed a little creepy and very egomaniacal.

One of the scariest insights gained during my formal educational process was that they were nearly all progressive liberal thinkers. I cannot recall a single person teaching me a conservative perspective of any kind; thus no balance and only partial truths. Near the end of my education, while working in the Baltimore City treatment system, I became a Democratic Socialist. I couldn't help it, I wasn't taught any other alternative. This is the problem we are experiencing today, some 30 years later. This imbalanced system teaches liberal ideology by presenting only the history and perspectives that advance those ideologies forward. They won't hire anyone who doesn't tow the party line; they even check party affiliation before interviewing applicants.

There is good news of sorts. Eventually, that brain washing fades as the realities of life set in and the ideology is proven false by time and experience. For the younger people reading, this is why your parents are probably conservative; their brain washing has faded; yours, not so much. The question is, why are we paying large sums of money for perspectives? Why are we being taught what to think and what to value when we should be being taught how to think critically? Is it any wonder that so many young people feel their lives are disordered?

Lemmingmanufacturing.gov

The government-run school systems are not balanced and they have no desire to be. They are constructed to perpetuate a very specific ideological agenda via a progressive liberal curriculum. This is irrefutable due to the reality that only 1 in 10 academics view themselves as "right leaning." There is no way to provide a holistic and unbiased educational experience in that setting. The few people who do see themselves as Republican or "right leaning" have views that are skewed by the contrast to their uber liberal counterparts within the establishment. This makes them only seem like they are more middle-of-the-road when in fact, they are probably just more logical right-leaning lefties. They are not middle-of-the-road they are just not "as" far left. Less than 0.75% view themselves as far right; yes, less than one percent. Those "right-leaning" professors may actually be teaching at religious universities and not in the public system.

In hindsight, I am not surprised that even with my own inquisitive intellect, rebellious nature and strong will, that I left my undergraduate learning process with a head full of socialistic and progressive beliefs. Every once in a while I can hear their repetitious voices spewing their unrealistic ideals in the back of my mind. I wonder if that's what happened in Germany during the Nazi era. I think the education system might actually owe me a refund for falsely advertising and misrepresenting what I paid for. I went to school to get facts and information, not biased revised perspectives or liberal ideologies.

Who MINDs?

Our college age children our being taught by people who are pure academics (people who live, work and socialize in the academic field). Most academics have never earned their own way in the real world. They make 100k + a year to echo forth curriculums authored by their tenured colleagues. They have great benefits, from graduation to retirement and lots of time off. Most have never struggled to survive. Most have little real world experience beyond being alive.

Have you ever looked up the word "tenure?" The word "tenure" is defined by Webster as; "the act, right, manner, or term of holding something such as a landed property, a position, or an office: especially a status granted after a trial period (to make sure you are in their echo chamber) to a teacher that gives protection from summary dismissal; (can't be fired) the right to keep a job, especially the job of being a professor at a college or university." (You get to keep the job for as long as you want it.)

Academics relay ideology mostly based on theory, spurned by a desire for a utopian society that can never really exist. They are people with little or no "real world" experience. Their only real experience exists in giving people theoretical perspectives. They have rarely personally applied their theories to the outside world in a successful manner. The outside world being a place where they wouldn't be the boss: A place where they would have to tolerate things that go against their programming and beliefs. This includes serving customers who are always right and the possibility of being fired. In the real world, the liberally trained and programmed graduate would most likely end up working for a conservative who they would think clueless.

Sad to say, most of the academics teaching today are taught by professors who do little more than profess for their entire lives. While there are many adjunct professors who do have real world experience they are only allowed to teach the curriculums and use the testing materials handed to them by the establishment's department heads. The majority of their real world experience goes undisclosed; with the exception of some self-affirming and ideologically reinforcing real-world examples.

The academic professors in our colleges today are really good at teaching people what to think but they are failing us because our young graduates barely know how to think, how to deduce or how to reason. There's a sad twist in this drama to which many of you will agree: Our children have it too easy today. All their human needs are being met for them. By the time they get to college they don't even have to learn how to think for themselves; they are just given their thoughts which they take right along with the rest of their entitlements. Some even seem relieved not to have to think, they just want the fancy liberal arts piece of paper certifying their echo chamber performance and pedigree. They no longer have to figure out what to think instead they wait for someone to tell them what to believe: That's easier and ideology SOUNDS just great.

The echo effect

The academics who teach at the state college level are locked into their echo chambers by tenure. They are almost never confronted by any information or data to which they don't already subscribe. They write papers for other academics to read and they only read the new ideology that their comrades have postulated. Most don't believe that information of any real value to them will come from any other outside source. They believe themselves to be the origins of all new evolutionary perspectives. They design research to prove their own views and design other research to disprove the outside-the-box perspective they disagree with. Their findings are then confirmed by their tenured friends and colleagues in the same echo chamber.

Sadly, many academics and professors never leave school. Most of the people involved in higher education today have never stepped outside of higher education; they go from high school to their Bachelor's degrees to their Masters degrees or straight onto their Doctorate degrees. Once they graduate, they

199

become professors. This academic allegiance is why they only let people with doctorates attain tenure; only a handful of staff teaching positions are given to people without doctorates; regardless of their brilliance, they can never become tenured. In many fields of study there are no practical reasons to attain a Doctorate unless you want to teach or do research which is most often still a part of academia. The reality is that poor people who can't afford to attain their doctorates are eliminated from access to these positions/jobs, leaving them to the "elite academics."

The leftist-party collusion of the academic is not always a conscious one. Most have simply never thought anything other than what they currently think. Their beliefs are never challenged by the system; they have never had their ideology tested by the real world outside of their echo chamber.

On occasion, these purveyors of the party line are confronted by a critically-thinking student who pokes holes in their lectures. These students rarely succeed at accomplishing little beyond wounding the professor's fragile ego. If this occurs in the classroom they may be ridiculed or even sanctioned by an egomaniacal academic who is unwilling to challenge the foundation of his or her own beliefs. Their egos disallow the possibility that "some kid" could have a new perspective or insight not already considered by the establishment. They really do believe that all the really "smart people" are in the system. The challenged academic reverts instantly to their echo chamber bully tactics and invite students who are in ideological concert (and who want a good grade) to "school" the dissenting student on their ridiculous notions. (When a professor gets intellectually stuck, they poll the audience and ask; "what do you all think of that statement.") The echo chamber's cultural inhabitants then berate and bully the inquisitive student into adapting their beliefs; at least if they want to look smart. The negative reaction felt by the dissenting student often leads to the limiting of their own critical thinking and insights in the future in order to achieve acceptance and a good grade. They are now forced to repress their real selves. Their only hope of being truly heard, may later surface in a dangerous or even deadly revolt.

Some of you may be thinking "Who cares, let them be, they'll grow up and grow out of it." The chamber effect will wear off!" King Oscar the II of Sweden once said "A man who has not been a socialist before 25 has no heart. If he remains one after 25, he has no brain." It just so happens to be around the age of 25 that the non-doctorate student finds himself out of the echo chamber and coming to grips with the real world's realities that force a shift toward a more realistic, non-ideological view of the world. This maturational shift happens because the real world is void of the echo chamber's thought safety. Other perspectives are allowed to be entertained; reality often forces its way into their conscious awareness. The only people who don't make this shift from progressive-ideological-socialist mob rule thinking to independent thinking are the people deeply entrenched in the echo chambers of their own words, definitions and perspectives; usually political, governmental and academic.

The people who teach have merely remained engaged in academics without real world exposure. They become the chosen sons of the educational institution that originally programmed them; the next generation of academic elite.

Be careful

There is an important reason why you should care about what is being taught in the government school system/s and that is because those ill informed students vote. They are often more motivated to vote because it's their first chance and because their teachers told them too. Every time one of them votes stupidly, a smart vote gets negated. Interesting that the current move from

201

the left is to have people vote even younger than 18; now you know why. The teens and youngsters of today grow up and vote 5-10 years from now. They can unwittingly influence the direction of a nation they know little about. Ironically, their votes can actually make it harder for you to pay for their college tuition. These new voters are emotionally motivated by their "new way of thinking" so much so that they can even convince their inattentive parents to vote with them for emotional reasons.

These young voters have been directed how to vote by the government sponsored coercion of the school system, by the mainstream media and by the behavioral conditioning of wanting good grades. Most of these fresh voters self-righteously believe that they are doing it for ethical and puritanical reasons but they are just sheeple being lead by wolves. These young minds need to be protected from themselves but only because we didn't protect them from subversive activity and the biased flow of one sided information. These fresh voters are not seen as wise enough to drink but it's OK for them to decide how a country should be run.

Alarmingly, young people today are more susceptible to peer-pressure then any generation before them. Peer-pressure-mongering bullies have 24-7 digital access to their brains. This is happening all around the world where technology has advanced but it is even more dangerous where technology and information is more strictly controlled (propaganda).

These are the same methods once used by tyrants throughout the ages, from the Egyptian pharaohs to today. These power-grabbing ideologies are still alive in places like China, South America, most of Europe; even Russia to a lesser degree. These country states all control their media.

It's simple deduction that the children literally ARE the future. Propaganda and perspective control is the origin of;

"teach the children what to think and they will think your way."
It only takes about 10 years to effect societal change using the
minds and perspectives of the young voting bloc.

Since when

So when does a nefarious entity start caring about what's in
the minds of its children; caring about what they believe? I want
to give you one consideration before I answer that. Since the
founding of the United States it was always viewed as "The
Great Melting Pot." Suggesting that "America" was the result of
diverse cultures blending together (assimilating) to form a
symphony of the best attributes of all the cultures of the world.
We all like that perspective right? It's what it means to be
uniquely American. This melting pot of culture "had" worked
well and things were going fine for a long time. I say "had
worked" well because there has been a collegiate shift away from
this melting-pot model. Did you old people miss that class?

Academia and its ideologues began programming the youth
of the US to believe (without proof) that multiple cultures could
stay intact while living in a single society. With the help of your
tuition and student loan payments, the US is now being viewed
by the left as a potential "Salad Bowl" and not a "Melting Pot."
The "Salad Bowl" is a fantastic place where separate ideologies
supposedly exist together in harmony while maintaining their
individual identities.

This "salad bowl" ideology is how the radical faiths are able
to force policy changes to suit their individual needs while
discounting others'. This is why we are having cultural
problems. The melting pot was a backward looking designation
of what was occurring; what was making America work. The
Salad Bowl ideology is just that Ideology; not reality based. It's
unproven utopian fantasy.

203

The salad bowl idea sounds good on paper but who decided to make this shift for our entire country? Did you? Did someone you know? Who decided it was better than the Melting Pot and did they purposefully leave some people out of the debate? Why? You can be pretty sure it happened in back rooms of academia and evolved into a fiction book written by an ideologue. That book was then turned into a civics lesson by the author with a lot of arguments about "how great it would be if only." NOT WORKING! The Melting Pot is what gave us our identity as Americans; the culture everyone in the world, wants to be a PART of. Unfortunately, due to in-grouping and out-grouping this theory only creates division. This is the modern day "separate but equal." (The same failed ideology once suggested by racist Southern Democrats of the past.) Cultural assimilation is our cultural identity. ASSIMILATION is necessary!

Chapter Eleven

TOTAL SYSTEM FAILURE

Splitting bi-polarization hairs

Democracies and democratic politics require polarization. In order for the political game to work, politics requires the division of a homogenized society. The reason is because individualized ideologies (too many different ones) become unwieldy and the momentum for change needs to be reinvented for every new issue because people won't be committed to a single side. This approach is a modification of the Parliamentary System.

The Electoral College in the US can only work in a two party system. As mentioned previously, if a viable third party were to evolve, it would be nearly impossible to collect the 270 electoral votes required to secure the presidency. For this reason the DC establishment will never allow a third party to evolve. The US government is designed as a two-party system.

The rationale for keeping the two-party system in place is rather simple. If you have a change you want to make, you just feed it through one of the progressive parties; the supposed "mechanism for change" is already in place. The system would work fine were it not for career politicians and their backroom deal making where they sell-out future votes for current ones. One party writes the laws and the other party plays the "straw dog" (just for show) because the backroom deals have already been made. Most times house and senate votes are just for show. A three party system cannot currently exist because it would collapse this agenda process. This could also destroy one of the existing parties and neither party is willing to take that risk. The current Electoral College would fail nearly every time in a three party system because neither side would be able to garner the 270 out of 583 electoral votes needed to win. No matter how many people want another party it's not going to happen. Even the Tea Party was eventually given a "side to be on." What we need to do is get rid of the Electoral College and its main stake holder, California, which has a 10% say in presidential elections despite there being 50 states.

Here is an example why the two-party-only system is in effect: If 90% of Americans were on one side of an issue (say the abolition of the IRS,) then the government would have no choice but to reform (unless there is tyranny). By using the politics of division, the powers-that-be can segment groups of voters into manageable sections based on other moral and philosophical beliefs.

If you believe that more than half the conservatives really care about abortion rights or you believe that more than half of liberals do care about it, then you have been fooled. That's just not true. A large number of conservative-minded people don't care one way or the other and a large number of liberals think abortion is over-utilized. The establishment has used these issues as wedge issues for their own agendas; namely to remain in power and divide the people. If you believe that all Republican are against gay marriage and that all Democrats support gay marriage then you're delusional. The easiest way for them to achieve this type of control, is to maintain a two-party system that feeds the populous with 10-second talking points.

Peace of the American Pie

Here is another popular polarization brain game. The concept of World Peace is a wonderful thing. World peace however is an ideological perspective that has NEVER existed in the real world. World Peace has never been a reality on the

206

planet, yet many people have been programmed to "fight" for it. (Fight for peace: I hope you see the implausibility here.)

Peace is a state experienced by the human mind and not a state of nations. Harmony is possible between two nations; it only exists for short periods of time between small numbers of variables (in-grouping and out-grouping). The Salad Bowl is out-grouping but its supporters scream for unity and peace. The same people who scream for the Salad Bowl structure, rage against Separate but Equal.

In Chinese the symbol for Harmony is merely an "And" symbol, as in; "this and that" existing together without canceling each other out or creating conflict for either. Nature, at its nature is violent; from "survival of the fittest" to tornadoes, hurricanes, volcanoes and earthquakes. Trying to be free of disaster is an ideology built on unreasonable fear. We either learn how to survive adversity or parish in the evolutionary cycle.

If mankind was capable getting along, it would have occurred during the feudal and medieval periods when resources were plentiful and land was free. When the people's needs were minimal, there was less conflict. Peace could not occur then, so it will not occur now. People who believe in World Peace will never transcend that notion because they won't accept the reality of people. They will always see man as falling short; they cannot see that violence and conflict are a natural occurrence.

The ancient tribes of Africa battled against one another. Native American Indians exterminated one another. The supposed peace loving Buddhists killed off the Taoists, some South American tribes ate one another and Pacific Island nations mounted naval assaults upon one another over vaginas. Outside of the human mind, Peace is an ideological concept not based on any proof or evidence. That's why it is called "Peace of MIND."

Every country and culture on the planet Earth has a set of identifiable characteristics and ideologies. In order for a group or nation to maintain is sovereignty it must maintain its character. Groups that enter into another group's boundaries or sovereignty must assimilate or they quickly overcome the structure in place. If the migrants choose not to assimilate and breed rapidly, the invaders could out-populate the current civil structure in a matter of 20 years. This is happening in Europe as we speak. Modern society is averaging 2.3 children while Muslims are averaging nearly 7 per couple; add multiple wives.

Let me give you an example of how ideology creates conflict and how it is contagion like. Let's say you moved to a new town and decided to join a local group of some kind. You brought your ideology with you. Would you expect to join that new group of people in their endeavor and then expect to change it into something other than what it was? Of course not, that would be foolish and it could even get you hurt. Why join the group if you don't like what it is doing? Why move there? You might start your own group then battle with that group for change. Where is the peace in that? Peace is acceptance while progressiveness and ideology are suggestions that things need to change. Liberal progressives invented the "Salad Bowl" concept as a change from the "The Great" Melting Pot."

People used to come to America to be AMERICANS, not to change America. The US was the "Great Melting Pot" which was about blending and fusing cultures together to form a symphony of the best attributes in order to become uniquely American. This was assimilation; like a stew. Academia began programming the youth with a false notion that multiple cultures could stay intact while living in a single society. The Salad bowl is essentially the end of what it means to be Uniquely American. It suggests that everyone just living in the same place is what

208

made America great. The fusion is what made America great. Remember, all ideology creates conflict and results in civil discord because ideology is not reality and progressive ideology is never satisfied.

You will be assimilated!

Assimilation is vital to maintaining any national structure. That is why all the nations of the Earth have immigration policies. These polices allow the assimilation process to occur over time by controlling the rate of entry. Europe's recent flood of refugees is creating major concerns as the new residents seek to bring their culture with them while staying separated from the real citizens and their existing culture. Assimilation means to join the current structure, often leaving behind other ideologies. Over history, every time one group has tried to dictate to another group, it started wars. That is the nature of man and the truth of the real world. Watch how fast I can make this happen. "Everyone should have a gun in their house." Discord is natural; and peace does not exist with discord, at least not for long.

Stop playing me

What if I told you that children's toys often represented their initiation into societal structures? Sure we all know about the types of boy-girl toys but what about the role behind the toy or the insertion of a desire to possess things via targeted advertising directed toward children. Remember when the Supreme Court made Camel cigarettes change the "Joe Camel" ads because they were cartoons? What about the cry for Lesbian Barbies and Gay Kens? (Wait, according to G.I. JOE Ken was always gay.) Think G.I. JOE had any symbolism for those of us who voluntarily joined the military post Vietnam?

Why do you think progressives try to control your children's toys; everything from guns to Barbies, cars to clothing, to making sure that your doll is a home owner? Toys are teaching

209

tools that define symbols, definitions and perspectives. Yep, ideology too! I hope your see the messaging there. How about a cool car Joey? What if Barbie had liked Corvettes or GIJOE liked Jeeps? How do you know they did? Every man has wanted a real life thing based on a toy he had, including Barbie.

You may decide if your child gets a certain toy or not but who is in control of your child wanting that toy? The simple answer is the media of any type. How about that iphone or Playstation? The PS2 was once amazing but now you need a PSXX. Peers, media (electronic and television) plant the desire for things in the mind along with the ideology behind them.

While parental modeling can stimulate drives in children, the educational system creates a desire for potential ideologies. The school system uses the very same tactics as TV marketers. Quite simply, indoctrination begins whenever environment and government influence a person by creating a perceived want or need, often using the earlier described systems of emotional attachment and emotional reaction. Even scarier, is the reality that these emotional reactions can be built into public education curriculums.

Here is an example of the direct programming liberals have been given. "If you care about the planet you are a democrat, because conservatives are stupid people who don't believe in (Man-Caused) global warming." There are countless videos of kids in school getting reamed by their teachers for being conservative. They never teach that the National Park System and the off-limits status of the North Slopes in Alaska were introduced by Republicans (conservatives). Republicans supposedly don't support the planet, yet they are the ones hunting, farming and not living in the big cities.

Did you know that the Republicans created the National Park System and nature preserves or that conservatives use 3 times more solar power per capita then liberals? Please tell me you knew that. No! Than that is effective polarization.

Unbiased my....!

If we step beyond the influence of media and realize that media entities are merely the pawns of nearly every government on Earth, we can make resolving these problems less convoluted. While TV and other media do influence your child before they get to school, first grade is where the government programming really begins. This is where they are forced to pay attention because they are now being graded on their attentiveness and compliance. (Or they'll tell your parents. Yep, they even use you as a threat to gain your child's allegiance.)

Doubt the government is in control? Which language is taught in every country around the world? It's a trick question. The answer is simple, the one chosen by the National or Federal government of every country on Earth. Which languages are on most of the TV stations since their inceptions? Simple, the languages allowed by the governments in power. Stop for a minute and consider if 51% of the population of the United States decided that Spanish should to be EVERYWHERE?

In the USA you actually need a special FCC (Federal Communication Commission) license granted for any broadcast network that wants to operate. Why, because they actually do own the air waves. If you start a station without their approval you will be shut down and fined in short time. They will claim it's about fees but they'll still tell you what you can and can't do on the air. They will pull your license if you curse too much, speak too much against the government or even if you just irritate them. In 2009, the Democrats in the House actually authored a Bill to limit conservative talk radio; claiming that an imbalance of REP/DEM content was the result of media bias and not a reaction to the free market. I guess they knew about media bias because most of it was liberally slanted. They didn't want fair and balanced, they wanted power.

This government's attempt to control the airwaves is the very reason why the US has the first amendment to begin with. The founders knew that speech and by extension the free press should be free in order for the people to be aware of their government's actions. This was long before any FCC REGULATION was even conceived of. None the less it is against the law to operate a radio or TV station without government approval despite this amendment. They claimed it was protection against sedition.

What the citizens of any country hear and learn (even the "free" US) is ultimately regulated by the "powers that be." The government can shut down any station they want, at their own discretion. It can be done without congressional or judicial intervention or review. The FCC works much the like the IRS and EPA. They are the government, but are treated as though they are somehow separate entities; mostly so they can act on their own outside of the confines of the Constitution.

Manipulation is simple; the more stringent the control of information, the higher the level of tyranny experienced by the populous. As an educational designer I can assure you that there is no such thing as a free media or an unbiased school system because all news "stories" and educational material have a goal and purpose in mind when they are created. Even if the goal is to expose the government, there's still an agenda.

Back to school

Let me give you a recent example of how the government can control the school system and possibly even history itself. One of the recent trends in public education (by public I mean government) is to do away with cursive writing and move toward teaching printed letters only. If you're like me, you may think that cursive writing is a form of expression that is uniquely

212

individualized; maybe even a tradition that should be maintained. Cursive is the way that all humans wrote English before the machines got involved. The focused attention toward printed letters came along with the printing press.

An interesting reality is that a child who cannot read cursive will not be able to read most of the direct accounts of history because historical documents in nearly all English-speaking countries are in cursive. (That would be really diabolical, wouldn't it?) But wait, there's more: a major problem with cursive writing is not about your children's ability to write it or the value of it; it is instead, about the inability of a computer to scan and interpret the content of it as efficiently (why signatures work). You see cursive writing is becoming more like a form of coded communication that takes longer for big brother's computer to examine. Key word searches are less accurate and harder to attain from cursive. Want to send a private email? Handwrite a letter, scan it and send it as a photo and you'll knock out about 99 percent of the traceable data algorithms at work. The people in power want to know your private thoughts and plans; "but just in case of an emergency."

Education, I mean programming, starts in the first grade because first-grade is when your children start learning data. It's when they start expanding upon their agreements on words, symbols, and definitions; where they start developing perspectives. First grade is when we surrender our children over to the government or the entity or our choosing, for the rest of their learning (I mean programming) process. Curiously, it is also the time when the government starts telling us what is best for our children, even to the point of mandating their participation, compliance and obedience. (We'll leave out the mandating of vaccines. Control the body, control the mind.)

First grade also happens to be the time in your child's life when your child truly begins to exert himself/herself and have influence over his or her peers. Unless you did some form of home schooling or sent your child off to kindergarten, first grade is when they really start learning the establishment's view of the world. This is when children are introduced to ideas outside of those given to them by their family of origin or their church (Sunday Schools start doing this earlier than public schools). First grade is when some of their perspectives are going to be redefined for the better and for the worse.

Do you think 3rd graders should be taught about gender identity and sexual preference; this is the current trend? Shouldn't their innocence be maintained for as long as possible? Isn't it the parent's choice to decide when education of a sexual nature should occur? Got Agenda?

It should also be noted that 1st grade is the tail end of the "formative years" but just in time to make a difference in how the individual will see the world. Accidental? Unless you object, intercede or are involved in the school system, this indoctrination will continue unabated until college graduation. After than it's the media's job to expand the echo chamber and to keep updating their programming. The reason you see mostly younger people at public demonstrations is because the older people have "wised-up" as their ideological programming faded.

You are not IMMUNE

Who contrives the news stories and information that you get? Is the information you get fed to you by those shiny young faces on the evening news: The same faces that were in the high school yearbooks 5 years earlier? The ones with the "LIBERAL Arts" and Communication Degrees handed to them in echo chambers by elite ideologues with social agendas. These young shiny often pretty programmed faces are now fronting the lines of mass media; echoing forth the sentiments of their programmers and leaders. Their editors always have the final say on content, usually making sure the new reporter "understands" the message the organization wants to present. Just read a few news media's mission statements: Most of them have done away with words like; objective, fair, thorough and unbiased: They have been replaced with, dynamic, progressive and insightful.

Earlier I mentioned "The Free Press;" it is referenced in the first amendment in the US constitution. The founders thought a free press (not attached to government) was necessary to prevent tyranny. Ben Franklin (a founding father) knew the potential power of information because he started the first Newspaper in the Colonies. Can you recall hearing about how dictatorial governments or régimes shut down the media in their countries in times of discord or up-rise, sometimes called news blackouts? Why would they do that if it wasn't a method of influencing the populous or to keep people from telling on the government?

As mentioned earlier: "Whoever controls the youth controls the future." The current structure makes colleges and media the foundation of all information. (It is really important for us to be aware of the government's attempts to REGULATE the internet: TO REGULATE INFORMATION. The world's governments have lost control of information and they want it back. They want to MANAGE the INFORMATION SUPER HIGHWAY and turn it into the Information Our-way.)

If you are a younger adult, use your critically thinking brain and consider this: Do you really think the government (i.e. colleges) are really so pure of heart, without any agenda at all? Really? Do you really think that if they thought they could gain an advantage that they wouldn't take it? The educational system will swear they are non-biased. They will never entertain the possibility of their being wrong. Have you ever seen a professor allow a student to correct them? There are no grassroots watchdog groups in place that are able to prevent the misuse of power in academia or in the media. That's your job!

"Trust, but verify" is a smart practice. If you get the "A" in class, it only proves that you gave the "right" answer and not necessarily the truth. Have you ever not gotten an "A" and thought you should have? Have you ever had one of those questions marked wrong when you just know that your response was correct? Is it possible that you were actually accurate and that the reason you didn't get the "A" was because you weren't towing the "party line" by giving their "right" answer? I promise you it happens; because power corrupts and because academia has way too much power: There are no checks on their power to influence. Your professor is way too isolated in their echo chamber to not let their use of power be corrupted. Getting the "A" is more often than not, a behavioral reward system for getting in lock step with "the people" (code for government). The attainment of an "A" is more about having the awareness they want you to have, than it is a reflection of your intellect.

Let's get personal

Almost 25 years ago, when I was in college I took a class called "The Effects of Drugs and Alcohol." I was assigned "The Benefits of Methadone" as a term paper topic. I argued with the professor because at the time (1990), I knew the reality of methadone on the streets, both its black market value and its addictive potential. The professor did not agree. After a brief discussion, I was told that I would write the paper and that it would be a "pro-methadone" paper or I would get a failing grade; which would, of course impact my dreams of a "4.0." So what did I do? I wrote that paper and got that "A." Writing it made me spend many hours changing my mindset to support something I didn't agree with. Having real data and facts prevented me from believing her ideology. Ten years later that same teacher admitted to me that she had worked in a methadone program during an internship and that my arguments against it during our conversations were quite valid.

We've all heard the stories about professors who even demanded that your answers reflect "what was taught in class." Have you heard professors state clearly that "the test will cover what was taught in class and unless you're here, you won't have the right answers?" Wait, what? The right answers are only available in class. I have personally had to fight their agendas many times in order to get my "A's" which I sometimes had to have to keep my scholarships. Comply, or lose your future.

All tests really do is determine how good we are at taking a test. A test determines how good we are at recalling what the teacher "said" in class or what we read out of a specific book. Tests that aren't mathematical or science based are merely proof that you can be in agreement with the words, definitions and perspectives of your teacher or school: That you can give the "right" answers. Eventually, even the most rebellious of minds fall into line or else they leave the education system. Maybe this is why some people don't like college; they just won't shape their minds around other people's ideologies. I love learning, but real education must be factual, reality-based and cover all the possible aspects of an issue in order for it to be true learning, not indoctrination. I do find it curious that there is a correlation between the common sense majority of yesteryear and the lack academia's influence in their lives: Now you know why your grandpa seemed so wise yet uninformed (un-programmed).

Ideology person-a-fied

Control the young mind and you will eventually control the popular culture. This used to take 20 years, but in today's high-tech fast-paced exchanges of information the amount of time it

217

takes to "get the message out" is shrinking every day. "Whoever controls the media, the images, controls the culture." (Allen Ginsberg) Ginsberg was a flaming progressive liberal ideologue who actually told on the establishment because he wanted to retaliate against the power-mongers who he felt slighted him. He disclosed many of the progressive's "dirty "little" secrets" as a way to have revenge for their misdeeds.

(The following topic is a perspective example. I am not suggesting you believe anything. I base my beliefs on truth and proofs alone. I postpone judgment when other possibilities exist.)

For insight purposes I ask the young "straight" reader this question: Do you believe that some people are "Gay?" Why? Seriously, I want you to construct an answer. What made them gay; evolution, genetics, environmental influences? (I didn't ask the gay community because as a therapist I know that people who are invested in an answer struggle to be open minded. If this bothers you too bad; we have freedom of speech and we won't be bullied.)

Do you have an answer? Now that you have a perspective in mind, let's go a little further with my question. Do you believe that Gay is a natural occurrence or a choice? Why? Has anyone proven either option to you conclusively? Has anyone proven it wasn't natural? (Think critically here, you are not being judged by the gay world. Despite popular pressures and the cultural bullies you have a right to your thoughts and beliefs.) Do you love nature and believe it is intelligent design or is all of life a random occurrence; perhaps even the creation of a higher being?

How about transgender? Is it a human male soul in a female body or is it a female soul in a man's body? Is it proof of the soul? Do you believe that nature has a course of its own that we may not all be aware of or did nature make a mistake when it comes to people who identify as "transgender?" Were they put

218

into the wrong body? Are Gay and transgender a third and forth sex coding of homosapians? (I only put these questions together because these groups have linked themselves together.)

Before some of you get your panties in a bunch, I want to be clear here once again. I said we will be kicking the elephant in its ass. That we would be going after issues that you might think are taboo or off limits. They are not! They don't get to decide that! You don't get to decide that! The only reason that these issues have become off-limits is because the people arguing for the perspective they favor are afraid of what might be uncovered. Much like the "Wizard of Oz" demanded that we not look behind the curtain. Nothing is off limits. I stated that I would use words accurately and with their true meaning. All I ask is that you suspend ideology and think rationally. Try to remove the emotional context from either side of the issue. (The LGBT community should be happy we are trying to understand.)

My points here are not about gay, lesbian or transgender issues. It is an attempt to make you go beyond what you think to determine why you think what you think. This topic is being used to clearly demonstrate how words, meanings, symbols and perspectives are formed and even coerced, without proofs; making them weak. I have no horse in the race other than reality and critical thinking. People will ultimately believe whatever they want to.

I have asked many gay and lesbian people these same questions hoping that they could furnish me with an answer that might convince me fully of their perspective. They almost never have a response outside of a personal awkwardness or an attack, usually based on the presumption that I do not have the right to question the issue. Yes I do! Yes we do! If it is something I see daily, then I have a right to try to understand it and make sense of it. (You should welcome our sincere effort.) Sometimes they outright try to paint themselves as my victim and see me as an aggressor, that I am somehow ignorant or hateful if I don't JUST believe what they want me to believe. Sorry! That is cultural bullying at its finest. In these instances, I am prejudicially denied my insight based on my not being "gay." Somehow they don't see the irony in that whole "being judged for what I believe" thing; they don't want me to judge, yet there they go again. If you wanted five wives, I would want to understand.

I believe in a divine intelligence in the Universe but I have no proof of a spirit of the Universe outside of my own personal evidential experiences. I do not go around making others adapt my beliefs strictly on the basis of my belief. Trying to make me feel bad is not evidence of your point, it's bullying. Sure, I've seen studies that may show brain differences and similarities upon dissection, but these studies do not show cause, only result. If I live an angry life my brain will develop differently than if I live a positive happy life, so will my body. Ideology is not proof.

I do however, find it interesting that many gay and lesbian people demand answers and proof of a religious nature but deny needing proof of their own beliefs because they "feel it" in their hearts. (A place with no thinking cells.) Believers in God feel it in their hearts that exact same way.

Curiously, the answer that they give me for how they know Gay is real is the same answer that people give me as their proof of God. Until proof is really incontrovertible, feelings that evolve from how we think are all that we have. There are studies that show biological differences in the religious, too. LGBT groups suggest that I believe their beliefs based on what amounts to faith yet they refuse to give this same level of importance and credibility for the proof of God and by extension the importance of beliefs about religion.

Personally, to me, God is not a feeling or an option. It is a fundamental part of my psyche, exactly like love or the belief that one is gay or transgender. If you are feeling hostile toward me right now then ask yourself how you can ask for my tolerance for your beliefs while not having tolerance for mine; when they are both based on foundations of the same proofs.

Personal attacks are the methods used by people without substance or facts. That won't happen here. You see, as a therapist I've seen people change their core concepts over and over again. From God to no God and back again. From straight to gay and even back again. I could not be a therapist if I didn't believe that changing core beliefs was possible. I may be stupid, ignorant, or even mean but that still does not provide any proof on your part; only fear and resistance to openly discussing the issue. These responses are all signs of denial and uncertainty.

Because I have witnessed these psychic-level changes, I rarely subscribe to "how" people "say they are" as a permanent aspect of who they are. If you do see yourself as Gay then I want you to reserve for me the right to be gay next year in the same way that I reserve the right for you to be straight. (Right now you may be using a "talking point," in your head: "It's not a choice." OK, prove it! With Facts! Using a talking point is not evidence it is merely ideology, programming and bullying.)

Here is some reality; recent research/studies show that only 42% of Americans believe "gay" is a form of nature. In 1985 that number was only 20%. These numbers drop significantly when you leave the United States and our educational system. Interestingly, 10% of the population refuses to answer that question. This, I am certain is due to the hand of the PC world and its cultural bullies. Funny, but when someone denies the existence of gay people as an act of nature then that person is made to feel like a bigoted hater. Yet, this is the majority's belief.

221

I'm not gay so it's really not my issue. Personally I want people to be healthy no matter what that looks like. What I want is for all of you to see how many of us mistakenly take speculation as fact; usually without proof. Prove "it" is real and causally related to the current conditions or prove that it is not. Believing something strictly because it's convenient is not proof.

I have yet to meet a straight person who believes that homosexuality is biological because of any actual proof; most have just been convinced to accept it. They have merely been convinced by others of its existence because of emotional blackmail and coercion. In the same vein, many religious people have no external or scientific proof of God either yet they want others to believe in God. What I distain is when people are forced to believe something or face ridicule and intolerance. Be it Gay or God or anything else.

And so we have it! Seeing ideology as truth and reality are the prime contagions of ideology. The pressuring to adopt unsubstantiated beliefs as truth, is bullying. Going along to avoid drama is pacification. Pacification is accepting something as the result of giving in to an argument without proof. This surrender is merely pacifistic thinking and weakness. It does nothing for the person forcing the issues and it is damaging to the person adopting the presumptions. My belief in something different from you is not hate. IT IS CALLED FREEDOM.

It is common for humans to passively go along with assumptions and presumption without first looking at both sides of an issue; this practice is, however, dangerous for everyone. How great would things be if you had real proof of God or Gay? How much more assured would we all be then. Not needing the answer, will not motivate you to find it. Interestingly, life seems to present us with these leaps of faith on all sides. You can still work on proving it; now you have a life's goal! You're welcome!

222

Full knowledge

Abraham Maslow commented that: "Full knowledge leads to right action. Right action is impossible without full knowledge." He was suggesting that hiding from one side of any issue leaves us with presumption, not knowledge. That knowledge is the result of thorough investigation. A person may be operating in the right manner but without what he defined as "full knowledge," that person just got lucky. He also suggested that if you have full knowledge, that you can't help but make the right decision, every time. The problem is that some people can just believe what they want to believe because they are able to hide from or ignore contrary evidence.

I suggest that you learn to embrace arguments against your beliefs no matter how vital your beliefs are to you. Operating on a false notion will eventually result in difficulties when you are forced to face reality later. Some say change becomes even harder later on in life; this works in the government's favor. Your confidence will increase dramatically when your beliefs can survive the process of scrutiny. Better to find out you are misinformed than to remain clueless.

Open-mindedness is not hearing an idea and passing judgment on its potential; it is instead, incorporating a concept into your thought processes and giving it time to filter through the personal motives for its place in your mind. Hearing something and passing judgment on it not open-mindedness. Being judgmental can make you judge-MENTAL. All you need is critical thinking and the energy to investigate the concept further and you will find confidence in your knowledge.

I want to also stress that the above formula also goes for the doubters of gay and lesbian realities. If you ask me if gay is real I have to say "yeah" but only because I know people who say they are and because we agree on a word but not necessarily its

223

cause or origin. If you ask me if a "Muslim" is real I have to say yeah, but only because there are people who say they are Muslims; I don't need to ask for proof!

Like most people, when I hear the word Gay (nowadays) I think same sex relationships but even this is an assumption on my part. I need to investigate exactly what that means to them when they say it. The definition must be clear to us both in order to communicate about it. Making it taboo makes it out of bounds; convenient! I can believe that someone has identified as "Gay" without needing them to validate their beliefs or provide evidence to prove it's real to me. That's called freedom. It's their business and not mine. If they want to talk about it with me we will have to come to an agreement on what the "Gay" word means. I believe that people will believe whatever they need to believe, usually based on fear or desire. If you're male and you want to sleep with men then just do it. You don't have to convince me of it for it to be "OK" for you. Just don't bully me into what I'm supposed to believe, so you feel better about it.

Since I know this an emotional topic, I will leave you all both straight and homosexual with a thought. For a very long time I could not imagine a reason that homosexuality might exist in nature. Everything in nature has a role, a part to play. Nature is a system of innumerable parts that work together; an ecosystem. Nature is focused on species evolution and the perpetuation of life; it's designed to adapt and overcome. Nature is designed to keep moving forward. I have struggled to find the role of homosexuality in nature since it is self-terminating; without a means for the trait to self-procreate. If it doesn't have a role in nature, then it is an anomaly or just a creation of man; of free will, of impulse.

In case you are interested my current philosophical argument (I'm not personally certain because proof is hard to come by) for the existence of the homosexual personas as a part of nature is that nature has found a way to control human pollutions and reduce offspring on its own. (If everybody on Earth was straight and breeding without contraception, we would have an even greater population problem.) Since nature struggles so much to control man and many believe man is a threat to nature, nature/God in its own wise way has found an avenue of population regulation. That is if gay is actually natural. If all humans procreated the Earth would eventually become overrun.

Since the homosexual cannot produce offspring without help, the gay human will not contribute to soaring populations without significant effort and intent to do so. I'm sure there are some gay people freaking out right now; judging something they never considered before but I am not asking you to believe this theory, I am only providing it for the straight people who often seek reasons for what they believe in before they change their world views: For the people who would feel better with reason.

Unfortunately, as great of an idea as this is (if I say so myself,) there is still no proof. This philosophical notion does work, whether people like it or not. Hopefully, the concept of being Gay is real and that convincing other humans it is real is not just a diabolical plan created by eugenicists seeking to control populations. (Now that's a conspiracy theory.)

In fact, if you believe in a loving God that would not want an animal/human to go unfulfilled, then perhaps that God would create such a solution to the overcrowding of his planet. My argument would make the condition real and important to the evolution and harmony of life on Earth. You work it out! I only arrived at this notion because I want reasons; I like things to make sense based on logic, not emotion. There is no proof proof; so I gave it my best shot and I will probably die with this belief. That is, unless you can show me evidence and not just conjecture; cause and not just effect. Don't show me the differences teach me how they evolved. I will continue to THINK CRITICALLY and not try to feel for my truths in the dark. (And yes I know about Kinsley and the xxy etc... All of which, are ideology and speculation.)

Real TRUTH

So how do we know if we have enough information to get to the real truth? The short answer is probably rarely or never. The point is to be open to allowing more information into your frame of reference. We may have enough information to adopt a perspective, but that is not usually enough to meet the burden of truth; not to be confused with the burden of PROOF. You see, like in the example above, we often only seek information until we are satisfied with what we find. Most often until we like what we find. We seek data only until we find the information necessary to resolve our anxieties about an issue. We settle on what suits us.

I really don't want to belabor the issue but it's quicker than developing another example. Let's get down and dirty again. Using the Pew Research findings above, it is clear that some people have a perspective that gay is a matter of science; that some people are and some people aren't gay. Others have the perspective that some people believe that they are gay but are not completely convinced that it is science. As the research shows the issue is equally split.

Until about 30 years ago, homosexuality was seen as a mental illness of delusion. It was in the DSM (Diagnostic and Statistical Manual) for mental health conditions; authored by the American Psychological Association. It has been removed for many decades now.

In contrast, many of the same arguments about Nature verses Nurture are made for other human conditions as well. The

Social Sciences are known as a "soft science" because it is impossible to prove many suppositions related to humans. Mostly because there are just too many variables to prove direct cause and effect. Still, to this day, there are mental health practitioners that disagree on cause and effect about many of the major mental health problems we face. They usually work from different paradigms (schools of thought or ideologies) which can still be refuted by other schools of thought (other ideologies).

My point here is that you might not be able to prove either side of a human issue yet many people demand that others see things their way based on their PERCEPTIONS only. If you can't prove, it you can't demand it. If you try to force an issue without irrefutable evidence then you are being a cultural bully and creating conflict.

Think about the dynamics of trying to MAKE someone believe what you want them to believe without any actual proof either way. Would that work for you, would you be willing to believe something important based just on someone else's belief in it? If I told you to vote for a specific candidate would that be enough? (Right now: There are people saying "yeah!")

Needing to get others to believe what we believe is a form of emotional illness; a form of codependent behavior. It suggests that the person forcing the issues does not have enough evidence to convince themselves, so they try to create consensus. This forced perspective-by-numbers is essentially the goal of Academia today; to get people to join with them in their beliefs, to create momentum toward legislation and thereby change things they don't see as rational. It is their method for working toward achieving Utopia even though Utopia has never existed outside of science fiction. This method is a perversion of power and a contagion of democratic thinking, brought to you by

227

academic ideologues who want their way and who will use propaganda to REAL-ize it.

Almost everyone knows that just because a majority of people believe something to be "right" does not make it any more right, yet that is democracy. This whole confused democratic process is a very strong argument for REAL libertarianism. Either way, you will eventually believe whatever you want to believe, thanks to a cognitive process known as "walling-off." "Walling-off" is an aspect of self-deception, a precursor to denial. The only thing that can change a person's mind is usually the first thing they will avoid; reality. (I write about this extensively in two of my other books on addiction and the family. You learn a lot about self-deception working with addicts for 30 years.)

The effort and fortitude required to examine proofs against a belief you have and the willingness to accept that you may have been wrong for years, is hard to come by. Most human psyches can't handle the type of self-imposed embarrassment that a major change of perspective can manifest. I suggest that you haven't been stupid or gullible, but instead you were lazy in seeking the real truth and that you got played by your own search for easy answers. How?

Cognitive Dissonance

The existence of Cognitive Dissonance (CD) makes getting the facts right the first time vital because the phenomenon suggests that it is harder to change our minds once we have adopted a belief: It's harder to think something new once you have become comfortable with your belief.

What Cognitive Dissonance suggests is that the avoidance of new thinking is actually a part of a human's emotional nature. Its human nature to become so invested in what we believe, that we don't want to (or can't) hear anything that would require us to

228

change our perspectives. We naturally seek to avoid emotional upheavals; especially those that might affect our world view.

Cognitive Dissonance is not an issue of willingness but instead, an issue related to anxiety. Knowing how things "are" makes us feel more secure; while uncertainty creates anxiety. We don't hold onto our old notions because we are hard-headed; we hold onto our old ideas because there is a sense of comfort in them; a sense of comfort in the familiar.

Here is the more technical definition. Cognitive Dissonance (CD) is the dynamic that occurs when a person faces conflicting information and attitudes about their beliefs or behaviors. CD produces a feeling of discomfort and anxiety when the new information would lead to a necessary change in how the individual operates; because it changes the foundation of their perspectives in a dramatic way. We avoid the new data or "new reality" in order to preserve order in our minds. We take precautions to protect our belief systems in order to reduce anxiety and preserve the familiar belief in place. (La, La, La, La, La; I'm not hearing you!) This anxiety factor is why some people become so animated and even mean-spirited (survival instinct) when we don't or "won't" agree with them. Our disagreement with them is seen as a threat to their whole belief structure. This is the mental illness of the ideologues.

While CD is not really denial, it is certainly the train that takes you to that state. This is another motivation for the "powers that be" to mold the young mind before it has adopted a way of thinking. It's too hard to change their minds later.

Festinger (1957) suggested that cognitive dissonance theory was motivated by an inner drive to hold on to our beliefs and avoid disharmony (or dissonance). He believed that the individual was driven to keep their beliefs in place due to a fear of being lost and uncertain about their environment. He believed that we seek consistency in our beliefs and attitudes in any given situation where new options present themselves. To keep it short; he also suggested that some people can become quite unhinged about keeping their belief. (Some of you may have experienced this during the reading of this book.) We usually refer to folks who respond with too much emotion about a subject as fanatics. Fanatics will start wars to maintain their notions. The irony is that they will kill to avoid dissention and dissonance; they kill to avoid disharmony.

Fringe holders of a belief, like middle-of-the-road Dems and Reps, are more inclined to recognize that they have made a mistake and label it as a "learning experience." Those persons at the extremes of any issue are more likely to reinterpret any contrary evidence they find: they are more likely to discredit the source of it in order to prove that they were right all along.

Pacification is giving into the bullies beliefs without having been provided evidence of the beliefs. It is easier to agree than to argue. Pacifists are people who experience less cognitive dissonance. To them it is easier to agree and change their notions than to face the conflict created by the fanatics.

Pacification is when you agree too easily because you have been conditioned that the fight is not worth it. It is the belief that resistance is a greater evil than fabricated ideology. Ideologues and progressives spend their entire lives getting you to the point of submission to their views. They are willing to change an entire institution and government to achieve these ends because they have convinced themselves that it is for the greater good. That is self-righteousness personified.

There is an unsettling phenomena that occurs when a person can no longer avoid oppositional truths or data that outright refutes their beliefs. They get defensive and discredit or "shoot the messenger" of the truth. They do this because it's easier to make you bad than themselves wrong. These people are usually convinced of their beliefs through sheer repetition and bullying.

As mentioned in the previous chapters, it doesn't matter what you believe or what evidence you have to the contrary, if you hear something enough times you will eventually believe it. This is known as the power of suggestion. Not being passively persuaded by repetition requires significant attention to the deceptive process; more attention and resolve than most people are willing to maintain. Add to this process our willingness to accept things as truth from supposedly trusted sources and we are often, literally blindsided.

Being able to trust a source is great but it creates this inherent blindside. The trusted person is able to fool you because you let your defenses down around them. It is actually quite difficult to guard against giving credibility where it doesn't belong. Time and repetition trump doubt. Not trusting is easier for those who are more negative, cynical and jaded. It is easier for negative bitter people to protect their thoughts; harder for caring positive people to remain suspicious and critical of what they are hearing.

Some people trust the Presidents of their countries so they believe their Presidents when they speak. If they voted for them, they are more likely to listen with a sense of conviction that their candidate is right and accurate when they speak; that their inability to accomplish things is the fault of the opposition. This is because they have an investment in their being the right person for the job. Their selection's failure would personalize that failure, so CD steps in and protects them. This is why some people will never admit they made a voting mistake.

Chapter Twelve

Re-MAKING HISTORY

Revisionist History

Shaping and controlling perspectives is the motivation for revisionist history. It is accomplished by integrating many of the techniques and concepts that we have identified thus far. Revisionist history is the revising of events, timelines, words, definitions and perspectives in order to falsely support and form otherwise unrealistic narratives (ideologies). Revisionist history is a nefarious process built on lies and deception. It is the purposeful erasing or withholding of data that might support opposing viewpoints or ideologies. (Much like the little known facts from earlier; that the Republicans freed the slaves; that the North was Republican and the South was where the Democrats held power prior to and during the civil war.)

Revisionists like Hitler, Stalin, Mao, Soros and many others before and after them used the dissemination of favorable and exaggerated historical events; often leaving out vital factors or events in order to control the perspectives of the populations. Revisionist history is a form of educationally based propaganda. All these fascists knew that if they could decide what history a child would learn they could then paint a picture in the mind of that child which would guarantee their ideological allegiance.

In a more innocent way, controlling information is how we create the notions of Santa Claus, the bogeyman, the Easter Bunny and the tooth fairy. The ingredients are; a trusted source, preferred data, ideology (a story) and repetition. (I am by no means suggesting that; Santa, the Tooth Fairy, and the Easter

233

Bunny aren't real. I believed in them when the propaganda and ideology were in place. I can't disprove their existence.)

Histrionic

Let's stop and think for a moment about who is in charge of which historical events are actually being taught. Think about who would want to preserve some information and leave other information out of the books and curriculums used to teach our children. Do you think this should be investigated? Should we find out who is really behind the curtain leading to these alterations in how history is portrayed? Do the unions protect the people who dishonestly disseminate information and keep them from being adjudicated? Should we know who is in charge of what is being taught in the class room? Who picks the books?

A teacher is directed by a department head that is supervised by a principal and the principal by a school board. That school board/system is regulated by either a government agency or a religious body. The scary truth is that the person who chooses the textbooks is usually just some individual sitting in a dark office somewhere, with a small textbook budget. They pick the books based on how they are marketed. If you want to influence history, you simply provide a nice looking product via a good sales team and reduce profits to get your book in place.

More often than not, someone usually chooses about three books for each subject and presents these choices to the school board as the "best" options being offered. Choices are usually made by appearance and by what meets the school's budget limitations. Throw in some payola (perks or gifts or trainings in nice vacation spots) to an underpaid school employee and it's actually quite easy to get your book on the board's table.

Sometimes there are state contracts with a specific publisher from which the purchaser can order the books. If that publisher has ideological leanings then you can bet that the items they make available will not be in opposition with their preferred accounts of historical events.

The question then becomes "who are these publishers" and even more important, who are these authors and educational designers? Might their personal beliefs dictate the final decisions available to the board? People like George Soros and his Open Source International (he changes the name every few years to hide his agendas) are often in place, to offer nearly free direction and support for educational bodies around the entire globe. (At the writing of this book, Russia was taking steps to remove the Soros foundations and their propaganda from their country.)

The truth is that most grade school teachers have "NO" say in the books they use, but they do have the capacity to alter lesson plans in order to focus on the history of their choosing (when not being supervised). Want to guess where the teachers learned their ideology from? It was most likely in one of those liberal Universities in the US where information is controlled by left-leaning liberals. Teachers ' colleges are almost all staffed by teachers and professors who are self-identified liberals.

There have been numerous legal cases of kickbacks or financial benefits for choosing one textbook over the other; from elementary school through college and even into corporate America. For this reason Texas has recently passed legislation that requires citizen oversight on public educational content.

If we really wanted to control the topics and history being taught, we might even provide the books for free via a philanthropic organization such as the one run by Soros. The donating organization then seems almost heroic because they saved the school money which they will happily spend elsewhere. If you were really serious about controlling the data, you might even try to get a seat on the school board where you could make your recommendations directly. Since the other people on the board are too busy to read all those books and because they respect your service and intellect, they will probably trust your opinion. In the end, whoever it is that decides which textbooks will be chosen has a LOT of power. They actually hold the power of the future in their hands.

Is it possible that we may be too trusting? Do you know who is in charge of your current educational structure? Do you know their names? Are they Conservative or Liberal thinkers? Is it the government? Are they Atheists or Creationists? Are they a huge corporation? Do you think this is important yet? I can assure you this: Common Core is the latest power-grab for the propaganda machine known as the public education system. It is an attempt to gain national power over what is being taught.

It is our duty to know what information our children are being taught. We cannot afford to surrender it over to a bureaucracy. The control of history and information is the very reason why some ideologues don't want you teaching your children at home. You're just not smart enough to do it because they think that you don't know "what" to teach them. They know about the power of data; they are afraid you might be developing a bunch of little anti-establishment rebels and militiamen.

Sadly enough, people pay more attention to what file they upload from the internet then they do to what programming their children are receiving. If you do not monitor and verify the information being taught, then you are the one at fault when your offspring and you disagree on "core" substantive issues. You are responsible for assuring that your children get the information necessary for them to form realistic and practical perspectives.

The history of history

Let's go back to that little angry twisted guy named Hitler. Have you ever stopped to think about all that he was able to achieve in regards to attaining power and control? If you're like me you may have been shocked by how many insane things he was able to convince so many people to do: How he was able to motivate people to follow him down his dark and twisted path. I want you to know his actual thoughts on the subject of education. He was not shy about telling people exactly how he was able to accomplish the absurd things that he did.

From early on, Hitler considered education to be a vital part of his plans for Nazi Germany. He started with flyers in a time when very few entities could afford to print and hand out free information. Only people with "extra money" could afford to buy or read papers. After getting in trouble for his techniques, he was arrested and wrote 'Mein Kamph" while in jail at Landsberg. In it Hitler wrote; "whoever has the youth has the future."

Some of you may remember the propaganda films with the kids all saluting him and the term "Hitler Youth." Children saw his movies in school (a rare treat for poor kids) and were taught how to salute him in their early childhood. (I'm realizing as I write this that there are people reading it under age 35 who may have never been exposed to the Hitler Youth information.)

By managing the minds of the children and by controlling information (truth,) Hitler assured himself and the Nazi party the blind allegiance of its youth; it's future. It is still a part of the Progressive's agenda to instruct children to go home and "inform" their parents about how they should think and what they should know. (Just like little Adolph.) When parents were less educated and when they had less access to information this was much easier. The programming of youth was also being done in both the 2008 and 2012 election cycles in the US. Elementary school children were actually singing songs about their future leader, even before he was elected.

One of the overall designs of Germany's education process was to convince the populous that Jews were bad and inferior.

They were also taught that they, the "Aryan Race" (as he taught them,) were superior. In actuality the term "Aryan" originates from the Sanskrit word "ārya;" an ethnic self-designation in India. It comes from a race not German Caucasian but Asian Indian. In classical Sanskrit it means "honorable, respectable, noble." It has nothing to do with a type of people, only an ideology. The terms swas-tik-a is a Hindu word/symbol as well; one that predates Germany as a country and one that is still used in China to represent purity and not fascism or communism. (Some Chinese characters have evolved from Sanskrit.)

You have been programmed to see the swastika symbol as a sign of hatred and control; it is not! Both groups of people (Chinese and Indian,) are what Hitler called "mudd people" because of their brown eyes. He looked down on the real inventors of the Arya culture. With enough education, revisionist history (propaganda,) Hitler was able to co-opt the symbol and change the meaning into something very different from what it actually represented. (Word, definitions and perspectives) This is the power of education and media control; also known as propaganda. (You knew this too, right?) I promise you that most of the people reading this book did not know these easy-to-find facts. See how it works? This is how Hitler turned the tide in only 10 short years; less time than has passed since 9/11.

In short, it goes like this: I teach you what I want you to know and because you don't have any contrary information you are forced to adopt a specific pattern of thinking because the data I presented seems logical.

Much like a person telling a lie, the perpetrator of propaganda only gives the student as much information as needed to make the point seem practical or logical. Most of you probably hate Arya-ns, not knowing they were actually Indians or the first organized society/community on Earth. (The same people who brought us yoga.) You might even picture Aryans as Skinheads. You might even be a Nazi who didn't know that you named yourself after a darker skinned brown eyed race. (I had to throw that in there.) If you doubt this information you may be experiencing the Cognitive Dissonance defined earlier.

If you know your WWII history you know that the children of Germany became his youth and no longer the children of their parents. Parents were forced to happily surrender their children over to his care. In fact, he also began a breeding program choosing soldiers with certain physical and character traits to mate with "good stock" German women. This meant forced intercourse and pregnancy so that he could make more babies to sustain his war programs while rewarding his soldiers with sex. That my friends, is a long-term goal, but perhaps the scariest part is that he was actually doing it and not just planning to.

Perhaps you've had the following experience. Have you ever looked at your children and thought; "this is not my child, what is wrong with you." Think about it for a minute. If you have children and they think differently from you, then how did that happen? Shouldn't they think just like you if you're teaching them your values? For some of you they do; congrats!

Hitler only had one real agenda; to insure total loyalty in the youth, the future. From their perspective he thought just like they did. They felt that their "leader" truly understood what was in their hearts. Of course they believed he understood them; he was the one who filled their hearts and minds with his ideology and his worldview. The German experience during this time is a clear example of how words, definitions and perspectives can be manipulated, controlled and managed through education and propaganda. The Germans weren't hateful people until they were taught hatred; generationally. When the Reich fell, it was as if a spell had been broken in the citizenry; as if they just woke-up!

239

Imagine what would happen if a college "professor" wanted to run for office today; all the young college students would relate to him in overwhelming numbers because they have been taught what the people in his ideological liberal framework have been professing. They would quickly and unquestionably, fall in to lockstep because, he thinks and speaks just like they do, or is that just like he does. Accident? Think about it! Check out Obama's ties to Soros and you will find that Soros is the man behind Obama's meteoric rise; powered by the young voter.

Suckers!!!

The people who are programmed by the control of data are not at fault. In every sense of the word "they don't know any better" because all they that "know" has been controlled through deception, indoctrination and coercion. In the case of Hitler, (Mao, Stalin and others) he simply taught the people what he wanted them to know; what to think and not how to think. Eventually they thought it and wanted it because his programming scheme worked. All the tyrants have trained their people on what things were important with short snippets of propaganda (talking points) that they wanted in the population's minds. Eventually, the people become convinced of a vision. In the case of Hitler, the effectiveness of this conditioning was so thorough that he was able to teach them who to hate. (We have that now.) So effective were his methods they eventually they even killed for him believing they were doing what they wanted to do. His plan was actually designed to last for 1000 years but it only took him about 10 years (8 to 18 years old for the children) to attain their undying support and allegiance.

Hitler wrote; "the first duty of the state was to care for the "physical well-being" and "physical development of the young." Sound familiar? Healthcare maybe? "It's real simple, <u>convince</u> the populous that you care about their mind, body or spirit and

240

they will trust that you will do the right thing for them in every other aspect of their lives." Health and safety are emotional scare tactics of the ugliest and most effective types.

Eugenicists are people who believe it is vital to control the Earth's population in both number and race. They originally sought to eliminate what were deemed the "weak and feeble-minded." Basically, this meant everyone from "inferior races," to alcoholics, to people with birth defects and yes even those with mental illness. Many Eugenicists were members of "high society" in the early 20th century. They wanted to take these concepts of control even further. Hitler was enamored with the leading Eugenicists of the time, Margaret Sanger. Like Hitler, the Eugenicists knew that if you could take control of the female's body they could then control her offspring. If you can gain the mothers trust from the physical or medical standpoint, her ear will be even easier to co-opt. They believed that if you can gain a mother's trust, she will later entrust you with her child's mind. Margret Sanger was the founder of Planned Parenthood. She was a leader in the Eugenics movement. She was hero to Hitler. (You knew that right? Read the Meehan Report on "How Eugenics led to Abortion," if Cognitive Dissonance isn't stopping you.)

Locus of control

Let's go back even further in the theories on mind control. Proverbs 22:6 "Train up a child in the way he should go: and when he is old, he will not depart from it." Again, this is not a political book per se, but it is certainly a book about motivation. Motivation evolves from perspectives which are built on words and definitions.

Most people today will readily admit that society is struggling. We have lost our healthy motivation and we have been programmed like "sheeple" to protest things we don't even really have an issue with. We spend our personal capital for someone else's beliefs because they feverishly suggested that if we don't care about the issue in question, we are flawed.

One might ask how our attention can be distracted; how that actually happens inside the human brain. Do you have feelings about a "Gay Pride Flag" or the "Virginia Battle Flag?" (Confederate flag) Really; those are your problems? Why do you care if you're not gay, live in the South or have ancestors who fought in the civil war as Democrats? I'll tell you why; because someone said you should. They suggested that if you didn't something bad was going to happen or there was something inherently wrong with your intelligence level. You were motivated by coercion and tricked into believing that you had to stand for or against something or else be ostracized as an uncaring prejudice bigot! This is polarization. This side or that side! You have to choose! WAIT!!! NO YOU DON'T!!! You don't have to choose or care; Vote for your real issues. If more people voted for economic issues we'd be better off now.

You have most likely been pushed to be either on the left or on the right; mostly because they are the only people doing the pushing. They may have even started you out with left of center and right of center but they still got you on their side. You may have even been co-opted and bullied by repetition to adopt certain issues, notions and beliefs without any proof. If you're gay then the left pushed for your gay rights so; "now that we got you your rights, you should show your loyalty by supporting our other efforts. We were there for you! It would be selfish of you not to be there for us!" That is coercion.

You don't owe "either side" anything because you gave them a vote once. If they stop serving your needs, you need to vote them out for someone who does. You can set term limits by voting. If you like the guy on the other side of the room, vote for him or her, that's real freedom. Party loyalty is not freedom, it is coercion. Don't be slave to "a party," emancipate yourself.

Future History

"Young ones are such easy targets." If it can happen to you, then your children will be more easily assimilated. Like it or not, our children are being programmed and reprogrammed; it's happening right now. All of us are being programmed all of the time and I can prove it!

Have you ever had a commercial jingle stuck in your head? Ever have your kid say they want something they saw on TV. Ever thought about a Viking River Cruise? (What is that; they're all dead?) There are people trying to mold and alter your perspectives every minute of every day. It's happening right now.

Our children have been programmed and yes, even me, the author of a book on how to not be programmed. Like I said earlier, it's not our fault. The only way to avoid this programming is to be vigilant. That or go off the grid like so many people are trying to do nowadays. We can't stop the programming in modern society but we can make it much harder than it is. Someone is going to feed us words, definitions and perspectives. We can be resistant by choosing who we trust more carefully. We can denounce repetitious messaging and demand proof.

Your child is going to be programmed and the only choice you have is, who is going to be doing the programming. Yes, they are your children, but if you teach them unrealistic ideologies they will struggle in the real world.

As alluded to earlier, telling your child to fight for peace on Earth is foolish. There has never been peace on Earth; there will always be conflict. Telling your kids that they can be successful without telling them how much hard work it will take is not doing them any favors. Teaching them that they deserve things

243

just because they were born will foster a sense of entitlement that can later lead to anxiety and depression issues.

There will always be people who want your family's allegiance; from altruistic charities to vulture-istic greed mongers. The use of language will always be co-opted for "someone's" personal, social, financial or political ambitions.

Racism and slavery are just an example. Racism has nothing to do with slavery. Slavery happens all around the world and often by people of the same race. Servitude was its original name and a lender could even collect a child as payment for an overdue debt. That child would be a servant and God knows what else. People have often been enslaved by people of different races; usually as a means of justifying their act of enslavement. Race is not relevant when it comes to slavery.

Freedom, not slavery, is the real issue. If you don't speak their PC language and support their PC issues then you're a hate-filled bigoted, old fashioned (not progressive) racist who doesn't KNOW (what we want you to know) better!

While it is morally incomprehensible to most, slavery is actually a legal issue of property. In early American and European history a black man (or any woman for that matter) could not own property. The concept of slavery in America was the result of greedy people seeking free labor; it was not racially motivated; it was greed. The word racism didn't exist then. Race and the presumed inferiority of a race were merely used as justification for it. As mentioned earlier, in America the black race was initially enslaved by a black man who sued for his right to own another black man Mr. John Casor.

The populous has always been fed the information that the leaders wanted them to have; from biblical times till right now. Men have always been persuaded to see things a certain way based on the control of information known as propaganda. The issue of race helps proves my point; that is why I raised it. Propaganda made it possible to justify the ownership of a human being and to murder countless others.

Back to the Future

Thus, the relationship between words, definitions and perspectives is clearly seen. Perspectives are attained through the control and manipulation of information. We can change peoples' perspectives by changing the meaning of words and the nature of language. Hopefully, you can see that just during the process of reading this book your perspectives have broadened. You might not buy all of what I'm selling but somewhere in your mind you are rethinking your perspectives. GOOD!

While I may not have changed your perspectives at all, I have brought insights to your perspectives; insights that some people on both sides of everything may not want you to have. Maybe the simple knowledge of splitting sides, known as polarization, will be enough to help you understand things more clearly. They may claim that this information is dangerous in the wrong hands. They believed they were doing you a favor by protecting you from it, from yourself. Scary!

I have used racism as an example to show you how things can be slanted, tainted and redirected to create favorable perspectives and victimization toward one group or another. If you have ever changed your mind about something important then you know that your mind can in fact, be changed for the better and for the worse.

When I was a child, I was programmed to believe that you grow up, you get married and you have kids. That was why they said you got married in the first place; marriage was for making babies and for growing families in a healthy way. As a child I can remember thinking that something happened in heaven when you conducted a marriage ceremony and that let heaven know you were ready for children. "Then the stork brought-cha!"

Before I was born people got married if they wanted to have "legal" sex or "legitimate" babies but being that I'm a child of the 60's that free sex Genie was already out of the bottle. Marriage is now, for the most part, in the government's view, a partnership contract only. The religion has been supposedly removed from it. That is a major change in societal perspective. The marriage perspective was changed by adding meaning and by stretching the space the word occupies in the dictionary. The word "Gay" now being defined as homosexual, has found its way into most dictionaries. Those dictionaries have therefore altered history (perhaps in a good way). As children are born and separated from history, they will at some point, not know that it wasn't always this way. This "unknowing" is a goal of revisionists.

Discriminating discernment

Discrimination is real, real natural. It is as natural as an act of love, compassion, anger or hatred. Just because something is distasteful or even hurtful, doesn't mean that it's not normal or that it is unnatural. The problem occurs when our use of discrimination is inhumane or "unreasonable." Fair is an ideology created by victims; fairness is not a force present in the universe, only in the dreams of man. Life is not fair and you can't legislate for something that is unattainable.

As mentioned earlier in this book, racism is actually the result of in-grouping and out-grouping. People naturally divide themselves into groups, from their favorite colors of colors to their favorite colors of people. People pick their favorite ice cream by using their ability to discriminate between flavors. Discrimination presents in many different forms and they are not all considered to be negative. You used your discernment skills while reading this book to help you determine what you do and don't "think" is accurate. Discrimination and discernment can be positive and necessary processes; even healthy judgment.

We experience discrimination all the time. The government and corporate America discriminate daily. Have you ever had a background check? How about those "innocent" little drop-down boxes that give you a religion to choose from; at least the ones that count. If you are not on the list in a drop down-box, you go to the "other" category. (Why are they asking your religious preference any way?) These boxes have always puzzled me because what it means is that some religions are more important based on how many people practice them publically.

There are many different languages in America beyond English, but Spanish is the only other language on product labeling and telephone directories? Discrimination? Who made Spanish the second language of the US? You? Why do we still press #1 for English, does that matter?

When my grandparents came to the US, they had to learn English; they believed that learning it made them "feel" more American. It was a way to assimilate into the culture; a way to a part of America. When they had to learn the language there wasn't an Information Super-Highway, a Rosetta Stone, Babbel or an app for that. It should be 10 times easier today but instead of letting immigrants experience that rite of passage and the ownership the process bestows, we enable new immigrants to be "separate but equal." We've institutionalized, separate but equal.

If we could remove the effects of the race baiters in today's culture, the reality is that language and race would not be half the problems they "seem" to be today. Thanks to the ideology of the progressive atheists, religions seem to be our problem now. In the modern world your religion is a much bigger issue than your race. We have a religious discrimination problem in the modern world. None of the world's religions are determined by race, but when you identify someone by their religion or when you denounce a religion, you are labeled as being a racist (RACE-ist). This is just utter nonsense. If you act against all religions you have Religious Intolerance. If you just don't like a particular religion, you are being prejudice. In all these cases you are certainly being intolerant of another person RIGHT to believe what they want to believe. You cannot hate other religions and then demand tolerance for yours; even if you religion is "Atheism." Words, definitions and perspectives.

Let's not forget the new buzz word used by the cultural bully labeling elite for any current form of dislike they see. Instead of accurately labeling it as out-grouping, the new word that they are attempting to co-opt (change the meaning of because racism is fading,) is "xenophobic." In case you didn't know; Xenophobia is a fear of people from other countries, but their working on changing that to fit their new narrative. The term Xenophobia does not suggest race or religion, but is instead defined as "a fear of people from different countries" (Foreigners). This is quite rare in the US because most of us are mutts anyway. Most of us have people at our Thanksgiving tables that are from other countries. (I guess my grandparents scare me!) In truth, the polarizing cults need a new hate word because of all the race-mixing and the crazy getting along that we've all been doing.

In the modern world, if you are prejudice or voice hostile intent toward a person of Jewish faith you are called anti-Semitic (not racial, the term instead means literally "anti Hebrew"). What is it called if you voice hostility toward Christians? Trick questions, it's called "OK," apparently, because somehow, you can't un-righteously hate on a Christian. Why not? Because no one's been able to figure out how to use the hostility of minorities toward majorities, to serve an agenda; they will.

One more manipulation of perspective to consider before we move on; most everyone has seen the bumper stickers "Free Tibet," supposedly to gather support for the ideological viewpoint that there is repression of Buddhism in Tibet. This is lunacy too, because Tibet is the center of Buddhism in the entire world. If it's repressed there, then what is being done to it in the US where it's rarely on a drop-down menu or in the Middle-east where you actually have a hard time finding a temple or even an observer? To take this false narrative idea a little further; Buddhists (believers in a form of Karma) were actually responsible for the systematic annihilation of all things Taoist: From the burning of scriptures, scrolls and books to the murder of every monk they could find. If their repression were real then wouldn't their repression just be Karma for doing to it to others years earlier? If there is repression of Buddhism in Tibet, then why do some Americans think it's their mission to prevent cosmic justice for a religion and history they don't understand?

If China, the supposed repressors of Buddhism in the world, weren't doing what they've been doing for centuries, then Tibet would be called Russia! Seems to me that China has actually preserved Buddhism, but it's hard to find the self-righteous demonization and polarization in that!

America may be the real repressor of Buddhism! I rarely see Buddhism, Taoism or Hinduism in a dropdown box on an online profile of any type in the US despite their numbers internationally. Do you ever see any languages other than Spanish on a label or hear another language offered on a phone menu option. No, you haven't? Is it possible it's just a way to garner Hispanic support at the voting booth? An easy way to get the Spanish speaking peoples of the world to vote left, because they are "seen" as the champions of the Hispanic plight. (More polarization) They had to come up with something because the

Hispanic values vote actually matches up much better with the Christian Right. Personally I've always been a little curious about exactly what percentage of the population you have to be in order to have your language considered? (He asks the lobbyists.)

More tainted discrimination: "Ethnicity" is not specifically related to people of Spanish decent; we all have an ethnic background and an ethnicity. Why is every other ethnicity washed out and why are other cultures not given "ethnic" representation? The term Ethnicity is defined as the ethnic quality or affiliation; a particular ethnic affiliation or group. (IN-GROUPING) Ethnicity is not strictly Hispanic, but the US government only recognizes one group when asking about ethnicity. Words, definitions and perspectives.

When someone says that Muslims are dangerous, they are not being racial. They are being either prejudice, bigoted or they are stereotyping. Discrimination for any reason is often called racism but discrimination is actually an important survival skill; just like stereotyping and profiling. All of these failures in perspective are the result of the PC culture and its agenda bullies.

That's right I said it! Stereotyping and profiling are normal too; everyone does it. Shaming people because they do is cruel and it is the very epitome of an ideological contagion. The cultural bullies that perpetuate these myths are the contagions this book warns of and exposes.

It is not stereotyping, discriminating or profiling that is the problem; it is what we do in reaction to the differences that we notice. There is my Jewish friend; I should say Happy Hanukah instead of Merry Christmas. It is insane to suggest there is anything wrong with this form of discriminating. Treating someone differently in a negative way as the result of any type of difference (not necessarily race based) is prejudice and may even be bigotry; UNLESS THEY APPRECIATE IT!

Have you noticed that you rarely hear the above terms prejudice or bigotry anymore? Why, because the word Racism would lose some of it power and status. Black victimhood would be reduced. The progressive goal has been to get you to see these words as one and the same. The reason is because people have a greater emotional response to Racism. It motivates by fear, to build allegiances with minority groups. Use of the word racism makes a victim seem real and it offers a champion available to support that victim's issue. In the US the term racism somehow suggests white-centered aggression thus everyone else but the white person becomes the worried victim.

Since the arguments for racism have diminished, the leftist progressives have now created "White-Privilege." Just another way to create a victim status for blacks; I guess they forget that there are more white people living below the poverty line than any other group. I guess they didn't want the privilege!

It is illegal to commit racist acts, but the laws that define racism in the US are very narrow. If however, I can get a person to "think" that other things are racist acts too, then I can get them emotional about these other issues. Through the use of propaganda, I can get them to believe that legal acts are illegal just because they are calling them racism. If they perceive things as racist, I can stir their sense of victimization all the way back to the time of the civil war. If I can't expand the constructs of racism the reactivity of it will eventually fade. This is the job of the race-baiters. If they don't "keep hate alive," the argument for the existence of racism will become watered down. If racism fades, it will reduce the level of victimization and outrage.

The white-to-black narrative must live-on because racism isn't such a big deal if everyone commits it. That would make it almost normal. The word racism is used to create outrage and imply that someone is still suffering due to the existence of slavery more than 150 years ago. Every time racism is re-experienced, it makes the period of slavery longer and more impactful. This race-baiting is an attempt to perpetuate Reparation Theology. By contrast; more people have died from alcohol use alone in the past 5 years than in the entire history of US slavery. Where is the outrage for that?

Committing actual/legal racist acts are a personal and spiritual dilemma for the individual. You are actually allowed to be a bigot in the US if you want to be but you are not allowed to commit an actual racist act. While I personally won't befriend a bigot, I will fight for their right to think any way they want. Our service-members die for that right nearly every day. Being a hater is your problem, but when you treat others wrongly in response to your beliefs, it then becomes a community's problem. You don't have the right to take away a right.

Once again I remind you that this chapter is not about racism at all. I know some of you are getting hung up there because that's how they want you to respond, emotionally. They want you to keep hatred, bigotry and prejudice all in one big pile called RACISM!!! The race-baiters want you to discredit insights like mine so that you can't hear them, because logic makes sense and it resolves emotional reactions. They want to preserve your emotional ideological programming.

Meaning spirits

A mean spirited notion you have in your heart or mind may be bigotry or prejudice but until you actually deny something based on race, racism has not taken place. If a black job candidate is given preference for any reason (a choice made based on race,) racism has occurred. Sure you can call it affirmative action, but what about all the other races and why are only blacks and whites singled out for the dynamic called affirmative action. Seems like favoritism and discrimination.

It is not fair for the individual to be caught up in the political/progressive remedy for problems of the past. The progressives are the ones making these issues seem more real than they are; the evidence to back that up is over overwhelming.

I know that this perspective is hard for some people to grasp because you have become emotionally invested in your beliefs about the issue (Cognitive Dissonance). You've been coerced into thinking what you think, simply by the use of language that has been conveniently redefined for you using a history that has been altered. Some of you have been shamed into accepting many other terms simply because you were not the perceived victim. The cultural bullies use these issues to make you feel bad if you don't believe what "they" believe. If you want real freedom, learn the truth! The truth will set you free, but first it may piss you off.

There is a difference between something institutionalized and something personalized. A thought or belief is not an action: Thus thoughts about racist acts are not racist actions and are therefore not illegal. If you think for 10 seconds that you are not going to hire this black kid and then you hire that black kid, you have proven yourself "not a racist."

I-S-M is used as a productive suffix in the formation of words denoting action or practice, state or condition, devotion or adherence as in; criticism, barbarism, despotism, plagiarism and yes, racism. The "ism" suggests that it is an act and not a thought. There is no such thing as racism in thought because thoughts are not actions. Once again, being made to feel bad or wrong for discriminating, stereotyping and profiling is a method of coercing people to support an agenda out of faux guilt. You can't call someone a racist because of what they think. Racism only exists in acts based on race alone.

253

Once again, my example here is not about racism, it's about language and its misuse. A white man cannot commit racism unless he denies a black man something he would give a white man. If he wouldn't hire a white man from New York and he doesn't hire a black man from New York, it is not racism, it is stereotyping. He must actually commit the act based on race for it to be racism A "racist" is a person who commits racism; (acts of racism) not a person who thinks about racial differences. Most employers just want good employees. Ideologues who have never owned a business don't understand this.

The ideologues that perpetuate this "racism-thought-myth" are WRONG and they know it. They want you to feel wrong so you don't put up resistance or speak out for truth. Ideologues who are threatened by your perspectives will attack you if you speak out, just like they did to Martin Luther King, Lincoln, Gandhi, JFK and even Reagan.

Prejudiced ways of thinking may make one a bigot but not a racist. It is an example of how language affects our beliefs and perspectives. Trying to make someone stop thinking about anything is a form of repression. Repression leads to major emotional/mental illness and sometimes extreme acts of rebellion and violence. You only need to consider the many acts of violence that now occur on academic grounds to realize that it is the speech repression in those places (in the PC world) that have repressed those voices. These are repressed voices of individuals who are exploding in acts of violence against those same thought police repressors.

Chapter Thirteen

THE MORAL OF THE STORY

"GET REAL AND LET OTHERS BE REAL, TOO!!!"

True You Perspective

Practice authenticity no matter how uncomfortable it may be. Be your true self and then make the adjustments necessary to improve your own perspectives. Don't let anyone keep you from learning and exploring both the positive and negative sides of your beliefs: That is where you will find the origins of your freedom. Do not fall prey to the power of suggestion because it is not reality. Be authentic or you will feel alone in the crowd. Embrace the perspectives of people who hate and you will see through their hatred to their own pain, insecurities and fears: You will see their weakness and your worth.

Being genuine is so rare these days

The fact that we can only trust some people is a sad state of affairs. The social pressures brought on by the cultural bullies are rapidly increasing as their methods are exposed through the implausibility of their ideology. As this happens they will become even more desperate than they are now. The lack of authenticity and the increase in personal insecurities is at an all time high. The sense of entitlement is growing and an all-out system failure will occur if reality is not restored.

Due to the manipulations of the ideologues, many people think they are owed things just because they breathe. If you really want your life to matter you are going to have to do something for someone else. Start by taking care of your own kids; then help others. That is when you will truly matter, because you will matter to them and the person you have aided.

Dishonesty, motivated by greed for personal prestige or political gain and the warped drive to fulfill selfish agendas have become institutionalized in the modern world. Greed is not good for anyone! Competitiveness is out-of-hand because insecurities are at an all time high. The concept that one person is better than another may be at the root of all our social problems, including racism and bigotry. Maturity comes with acceptance and with the realization that control in an illusion. Maturity shows interest in things that are unique.

We must love who we love and it's our choice to hate who we hate, but careful because hate is contagious. World peace has never existed and it never will. World peace goes against the nature of man because he is fearful, competitive and selfish. Want to make someone feel great, make them more relevant. Want to make someone hurt, want to make them dangerous; make them think they are irrelevant.

Feelings Aren't Facts

Feelings aren't facts. They are real, but they are not facts. I can walk into a room full of people and feel unwanted or disliked. Meanwhile everyone in the room may actually be glad to see me. The reverse can also be true: I can walk into a room and feel loved, but in fact the whole room could be really bothered by my presence. Either way, I feel what I am feeling; the truth is not required to be in concert with what I'm feeling. I must have thoughts about an issue before I can feel anything. My thoughts about an issue can be dead wrong, making my feelings illusionary, even delusional.

We feel the way feel because we think the way we think. We can often feel threatened when we are not and we can even feel safe when we aren't. This inconsistency is the fuel of the cultural bullies. They prey on our emotional reactions. We are powerless over feelings related to past trauma. That is nature's way. While we can work toward having different feelings and reactions, the fact is (with the exception of the information being fed to my senses) the actual environment has little to do with what we are feeling inside. The environment is merely a trigger of our past emotional programming. Our fears are much greater than their realities. Don't believe the lie that fear tells!

The Pacification Contagion

Remember when we were strong? When we stood up for our values and respected each other's beliefs and when we were not threatened by differences? Remember when strength was admired as a virtue, not as a threat. Remember when we didn't have an epidemic of anxiety disorders, ADHD, depression, hurt feelings and neurosis. Ever heard stories about how tough our grandparents were, how they persevered through anything and everything? I do! I miss that about US!

Let me start by saying that getting to this point of confusion is not really our doing, but moving forward, that's all on us. That's right! I said it! We are now responsible for our entire world! Attempting to ignore lies and allow deceit to go unchecked will no longer suffice. Humans are responsible for humanity. Standing up and speaking out is the only way to restore our voice and by extension, our freedoms.

No More Excuses

No more waiting and no more entitlement. You don't deserve squat until you earn it. You get nothing for free; not respect, not trust, not reliability and not value to our society. (If you are whining right now about your value as a person, then you better keep reading.) I said to "OUR SOCIETY!" If you want to be a part of society, then you owe that society the real you and your true voice. If you want to say something, you must be able to say it. Presume that you have to "give a damn." You are stronger and valuable than you think.

257

This book has informed you about what this therapist sees as the real problems in and threats to, our society. My hope is that knowing what it has shown you will provide for you a way to start living in a solution. You see, I know you can handle the truth, because you're made up of the same stuff that once fought tiger and bears. Remember the saying, "Sticks and stones can break my bones but words will never hurt me?" I'm a therapist! If you are over 18 and you stay around people who are negative, then that's on you. Words from strangers can't hurt you unless you want to be offended. The only real hate speech is against truth; it lives in words that foster lies. SPEAK TRUTH!

It's time to stand up for your right to think how you think, feel what you feel, love who you love, like what you like and believe what you believe without letting the cultural bullies tell you how to be. No one man or woman can judge your beliefs or your perspectives without selling out their own. There is a caveat; you have to give everyone else the same rights without trying to censor them because you don't like what you hear. We are not 12! The truth is the truth and political correctness is an ideological LIE designed to silence you and rob you of your voice. The "Silent Majority" will no longer be silent!

In this book I have identified for you the stumbling blocks of thousands of people who I have worked with personally. It is an accounting of what I see happening all around us in the modern world. I've witnessed the contagion of ideology first hand and so have you. I have seen how this false racial narrative has stunted the growth of young black men because they were not motivated to survive and overcome, but to give up and hate back.

As the title of this book suggests, the Politically Correct ideologue police have imprisoned your heart, your mind and your soul. They have infected your brain and your heart. It is time to reclaim your individuality and our true identity as a nation. It's time to care about what you want to care about and not be coerced into selective outrage that only serves someone else's agenda. If hearing or saying "Merry Christmas" is a problem for you, you have a bigger problem than Merry Christmas. That problem has nothing to do with Christmas; it's a problem of hatred in your heart. If so, there probably isn't any hope for you without serious psychological help!

I believe that by letting people convince you of how you should be is the very reason why many of you often feel lost and alone. Intimacy is letting someone, anyone, everyone, know what and how you really think and why.

Stop being a little bitch (that's for the men). Stop whining like a little baby (that's for the women). Your feelings aren't facts. Get it straight (that's not a sexual preference issue). Stop talking about what other people do and start doing something about your current station in life. If you have a sense of entitlement, then other people helping you is your problem. If you are sensitive, then trying to get others to adjust to your needs will leave you sad and alone. If you are scared, then other people protecting you is going to be your downfall; self-reliance is your solution.

Acculturation

In order for any group to retain its identity, it needs to control the rate at which new members enter that group. It doesn't matter if it's your family, your neighborhood or your country. Too many new people entering the group too quickly will change the culture of that group, no matter the size; from study group to nation state. If you don't want to be a part of a group, then stay away from it. Don't move to Rome and expect to live any other way, than like the Romans. When in Rome do as the Romans do. When in the United States do as the Americans do.

259

Don't be bullied

Don't be pressured to feel shame or guilt. Shame has no purpose other than to make a person believe they are wrong or defective. Guilt is an internal mechanism; people either have it or they don't. PUSH BACK!!! HARD!!!!! Assert yourself!

Be critical and mindful of propaganda

Propaganda is the control of information. Information has always been controlled by people with agendas. If you get information from any one source, you get agendas. My agenda is to make you see agendas. The only way to see through an agenda is to look all the way through it, to look for more data, to remove emotion and think logically.

Escape the Echo Chamber!

Embrace diversity and differences, not according to race, according to perspective. Thinking that people of one race all see something the same way is bigotry and stupidity. Challenging information makes your perspectives stronger. The avoidance of contrary thoughts and insights weakens your perspectives.

Make sure that the source of your information is trusted, that it provides all the facts; good and bad. Remember that all educational curriculums have agendas and a desired end-state perspective for the learner. Remember that because "we don't know what we don't know" we can be manipulated and co-opted. Avoid grouping-up unless you're playing a game.

Learn the Solution's Problems First

Beware of people offering with quick fixes in times of crisis because they maybe the instruments of the crisis in the first place. Learn about people like Cloward and Pivens, as they set and outlined the foundation for how the progressive ideologues operate. These create crisis, then "Never let a crisis go to waste."

Be suspicious of large permanent solutions to temporary problems; they often cause more problems than they remedy.

Find out Who's in Charge

Learn who is in charge of things like curriculum design. Mind whose minding the children. Avoid the trap of reelection. If they didn't get it done the first time, they probably can't do it. Your vote is a term limit. If you are not a politician, run for office; we need authentic people representing us. Read your child's schoolbooks and make sure that they provide programs of study that reflect your values, too.

Quick, easy and convenient answers are rarely answers at all: Most of the time they are only speculation and ideology. Ideology is a dream state of how someone envisions something should be; not how it can be. When you hear cries for things such as rights and about violations of those rights, pay close attention as you may be getting "played."

Learn from and Preserve History

Most of the human ideas about man have already been discovered, tried, tested, proven or disproven. Look to the past to learn how things truly are and how people actually relate to one another. Peace is in the hearts of men and not in their interactions; that is harmony and it is fleeting. Efforts to erase history are happening all around us; from the removal of statues in the public square to the distain for religion and God. History is not always pretty, but it is always a reminder of reality. Forget history and you will repeat it. Push back hard against those who wish to alter the consciousness of man by changing who he was.

Don't Suffer Potential Inconvenience

Wait until you actually experience a hardship to feel the pain of it. Be careful of those who want you to fear potential problems that may or may not exist. Guard against allowing other people to motivate you out of fear or of a wrong that may

261

never happened. Ask for proof and take each event as it stands on its own merits. Remember; fear lies!

Ideology is not Practicality

When someone wants you to embrace their change (progressiveness,) they will try to create an emotional need where one doesn't exist. Remember that all of their little schemes have already been tried; nearly all have failed.

Ideology creates conflict because it demands change. New ideology is inherently negative. People hate change and always suffer when change is unnecessary or motivated by selfish, narrow minded people who can't see outside of their own little echo chamber.

LET FREEDOM RING!
MAKE THEM HEAR YOU!!
KEEP AN EYE ON THOSE IN POWER!!!
BE REAL, BE AUTHENTIC!!!!
PROTECT ALL FREEDOM AND YOU'LL BE FREE!!!!!

References

Aronson, E., & Mills, J. (1959). The effect of severity of initiation on liking for a group. The Journal of Abnormal and Social Psychology, 59(2), 177.

Aubrey, T. trans, 1972 (1954). Herodotus, The Histories. London, New York: Penguin Books.

Benson, A (2012). Who Originated the Term "Racist" And Why? Posted on October 18, 2012 By Al Benson Jr. https://revisedhistory.wordpress.com/2012/10/18/who -originated-the-term-racist-and-why/

Biography.com Editors Leon Trotsky Biography, The Biography.com website http://www.biography.com /people/leon-trotsky-9510793 Access Date January 23, 2016 Publisher A&E Television Networks

Cook, J. (2015) Do high levels of CO2 in the past contradict the warming effect of CO2? Retrieved December 5, 2015 from https://www.skepticalscience.com/print.php?r=77

Cooper, R. W. (2011) [1947]. The Nuremberg Trial. London: Faber & Faber.

Evans, R. J. (2003). The Coming of the Third Reich. Penguin Group. ISBN 978-0-14-303469-8

Festinger, L. (1957). A Theory of cognitive dissonance. Stanford, CA: Stanford University Press.

Festinger, L. (1964). Conflict, decision, and dissonance (Vol. 3). Stanford University Press.

Freedman, A. (2013) The Last Time CO2 Was This High, Humans Didn't Exist. Retrieved November 5,2015 from http://www.climatecentral.org/news/the-last-time-co2- was-this-high-humans-didnt-exist-15938

Glanville, J. (2008). "The big business of net censorship". The Guardian (London). Retrieved 26 March 2014.

Goebbels, Joseph (September 1935). "Jews will destroy culture". Nazi Party Congress at Nuremberg.

Godwin, Mike (2003). Cyber Rights: Defending Free Speech in the Digital Age. MIT Press. pp. 349–352.

Hahn, R. (2002) "The False Promise of 'Full Disclosure'," Policy Review, Hoover Institution.

263

Hale, O. J. (1973). The Captive Press in the Third Reich. Princeton, NJ: Princeton University Press. ASIN B0011UXVDG. ISBN 0-691-00770-5.

Jaschik, S (2012) Moving further to the left. Retrieved January 10, 2016 from https://www.inside highered.com /news/2012/10/24/survey-finds-professors-already-liberal-have-moved-further-left.

John Casor. (n. d.)In Wikipedia. Retrieved August 2015 from https://en.wikipedia.org/wiki/John_Casor

Longerich, Peter (2015). Goebbels: A Biography. New York: Random House.

Masci, D. (2015). Americans are still divided on why people are gay. Retrieved November 2015, from http://www.pew research.org/fact-tank/2015/03/06/americans-are-still-divided-on-why-people-are-gay/

Marlin, R. (2002). Propaganda and the Ethics of Persuasion. Broadview Press. pp. 226–227.

Meehan, M. (2002) Hw eugenics and population control led to abortion. Retrieved September 11, 2015. From http://www.meehanreports.com/how-led.html

McCarthy, J (1950). Speech Explaining the Communist Threat http://teachingamericanhistory.org/library/document/ speech-explaining-the-communist-threat/

Overy, R. (2001). Interrogations: The Nazi Elite in Allied Hands. London: Allen Lane.

Pacification (2011). In Merriam-Webster.com. Retrieved December 11, 2015 from http://www.merriam-webster.com/dictionary/pacification

Paul, R. & Elder, L. (2008) The Miniature Guide to Critical Thinking Concepts and Tools, Foundation for Critical Thinking Press.

Rowland, D. (2005). Information Technology Law. Routledge-Cavendish. pp. 463–465

Ryan, C. (2013). Language Use in the United States: 201. Retrieved December 2015 from https://www.census.gov/prod/2013pubs/acs-22.pdf

SAXENA, V. (2015). Fact: Blacks Murder More Whites Than Whites Murder Blacks. Retrieved December 6, 2015 from http://downtrend.com/vsaxena/blacks-murder-more-whites-than-whites-murder-blacks

Slck, M (2015) Signs and practices of a cult. Retrieved December 12, 2015 from Https://carm.org/signs -practices-of-a-cultPsychology.

Shaw, B (1903). Man and Superman. Cambridge, Mass.: The University Press, 1903; Bartleby.com,De Sélincourt,

Spiegelhalter, D. (2015). Is 10% of the population really gay? http://www.theguardian.com/society/2015/apr/05/10-per-cent-population-gay-alfred-kinsey-statistics

Wright, Q. (1946). "The Nuremberg Trial". Annals of the American Academy of Political and Social Science 246: 72–80.

United Nations (2015) 2015 Revision of World Population Prospects. Retrieved January 1, 2015 from http://esa.un.org/unpd/wpp/

Volkogonov, D. (1994). *Lenin. A New Biography*, translated and edited by Harold Shukman, New York: The Free Press.

CPSIA information can be obtained
at www.ICGtesting.com
Printed in the USA
LVHW051327150321
681564LV00014B/614